THE SENIOR  Y0-BXH-357

COLLECTION EDITOR:

GILLDA LEITENBERG

# TRAVEL AND TOURISM

EDITED BY JERRY WOWK

AND CAROL MAYNE

To Loverne, Odessa and Anthony:
"Because of you, I am what I am and I have this moment.
Without you, it would not be possible."
Source "Because of You, Kyushu" by Rita Ariyoshi

McGraw-Hill Ryerson Limited

Toronto • Montreal • New York • Auckland • Bogotá
Caracas • Lisbon • London • Madrid • Mexico • Milan
New Delhi • Paris • San Juan • Singapore • Sydney • Tokyo

**Travel and Tourism**
**The Senior Issues Collection**

ISBN 0-07-551704-3

1 2 3 4 5 6 7 8 9 10   BG   4 3 2 1 0 9 8 7 6 5

Printed and bound in Canada

**Canadian Cataloguing in Publication Data**
Main entry under title:

Travel and Tourism

(The Senior issues collection)
ISBN 0-07-551704-3

1. Readers (Secondary). 2. Readers — Travel.
I. Wowk, Jerry. II. Mayne, Carol. III. Series.

PE1127.T7T73 1994    808'-0427    C94-932371-3

Editor: *Kathy Evans*
Supervising Editor: *Nancy Christoffer*
Permissions Editor: *Jacqueline Donovan*
Copy Editor: *Judith Kalman*
Proofreader: *Gail Marsden*
Designer: *Mary Opper*
Typesetter: *Pages Design Ltd.*
Photo Researcher: *Elaine Freedman*
Cover Illustrator: *Daphne McCormack*

The editors wish to thank reviewer Freda Appleyard for her comments and advice.

This book was manufactured in Canada using acid-free and recycled paper.

# Contents

# Introduction

*"Once upon a time in a land far away..."*

*How familiar are those words that—from the time we first listened to stories and then read them for ourselves—magically and imaginatively transported us to distant places where adventures and excitement awaited. Through books, stories told to us by family and friends, movies, and television shows we have all, at one time or another, travelled to unique destinations and experienced incredible journeys into the past, the present, and the future.*

*The mystique that surrounds travelling appeals to us both in our dreams and in our realities. Magic carpets, time machines, supersonic jets, river rafts—how we long to go "someplace" to experience the almost indescribable thrill that accompanies new discoveries and adventures. Each of us has felt the stirring—the longing and desire— to seek landscapes that are different from the ones we inhabit. We have all planned—and for some of us, we have been fortunate to experience—trips to explore far-away islands; to scale rugged mountain peaks; to delve into the mysteries of the oceans' depths; to investigate the distinct nuances of many cultures. Some of us have travelled extensively to other countries; others of us have ventured only as far as a neighbouring town or city; still others have trekked through the mountains, deserts, fields, and plains without ever leaving our homes, relying solely on the images and adventures brought to life by travel writers. Regardless of where the miles have taken us—physically and imaginatively—we have all been affected, in some way, by travel experiences. This anthology is intended to provide each of its readers with a travel opportunity—an opportunity to become an "armchair traveller," to be whisked away to "somewhere else" and, through an empathetic sharing of those events, to understand better how such experiences lead us to make discoveries about ourselves and the world.*

*The majority of travellers' tales you will encounter in this anthology contain common themes: the appeal of the open road; the urge to take risks; the search for growth and expanding one's horizons; the fear of failure, of returning home before the experience is complete; the trials of illness and homesickness, arrivals and departures; the joys—and occasional tribulations—in discovering new friends and cultures; the frustration when "the best laid plans" go awry; the opportunities to explore the unbeaten track; the forging of new bonds and relationships; the challenge of pushing oneself to the limit; the supreme triumph of being able to say, "I did it."*

*Travel also involves interaction with other people. No travel adventure, even those touted as being "solo adventures," could have been accomplished without the assistance or intervention of other people. The importance of those human relationships and contacts cannot be underestimated. In this anthology, you will also examine other complex and far-reaching issues linked to travel: tourism, the travel industry, ecotourism, strategies for travelling, globalism.*

*When you have embarked on the various travels in this anthology, you will see one of the key elements: the traveller returns from his or her journey a "changed" person, usually in a positive sense. While travel destinations may have been disappointing, or the adventures fraught with unpleasant circumstances, most of the travellers feel positive about what they did, or attempted to do. Others, during the course of the adventure, vacillated between good and bad feelings concerning their voyages. The urge to turn back to safer ground, to give up on the trek, in the face of inner conflicts with loneliness and isolation and external conflicts with cultures and nature, was often incredibly strong. Yet so were the wills of these travellers.*

*While we were compiling the selections in this anthology, we became amazed at the connections we drew between our own travel experiences and those we read about. The more travel writing we read, the more we discovered that travel has a universal effect on people. Whether we actually travel to a specific destination, or travel vicariously through travellers' tales, our very willingness to step "beyond" ourselves is a sign of growth, of seeking ways to expand our personal universes. Travel challenges us to grow, to learn, and to change as it broadens and deepens our awareness of people, places, and events.*

*We hope that this anthology provides you with abundant opportunities to reflect on the importance of travel in your own life and in the lives of others. It has been said that: "A journey of a thousand miles must begin with a single step." Whether your travels are extensive or limited, we invite you to take that "single step" and embark on some fascinating voyages and explorations.*

*Carol Mayne and Jerry Wowk*

# Thoughts
# on
# Travel

~

I am traveller. I have a destination but no maps. Others perhaps have reached that destination already, still others are on their way. But none has had to go from here before—nor will again. One's route is one's own. One's journey unique. What I will find at the end I can barely guess. What lies on the way is unknown. How to go? Land, sea or air? What techniques to use? What vehicle?
— *P.K. Page*

On the old highway maps of America, the main routes were red and the back roads blue. Now even the colors are changing. But in those brevities just before dawn and a little after dusk—times neither day nor night—the old roads return to the sky some of its color. Then, in truth, they carry a mysterious cast of blue, and it's that time when the pull of the blue highway is strongest, when the open road is a beckoning, a strangeness, a place where a man can lose himself.
— *William Least Heat Moon*

The beckoning counts, and not the clicking latch behind you: and all through life the actual moment of emancipation still holds that delight, of the whole world coming to meet you like a wave.
— *Freya Stark*

I am not much of an advocate for traveling, and I observe that men run away to other countries because they are not good in their own, and run back to their own because they pass for nothing in the new places. For the most part, only the light characters travel. Who are you that have no task to keep you at home?
— *Ralph Waldo Emerson*

Without stirring abroad,
One can know the whole world;
Without looking out of the window
One can see the way of heaven.
The further one goes
The less one knows.
— *Lao Tsu*

I had believed that my homeland was the whole world, just as when I was a child I believed that our street was the whole homeland. As I grew up so the street grew smaller. But when my being reached out beyond the homeland, the earth shrank and new feelings, that I was larger than before, filled me.
— *Nawal el Saadawi*

For my part, I travel not to go anywhere but to go. I travel for travel's sake. The great affair is to move; to feel the needs and hitches of our life more nearly; to come down off this feather-bed of civilisation, and find the globe granite underfoot and strewn with cutting flints.
—*Robert Louis Stevenson*

Joe Talirunili *Migration* c. 1976

*from*

# Song
# of the Open Road

~

**BY**

**WALT**

**WHITMAN**

I
Afoot and light-hearted I take to the open road,
Healthy, free, the world before me,
The long brown path before me leading wherever I choose.

Henceforth I ask not good-fortune, I myself am good-fortune,
Henceforth I whimper no more, postpone no more, need nothing,
Done with indoor complaints, libraries, querulous criticisms,
Strong and content I travel the open road.

The earth, that is sufficient,
I do not want the constellations any nearer,
I know they are very well where they are,
I know they suffice for those who belong to them.

(Still here I carry my old delicious burdens,
I carry them, men and women, I carry them with me wherever I go,
I swear it is impossible for me to get rid of them,
I am fill'd with them, and I will fill them in return.)...

5
...I inhale great draughts of space,
The east and the west are mine, and the north and the south are mine.

New Brunswick

# Peopling the Landscape

**BY**

**MARK**

**SALZMAN**

~

once had a college English teacher who said that the most important element in travel writing was "a strong sense of place." She assigned us to go visit an unfamiliar place and write about it. I chose the woods behind the Yale Bowl and described the rocks, trees and moss as "strongly" as I could. I was bored stiff by the assignment and wondered why anyone would waste time describing a place when we have photographs to do that for us. At that time I thought travel books were tourist diaries written by people who had nothing better to do than wander around poor countries and gush about the friendly natives, the quaint architecture and the fresh bread.

Then, several years later, I ended up teaching English at a medical college in China and wrote a book about it called *Iron and Silk*. To my surprise, I started finding my book in the Travel section of bookstores. At first I didn't attach much significance to that because I also found it under Social Sciences, Biography, History, Sports: Martial Arts, and Eastern Mysticism. But when I was invited to give one of the talks in this series [at the New York Public Library] I began to rethink my definition of travel writing.

I didn't go to China with the intention of traveling around the country and then writing about it. I had grown up with an interest in China from watching kung fu movies when I was a teenager—the kind where enlightened monks do back handsprings and then pause in midair just long enough to plant a spear in the forehead of an evil warlord. That sort of thing appealed to me, so I started studying martial arts. Later, when I went to Yale, I learned to speak and read and write Chinese, hoping that Chinese philosophy would improve me. Unfortunately, reading Chinese philosophy in the original didn't improve me any more than reading it in translation had. I remember opening the *Tao Te Ching,* a classic philosophical text, and being able to read in classical Chinese: "The world originates in Being. And Being originates in Nonbeing." And nothing happened—no brilliant insights, no oneness with the universe, no peace of mind. Meanwhile all my friends were getting high-paying starting positions at investment banks. (They're in jail now, but at the time I was very jealous.)

Toward the end of my senior year I signed up for a job teaching English in Hunan. I had never thought about actually going to China, because my interest had always been in traditional Chinese art and philosophy, not in socialist reconstruction. But since I had learned the language and was no longer using it to read books about Being and Non-being, I thought I should give China a try. I also hoped that I could study with a martial arts teacher in China, but I didn't count on it because I had been told that Chinese teachers were very conservative—they wouldn't teach a foreigner because foreigners are lazy and decadent. Well, we know that's pretty much true, but I didn't want *them* to know it, so when I got to Hunan I pretended to be very upright and disciplined. I got up early every morning and did push-ups and hoped that one of the teachers would see me. And eventually one of them did.

At the end of two years I went back home and I still didn't have any idea what I wanted to do with my life. I wasn't qualified for anything. My only job offer came from an uncle in Chicago who is a contractor. He paves roads, and he was interested in having me translate for his company—they wanted to pave China. But somehow that didn't appeal to me. Then one day a friend of mine said, "You ought to write about your martial arts teacher, the 'Iron Fist.' You're always talking about him, and it would make a great little short story." So I said O.K., and I went and wrote the story, and my friend liked it. He said he had a friend in New York who had just started a job in either publishing or banking—he couldn't remember which—and he asked if he could send the story to her. Luckily, it turned out to be publishing, and a few weeks later she called and asked if I had any more stories about my experiences in China....

Now at no time did I think what I was doing was travel writing. I had gone to one place in China and lived there for two years and come home; I never accumulated much travel detail. Besides, I don't like travel; it's such a hassle—buying tickets and finding hotels and arguing about where to change buses. Tourists with backpacks and sandals are always saying, "You simply must see the Purple Phoenix Pagoda, it's incredible." So you get into a truck full of people and their sacks of grain and chickens, and after forty-five minutes you get off and walk through a lot of mud to find a concrete gazebo painted purple. Or a rock that an emperor in the Ming dynasty stood on when he made a speech. That's not my idea of enjoyment, so I didn't become a good collector of places when I was in China, and the places I did visit made very little impression on me....

I'm an impatient reader as well as an impatient writer. I get bored by lengthy descriptions, which explains why I never liked nineteenth-century novels. *Tess of the D'Urbervilles* has about ninety pages of good story in it; all the rest is heath and flowers and strands of hair brushing against cheeks, and it puts me right to sleep. For me, a sense of place is nothing more than a sense of people. Whether a landscape is bleak or beautiful, it doesn't mean anything to me until a person walks into it, and then what interests me is how the person behaves in that place. To show you what I mean, I'd like to tell you a few "travel" stories.

My father is an amateur astronomer; stick him in a field on a clear night where there aren't any city lights nearby and he's a happy man. He used to wake us kids up in the middle of the night just to see some fuzzy speck through his telescope that he insisted was a globular cluster or a spiral galaxy. You can imagine how excited he was when he heard that in 1970 there was to be a total eclipse of the sun that would be visible along the coast of Virginia. For a year in advance he planned a drive down there from our home in Connecticut. He would spread maps all over the living room and just stare at them over and over, even though I-95 would take us the whole way.

Finally the big moment arrived. I was only ten and my brother was eight, but my father didn't want us to miss it. He woke us at one o'clock in the morning and put us in the back of the Volkswagen bus and we drove all night. It was such an adventure! I remember stopping at a gas station at around four in the morning so that Dad could fill his thermos with coffee. When you're a kid, just smelling coffee makes you feel grown-up. Smelling it in the middle of the night in a car on the highway made me feel like the ancient mariner.

We drove and drove, saw the sun come up in Maryland, and arrived at the Cape Charles beach at around ten-thirty. We had a few hours to kill, so my brother and I paced up and down the beach, collecting crab claws for our baby sister and poking at a gull skeleton that convinced us we were at the edge of the world. We waited and waited, and I wasn't exactly sure what we were waiting for because I was just a kid. I knew that something was going to happen to the sun, but I didn't know what. Well, we were just standing there, and all of a sudden we saw it coming across the ocean—the shadow. When the moon blocks out the sun it casts a shadow on the earth, and it was just our luck that the shadow was moving west, across the water and toward us. The shadow raced over the ocean like a wall of darkness. It was such a distinct line. The sky was full of gulls, and when that line of blackness hit them they dropped like stones into the water as if they had been shot, and went silent. It was the most extraordinary thing. The wall kept coming toward us, and then *boom!*

I don't know how many of you have seen a total eclipse, but what happens is that the whole sky goes ultramarine. It's like those paint sets you get as a kid. There's always a blue, and you use it to paint the sky, but it never looks like the sky—what sky is that blue? Well, *this* sky is that blue. It's so rich and deep that the stars come out, while the horizon is a luminous red. Overhead there's a soft white glow, and right in the middle of that is the blackest disk you've ever seen, which is the moon in front of the sun. It's pure science fiction.

Anyway, here it was, the moment of a lifetime, and I suddenly noticed that my father was talking to somebody. After all that planning and staring at all those Rand McNally maps he wasn't looking at the eclipse; he was pleading with a family that was standing right next to us. At the instant of totality these people had turned around and were facing the other way. Somebody had told them that if you look at an eclipse it will hurt your eyes, which isn't true; it's *before* totality that you mustn't stare at it. But when it's total all the harmful rays are blocked, and you're just missing the greatest thing in your life. So my father was pleading with these people: "Turn around! Look at it! It's safe, I promise you—I wouldn't let my children look at it if it wasn't safe!" And they thought he was some kind of nut. "Don't listen to that crazy man," the parents told their kids, and they waddled them away, off the beach. They never did turn around.

Of course the eclipse was spectacular, but if that had been the only thing that happened that day I don't think I would remember it so clearly. But the fact that this family came all the way to "see the eclipse" and then didn't dare look at it: the wasted opportunity made that velvet-black disk even more rare and spectacular. It also told me so much about my father. Totality only lasts about two minutes, and he wasted a minute of it trying to get those people to see it....

On a trip to China to travel the Silk Route, Stuart Stevens and I were in the Takla Makan Desert on our way to Kashgar, which is near the Afghanistan border. We were taking a three-day bus ride across the desert, and on the second day the bus broke down. Typical me, I groaned and predicted that we would be stuck there until the next bus came, which wouldn't be for a week. Stuart said, "Are you kidding? I'm going to stop an army truck and we'll ride with them." I said, "No way they'll stop for us." But pretty soon Stuart saw an army truck coming down the road—it was the only road for hundreds of miles in any direction—and stopped it by throwing himself on the hood. The driver got out. He was a Uighur—they're Turkish-speaking Moslems who constitute the majority of people living in Chinese Turkestan; many of them have light-colored hair, blue eyes and aquiline noses.

Stuart grabbed the driver and said to me, "Tell him he's going to take us to Kashgar." I said to the driver, "My friend thinks you're going to take us to Kashgar," and the driver, to my surprise, said O.K. But he said there was room for only one passenger in the front of the truck and he wanted me to sit up there because I could speak Chinese. Stuart had to get in the back, which was open, and roll himself up in a giant piece of canvas to protect himself from the cold.

We got started and the driver said, "There's something you must understand: I don't stop my truck. We will drive all night until we reach Kashgar." Kashgar was hundreds of miles away, through a desert that didn't have any gas stations; I didn't see how that was going to work. The driver said, "I am Ali, King of Trucks! I never stop my truck!"

Kashgar, China

And sure enough, several hours later when the gas gauge said empty, he asked me if I knew how to drive. I said I did. He handed me the wheel, opened the driver's side door, crawled out onto the running board and flung himself into the back of the truck, where he had two fifty-gallon [227 L] drums. He sucked some gas into a tube to create a siphon and then stuck the tube into the gas tank. Meanwhile I kept driving the truck over a dirt road at forty miles an hour [64 km/h] in pitch darkness.

Later that night Ali got drowsy, so he just curled up in his army coat and fell asleep. So here I was, driving a huge army truck through a totally desolate place: it looked like the surface of the moon, with no sign of vegetation or animal life. Suddenly we came to a military checkpoint—there are a lot of them in this region because the Takla Makan Desert is where China does most of its nuclear testing. The guard was a Han Chinese. I yelled at Ali and shook him, but he was out. The guard shined a flashlight in at me and I rolled the window down. "Where are you from?" he demanded. "Urumqi," I said, which is the capital of Xinjiang province. "Where are you going?" he asked. "Kashgar," I said. He asked me what sort of person I was. I told him I was a Uighur. He grunted and waved me on.

I thought that was the end of the adventure. But about an hour later the truck started to make strange noises and I saw that the engine temperature gauge was as high as it could go. I shook Ali awake and asked him what to do. "My radiator has a leak," he said. "I have to put water in it." I asked him if he had any water. "No," he said, "but that's no problem." With the truck still going, he got out and climbed up on the hood. "Never stop the truck!" he called back to me.

After a few minutes he climbed back down onto the running board and said, "Drive off the road here and make a slow circle and come back to the road up ahead. I'll meet you there." He pointed to where he wanted me to rejoin the road. Then he grabbed a couple of metal containers and jumped off the truck and ran across the sand. I saw that he had found a frozen riverbed. He broke the ice and filled the containers with water while I drove a slow circle in the desert. When I got back to the road he jumped up on the truck (I didn't stop), opened the hood, poured the icy water from the containers into the engine, closed the hood and swung himself back into the passenger seat. "I am Ali, King of Trucks!" he said, then went back to sleep.

The best piece of travel literature I know isn't a book. It's a documentary film called *For All Mankind*. The man who directed it is a writer who went to Houston ten years ago on the tenth anniversary of the moon landing. He visited NASA's film library and saw some footage that the astronauts shot during their trips to the moon and he thought, "Why doesn't anyone do something with all this?" So he spent ten years looking at six million feet of film and editing it and organizing it so that you feel you're along with the astronauts on their journey. The film begins with them putting on their space suits and takes them to the moon and back.

When I went to the movie I expected to be impressed by the photography and the magnitude of the whole thing—imagine watching a bunch of guys get strapped to a tower of explosives and ride it to the surface of the moon. I wasn't disappointed—I saw the movie six times in a row. But for me the most incredible moment wasn't the sight of the rocket taking off, or the moon getting closer, or even the earth getting farther away. It was seeing the astronauts on the surface of the moon, skipping like little boys and singing, "I was walking on the moon one day." Here they were, two superbly trained test pilots, goofing around to the point of stumbling and falling down, even though the slightest puncture in their suits would have killed them. In another scene you see the astronauts tossing pens back and forth in their zero-gravity spacecraft while technicians down on earth keep imploring them over the radio to get back to work. The astronauts say they were having so much fun they could hardly concentrate on flying the capsule.

They got to participate in the greatest travel adventure of all time, and you'd think they would have felt like heroes up there. But instead they say they felt insignificant. They saw that life as we know it is a thin film of activity stretched over a spinning rock hanging in the middle of limitless space. They say that time itself lost all meaning. And you can see it in the way they behave; their sense of the immediate fleeting moment transforms the simplest tasks like picking up rocks into unforgettable gestures. That's what really got to me—their sense of how precious that time was. I could watch a hundred hours of pictures of outer space and it wouldn't do much for me. But the sight of those men in their big white suits hopping on the moon gave me a real sense of place—of what I might have felt if I had been there myself. That's good travel literature.

# Passports to Understanding

~

**BY**

**MAYA**

**ANGELOU**

Human beings are more alike than unalike, and what is true anywhere is true everywhere, yet I encourage travel to as many destinations as possible for the sake of education as well as pleasure.

It is necessary, especially for Americans, to see other lands and experience other cultures. The American, living in this vast country and able to traverse three thousand miles east to west using the same language, needs to hear languages as they collide in Europe, Africa, and Asia.

A tourist, browsing in a Paris shop, eating in an Italian ristorante, or idling along a Hong Kong street, will encounter three or four languages as she negotiates the buying of a blouse, the paying of a check, or the choosing of a trinket. I do not mean to suggest that simply overhearing a foreign tongue adds to one's understanding of that language. I do know, however, that being exposed to the existence of other languages increases the perception that the world is populated by people who not only speak differently from oneself but whose cultures and philosophies are other than one's own.

Perhaps travel cannot prevent bigotry, but by demonstrating that all peoples cry, laugh, eat, worry, and die, it can introduce the idea that if we try to understand each other, we may even become friends.

*from*

# Sunrise
# with Seamonsters

BY

PAUL

THEROUX

There are two sorts of people who like trains—the railway buff and the joy-rider. There are also two sorts of travelers.

There are those whom we instantly recognize as clinging to the traditional virtues of travel, the people who endure a kind of alienation and panic in foreign parts for the after-taste of having sampled new scenes. On the whole travel at its best is rather comfortless, but travel is never easy: you get very tired, you get lost, you get your feet wet, you get little co-operation, and—if it is to have any value at all—you go alone. Homesickness is part of this kind of travel. In these circumstances, it is possible to make interesting discoveries about oneself and one's surroundings. Travel has less to do with distance than with insight; it is, very often, a way of seeing. The other day I was walking through London and saw an encampment of gypsies on a patch of waste ground—the caravans, the wrecked cars, the junked machines, the rubbish; and children wandering through this cityscape in metal. This little area had a "foreign" look to me. I was curious, but I didn't investigate—because, like many other people, I suppress the desire to travel in my own city. I think we do this because we don't want to risk dangerous or unpleasant or disappointing experiences in the place in which we live: we don't want to know too much. And we don't want to be exposed. As everyone knows, it is wrong to be too conspicuously curious—much better to leave this for foreign places. All these are the characteristics of a person with a traveling mind.

The second group of travelers has only appeared in numbers in the past twenty years. For these people travel, paradoxically, is an experience of familiar things; it is travel that carries with it the illusion of immobility. It is the going to a familiar airport and being strapped into a seat and held captive for a number of hours—immobile; then arriving at an almost identical airport, being whisked to a hotel so fast it is not like movement at all; and the hotel and the food here are identical to the hotel and the food in the city one has just left. Apart from the sunshine or the lack of, there is nothing new. This is all tremendously reassuring and effortless; indeed, it is possible to go from—say— London to Singapore and not experience the feeling of having traveled anywhere.

For many years, in the past, this was enjoyed by the rich. It is wrong to call it tourism, because businessmen also travel this way; and many people, who believe themselves to be travelers, who object to being called tourists. The luxury travelers of the past set an example for the package tourists of today: What was the Grand Tour but a gold-plated package tour, giving the illusion of gaining experience and seeing the world?

In this sort of travel, you take your society with you: your language, your food, your styles of hotel and service. It is of course the prerogative of rich nations—America, western Europe, and Japan.

It has had a profound effect on our view of the world. It has made real travel greatly sought-after and somewhat rare. And I think it has caused a resurgence in travel writing.

As everyone knows, travel is very unsettling, and it can be quite hazardous and worrying. One way of overcoming this anxiety is to travel packaged in style: luxury is a great remedy for the alienation of travel. What helps calm us is a reminder of stability and protection— and what the average package tourist looks for in foreign surroundings is familiar sights. This person goes to China or Peru and wants to feel at home. Is this a contradiction? I suppose it is, but we must remember that in the past the very rich went from castle to castle or court to court; from the court of George III in London to the court of The Son of Heaven in Peking. It is much the same among certain travelers today. I was once in Siberia, and I recall an Australian saying to me in a complaining way, "It's cold here!" In Peru an American woman said to me, "I hate these hills—they're too steep." We were in the Andes. And not long ago, in China, a woman said to me, "I've been all around the world—Madagascar, the Galapagos Islands, Arabia, every-where—and I didn't walk. I never walk. I hate to walk. I never go to places where I have to walk. But I've been everywhere."

This is actually quite extraordinary. For that woman, travel is a sedentary activity. She has been carried across the world. She is the true armchair traveler.

It is easy to laugh at her, but her kind of traveling is very popular. Travel nowadays is seen to be a form of repose: most people you see in travel posters are lying down in the sunshine, or sleeping in a lounge chair, or just sitting. In a sense, Abroad is where you don't have to do anything but loaf. I realize that a great confusion has arisen because we regard travel and a vacation as interchangeable. But really there is no connection at all between being alone in upcountry Honduras and, on the other hand, eating fish and chips in Spain. For a person with two weeks' vacation, travel—in its traditional sense—would be unthinkable; which is why parts of Spain have become Blackpool with sunshine—it's more restful that way. I don't blame people for craving that, but I do object when it is regarded as travel.

# The Terminal Man

### BY

### ALBERTO

### MANGUEL

~

For certain mortals, the purpose of travel has become arriving. For them, eager in reaching the end, there is no thrill in anticipation. Waiting rooms, which offer vast possibilities as social salons or public houses, are for these hurried unfortunates new tenements of hell. For them, the ideal form of transportation is Dorothy's pair of magic shoes, which, I understand, zoomed her from Oz to Kansas "so swiftly that all she could see or feel was the wind whistling past her ears."

Ever anxious to improve on the universe, my fellow travellers love speed because it seems to deny space. Europe, they argue, is not an ocean away, merely 3 1/2 hours by the Concorde. The realization that the ocean is 106 million square kilometers escapes them, as it escaped Gulliver in Lilliput.

I'm glad to say that, in spite of their haste, space stands fast. Faraway places remain far away, and the breathlessness with which we can reach them doesn't bring them any nearer. For me, at least, much of their attraction is in the fact that they *are* far away, like the moon; that they require exertion to be reached. *Travel*, the dictionary reminds us, comes from *travail,* work. And waiting rooms provide a pause.

Once, at about five in the morning, at the airport of Saint-Denis on Réunion Island, in the Indian Ocean, I was told by an attendant (who seemed to be running the airport all on her own, as if the place were a family concern) that my flight to Paris had been delayed "for an indeterminate time." Grumpy and sandy-eyed, I sat down and turned to my fellow unfortunates.

They were a French family: the father, the mother and two girls of 7 or 8. I started mumbling the usual inane clichés: "Travelling is getting to be impossible." "They could at least put up comfortable chairs," etc. I find clichés extremely useful when complaining.

"Actually," the father interrupted, "we don't mind waiting. You see, we came to Réunion just because we wanted to be in Réunion. So we don't mind spending a little more time here."

The mother smiled, "We wanted the girls to see the place where the feather came from."

"Papa, show him the feather," said one of the girls.

The father put his hand inside his breast pocket and pulled out a folded piece of plastic. He opened it carefully. Inside was a yellowish, slightly curved feather.

"My grandfather gave me this, and he had it from his grandfather. Can you guess what it is?" asked the first girl. "It's a dodo's feather. The last of the Réunion dodoes was killed over 200 years ago."

"Touch it," said the other girl.

I did. It felt stiff and coarse, like a dry leaf. It belonged to something that had vanished forever.

At Saint-Denis, being shown a dodo's feather; at Heathrow, meeting a man who had met a friend of Kafka's; at Mirabel, watching a group of nuns move slowly through a snowstorm, as if they were levitating; not always, but sometimes the wait is rewarding. Time regains an easier pace; places are put into perspective. The site we are leaving, the site we intend to reach, granted a moment of recollection, become memory and longing. The waiting room—the maligned, avoided waiting room—grants us that moment.

# The
# Return

~

**BY**

**ALISTAIR**

**MACLEOD**

t is an evening during the summer that I am ten years old and I am on a train with my parents as it rushes toward the end of eastern Nova Scotia. "You'll be able to see it any minute now, Alex," says my father excitedly, "look out the window, any minute now."

He is standing in the aisle by this time with his left hand against the overhead baggage rack while leaning over me and over my mother who is in the seat by the window. He has grasped my right hand in his right and when I look up it is first into the whiteness of his shirt front arching over me and then into the fine features of his face, the blueness of his eyes and his wavy reddish hair. He is very tall and athletic looking. He is forty-five.

"Oh Angus, sit down," says my mother with mingled patience and exasperation, "he'll see it soon enough. We're almost there. Please sit down; people are looking at you."

My left hand lies beside my mother's right on the green upholstered cushion. My mother has brown eyes and brown hair and is three years younger than my father. She is very beautiful and her picture is often in the society pages of the papers in Montreal which is where we live.

"There it is," shouts my father triumphantly. "Look Alex, there's Cape Breton!" He takes his left hand down from the baggage rack and points across us to the blueness that is the Strait of Canso, with the gulls hanging almost stationary above the tiny fishing boats and the dark green of the spruce and fir mountains rising out of the water and trailing white wisps of mist about them like discarded ribbons hanging about a newly opened package.

The train lurches and he almost loses his balance and quickly has to replace his hand on the baggage rack. He is squeezing my right hand so hard he is hurting me and I can feel my fingers going numb within his grip. I would like to mention it but I do not know how to do so politely and I know he does not mean to cause me pain.

"Yes, there it is," says my mother without much enthusiasm, "now you can sit down like everybody else."

He does so but continues to hold my hand very fiercely. "Here," says my mother not unkindly, and passes him a Kleenex over my head. He takes it quietly and I am reminded of the violin records which he has at home in Montreal. My mother does not like them and says they all sound the same so he only plays them when she is out and we are alone. Then it is a time like church, very solemn and serious and sad and I am not supposed to talk but I do not know what else I am supposed to do; especially when my father cries.

Now the train is getting ready to go across the water on a boat. My father releases my hand and starts gathering our luggage because we are to change trains on the other side. After this is done we all go out on the deck of the ferry and watch the Strait as we groan over its placid surface and churn its tranquillity into the roiling turmoil of our own white-watered wake.

My father goes back into the train and reappears with the cheese sandwich which I did not eat and then we go to the stern of the ferry where the other people are tossing food to the convoy of screaming gulls which follows us on our way. The gulls are the whitest things that I have ever seen; whiter than the sheets on my bed at home, or the pink-eyed rabbit that died, or the winter's first snow. I think that since they are so beautiful they should somehow have more manners and in some way be more refined. There is one mottled brown, who feels very ill at ease and flies low and to the left of the noisy main flock. When he ventures into the thick of the fray his fellows scream and peck at him and drive him away. All three of us try to toss our pieces of cheese sandwich to him or into the water directly before him. He is so lonesome and all alone.

When we get to the other side we change trains. A blond young man is hanging from a slowly chugging train with one hand and drinking from a bottle which he holds in the other. I think it is a very fine idea and ask my father to buy me some pop. He says he will later but is strangely embarrassed. As we cross the tracks to our train, the blond young man begins to sing: "There once was a maid." It is not the nice version but the dirty one which I and my friends have learned from the bigger boys in the sixth grade. I have somehow never before thought of grown-ups singing it. My parents are now walking very fast, practically dragging me by the hand over the troublesome tracks. They are both very red-faced and we all pretend we do not hear the voice that is receding in the distance.

When we are seated on the new train I see that my mother is very angry. "Ten years," she snaps at my father, "ten years I've raised this child in the city of Montreal and he has never seen an adult drink liquor out of a bottle, nor heard that kind of language. We have not been here five minutes and that is the first thing he sees and hears." She is on the verge of tears.

"Take it easy, Mary," says my father soothingly. "He doesn't understand. It's all right."

"It's not all right," says my mother passionately. "It's not all right at all. It's dirty and filthy and I must have been out of my mind to agree to this trip. I wish we were going back tomorrow."

The train starts to move and before long we are rattling along the shore. There are fishermen in little boats who wave good-naturedly at the train and I wave back. Later there are the black gashes of coal mines which look like scabs upon the greenness of the hills and the blueness of the ocean and I wonder if these are the mines in which my relatives work.

This train goes much slower than the last one and seems to stop every five minutes. Some of the people around us are talking in a language that I know is Gaelic although I do not understand it, others are sprawled out in their seats, some of them drowsing with their feet stuck out in the aisle. At the far end of the aisle two empty bottles roll endlessly back and forth clinking against themselves and the steel-bottomed seats. The coach creaks and sways.

The station is small and brown. There is a wooden platform in front of it illuminated by lights which shine down from two tall poles and are bombarded by squads of suicidal moths and June bugs.

Beneath the lights there are little clusters of darkly clad men who talk and chew tobacco, and some ragged boys about my own age who lean against battered bicycles waiting for the bundles of newspapers that thud on the platform before their feet.

Two tall men detach themselves from one of the groups and approach us. I know they are both my uncles although I have only seen the younger one before. He lived at our house during part of the year that was the first grade and used to wrestle with me on the floor and play the violin records when no one was in. Then one day he was gone forever to survive only in my mother's neutral "It was the year your brother was here," or the more pointed "It was the year your drunken brother was here."

Now both men are very polite. They shake hands with my father and say "Hello Angie" and then, taking off their caps, "How do you do" to my mother. Then each of them lifts me up in the air. The younger one asks me if I remember him and I say "Yes" and he laughs, and puts me down. They carry our suitcases to a taxi and then we all bounce along a very rough street and up a hill, bump, bump, and stop before a large dark house which we enter.

In the kitchen of the house there are a great many people sitting around a big coal-burning stove even though it is summer. They all get up when we come in and shake hands and the women put their arms around my mother. Then I am introduced to the grandparents I have never seen. My grandmother is very tall with hair almost as white as the afternoon's gulls and eyes like the sea over which they flew. She wears a long black dress with a blue checkered apron over it and lifts me off my feet in powerful hands so that I can kiss her and look into her eyes. She smells of soap and water and hot rolls and asks me how I like living in Montreal. I have never lived anywhere else so I say I guess it is all right.

My grandfather is short and stocky with heavy arms and very big hands. He has brown eyes and his once red hair is almost all white now except for his eyebrows and the hair of his nostrils. He has a white moustache which reminds me of the walrus picture at school and the bottom of it is stained brown by the tobacco that he is chewing even now and spitting the juice into a coal scuttle which he keeps beside his chair. He is wearing a blue plaid shirt and brown trousers supported by heavy suspenders. He too lifts me up although he does not kiss me and he smells of soap and water and tobacco and leather.

He asks me if I saw any girls that I liked on the train. I say "No," and he laughs and lowers me to the floor.

And now it is later and the conversation has died down and the people have gradually filtered out into the night until there are just the three of us, and my grandparents, and after a while my grandmother and my mother go upstairs to finalize the sleeping arrangements. My grandfather puts rum and hot water and sugar into two glasses and gives one to my father and then allows me to sit on his lap even though I am ten, and gives me sips from his glass. He is very different from Grandpa Gilbert in Montreal who wears white shirts and dark suits with a vest and a gold watch-chain across the front.

"You have been a long time coming home," he says to my father. "If you had come through that door as often as I've thought of you I'd've replaced the hinges a good many times."

"I know, I've tried, I've wanted to, but it's different in Montreal you know."

"Yes I guess so. I just never figured it would be like this. It seems so far away and we get old so quickly and a man always feels a certain way about his oldest son. I guess in some ways it is a good thing that we do not all go to school. I could never see myself being owned by my woman's family."

"Please don't start that already," says my father a little angrily. "I am not owned by anybody and you know it. I am a lawyer and I am in partnership with another lawyer who just happens to be my father-in-law. That's all."

"Yes, that's all," says my grandfather and gives me another sip from his glass. "Well, to change the subject, is this the only one you have after being married eleven years?"

My father is now red-faced like he was when we heard the young man singing. He says heatedly: "You know you're not changing the subject at all. I know what you're getting at. I know what you mean."

"Do you?" asks my grandfather quietly. "I thought perhaps that was different in Montreal too."

The two women come downstairs just as I am having another sip from the glass. "Oh Angus what can you be thinking of?" screams my mother rushing protectively toward me.

"Mary, please!" says my father almost desperately, "there's nothing wrong."

My grandfather gets up very rapidly, sets me on the chair he has just vacated, drains the controversial glass, rinses it in the sink and says, "Well, time for the working class to be in bed. Good-night all." He goes up the stairs walking very heavily and we can hear his boots as he thumps them on the floor.

"I'll put him to bed, Mary," says my father nodding toward me. "I know where he sleeps. Why don't you go to bed now? You're tired."

"Yes, all right," says my mother very gently. "I'm sorry. I didn't mean to hurt his feelings. Good-night." She kisses me and also my grandmother and her footsteps fade quietly up the stairs.

"I'm sorry Ma, she didn't mean it the way it sounded," says my father.

"I know. She finds it very different from what she's used to. And we are older and don't bounce back the way we once did. He is seventy-six now and the mine is hard on him and he feels he must work harder than ever to do his share. He works with different ones of the boys and he tells me that sometimes he thinks they are carrying him just because he is their father. He never felt that way with you or Alex but of course you were all much younger then. Still he always somehow felt that because those years between high school and college were so good that you would both come back to him some day."

"But Ma, it can't be that way. I was twenty then and Alex nineteen and he was only in his early fifties and we both wanted to go to college so we could be something else. And we paid him back the money he loaned us and he seemed to want us to go to school then."

"He did not know what it was then. Nor I. And when you gave him back the money it was as if that was not what he'd had in mind at all. And what is the something you two became? A lawyer whom we never see and a doctor who committed suicide when he was twenty-seven. Lost to us the both of you. More lost than Andrew who is buried under tons of rock two miles beneath the sea and who never saw a college door."

"Well, he should have," says my father bitterly, "so should they all instead of being exploited and burrowing beneath the sea or becoming alcoholics that cannot even do that."

"I have my alcoholic," says my grandmother now standing very tall, "who was turned out of my Montreal lawyer's home."

"But I couldn't do anything with him, Ma, and it's different there. You just can't be that way, and—and—oh hell, I don't know; if I were by myself he could have stayed forever."

"I know," says my grandmother now very softly, putting her hand upon his shoulder, "it's not you. But it seems that we can only stay forever if we stay right here. As we have stayed to the seventh generation. Because in the end that is all there is—just staying. I have lost three children at birth but I've raised eight sons. I have one a lawyer and one a doctor who committed suicide, one who died in coal beneath the sea and one who is a drunkard and four who still work the coal like their father and those four are all that I have that stand by me. It is these four that carry their father now that he needs it, and it is these four that carry the drunkard, that dug two days for Andrew's body and that have given me thirty grandchildren in my old age."

"I know, Ma," says my father, "I know that and I appreciate it all, everything. It is just that, well somehow we just can't live in a clan system anymore. We have to see beyond ourselves and our own families. We have to live in the twentieth century."

"Twentieth century?" says my grandmother spreading her big hands across her checkered apron. "What is the twentieth century to me if I cannot have my own?"

It is morning now and I awake to the argument of the English sparrows outside my window and the fingers of the sun upon the floor. My parents are in my room discussing my clothes. "He really doesn't need them," says my father patiently. "But Angus I don't want him to look like a little barbarian," replies my mother as she lays out my newly pressed pants and shirt at the foot of the bed.

Downstairs I learn that my grandfather has already gone to work and as I solemnly eat my breakfast like a little old man beyond my years, I listen to the violin music on the radio and watch my grandmother as she spreads butter on the top of the baking loaves and pokes the coals of her fire with a fierce enthusiasm that sends clouds of smoke billowing up to spread themselves against the yellowed paint upon her ceiling.

Then the little boys come in and stand shyly against the wall. There are seven of them and they are all between six and ten. "These are your cousins," says my grandmother to me and to them she says, "this is Alex from Montreal. He is come to visit with us and you are to be nice to him because he is one of our own."

Then I and my cousins go outside because it is what we are supposed to do and we ask one another what grades we are in and I say I dislike my teacher and they mostly say they like theirs which is a possibility I have never considered before. And then we talk about hockey and I try to remember the times I have been to the Forum in Montreal and what I think about Richard.

And then we go down through the town which is black and smoky and has no nice streets nor flashing lights like Montreal, and when I dawdled behind I suddenly find myself confronted by two older boys who say: "Hey, where'd y'get them sissy clothes?" I do not know what I am supposed to do until my cousins come back and surround me like the covered wagons around the women and children of the cowboy shows.

"This is our cousin," say the oldest two simultaneously and I think they are very fine and brave for they too are probably a little bit ashamed of me and I wonder if I would do the same for them. I have never before thought that perhaps I have been lonely all of my short life and I wish that I had brothers of my own—even sisters perhaps.

My almost-attackers wait awhile scuffing their shoes on the ashy sidewalk and then they separate and allow us to pass like a little band of cavalry going through the mountains.

We continue down through the town and farther beyond to the seashore where the fishermen are mending their gear and pumping the little boats in which they allow us to play. Then we skip rocks on the surface of the sea and I skip one six times and then stop because I know I have made an impression and doubt if I am capable of an encore.

And then we climb up a high, high hill that tumbles into the sea and a cousin says we will go to see the bull who apparently lives about a mile away. We are really out in the country now and it is getting hot and when I go to loosen my tie the collar button comes off and is forever lost in the grass through which we pass.

The bull lives in a big barn and my cousins ask an old man who looks like my grandfather if he expects any cows today. He says that he does not know, that you cannot tell about those things. We can look at the bull if we wish but we must not tease him nor go too close. He is very big and brown and white with a ring in his nose and he paws the floor of his stall and makes low noises while lowering his head and swinging it from side to side. Just as we are ready to leave the old man comes in carrying a long wooden staff which he snaps onto the bull's nose ring. "Well, it looks like you laddies are in luck," he says, "now be careful and get out of the way." I follow my cousins who run out into a yard where a man who has just arrived is standing holding a nervous cow by a halter and we sit appreciatively on the top rail of the wooden fence and watch the old man as he leads out the bull who is now moaning and dripping and frothing at the mouth. I have never seen anything like this before and watch with awe this something that is both beautiful and terrible and I know that I will somehow not be able to tell my mother to whom I have told almost everything important that has happened in my young life.

And later as we leave, the old man's wife gives us some apples and says, "John you should be ashamed of yourself; in front of these children. There are some things that have to be but are not for children's eyes." The chastised old man nods and looks down upon his shoes but then looks up at us very gravely from beneath his bushy eyebrows, looks at us in a very special way and I know that it is only because we are all boys that he does this and that the look as it excludes the woman simultaneously included us in something that I know and feel but cannot understand.

We go back then to the town and it is late afternoon and we have eaten nothing but the apples and as we climb the hill toward my grandparents' house I see my father striding down upon us with his newspaper under his arm.

He is not disturbed that I have stayed away so long and seems almost to envy us our unity and our dirt as he stands so straight and lonely in the prison of his suit and inquires of our day. And so we reply as children do, that we have been "playing," which is the old inadequate message sent forth across the chasm of our intervening years to fall undelivered and unreceived into the nothingness between.

He is going down to the mine, he says, to meet the men when they come off their shift at four and he will take me if I wish. So I separate from my comrade-cousins and go back down the hill holding on to his hand which is something I do not often do. I think that I will tell him about the bull but instead I ask: "Why do all the men chew tobacco?"

"Oh," he says, "because it is a part of them and of their way of life. They do that instead of smoking."

"But why don't they smoke?"

"Because they are underground so much of their lives and they cannot light a match or a lighter or carry any open flame down there. It's because of the gas. Flame might cause an explosion and kill them all."

"But when they're not down there they could smoke cigarettes like

Grandpa Gilbert in a silver cigarette holder and Mama says that chewing tobacco is a filthy habit."

"I know but these people are not at all like Grandpa Gilbert and there are things that Mama doesn't understand. It is not that easy to change what is a part of you."

We are approaching the mine now and everything is black and grimy and the heavily laden trucks are groaning past us. "Did you used to chew tobacco?"

"Yes, a very long time ago before you were ever thought of."

"And was it hard for you to stop?"

"Yes it was, Alex," he said quietly, "more difficult than you will ever know."

We are now at the wash-house and the trains from the underground are thundering up out of the darkness and the men are jumping off and laughing and shouting to one another in a way that reminds me of recess. They are completely black with the exception of little white half-moons beneath their eyes and the eyes themselves. My grandfather is walking toward us between two of my uncles. He is not so tall as they nor does he take such long strides and they are pacing themselves to keep even with him the way my father sometimes does with me. Even his moustache is black or a very dirty grey except for the bottom of it where the tobacco stains it brown.

As they walk they are taking off their headlamps and unfastening the batteries from the broad belts which I feel would be very fine for carrying holsters and six-guns. They are also fishing for the little brass discs which bear their identification numbers. My father says that if they should be killed in the underground these little discs would tell who each man was. It does not seem like much consolation to me.

At a wicket that looks like the post office the men line up and pass their lamps and the little discs to an old man with glasses. He puts the lamps on a rack and the discs on a large board behind his back. Each disc goes on its special little numbered hook and this shows that its owner has returned. My grandfather is 572.

Inside the adjoining wash-house it is very hot and steamy like when you are in the bathroom a long, long time with the hot water running. There are long rows of numbered locks with wooden benches before them. The floor is cement with little wooden slatted paths for the men to walk on as they pass bare-footed to and from the noisy showers at the building's farthest end.

"And did you have a good day today Alex?" asks my grandfather as we stop before his locker. And then unexpectedly and before I can reply he places his two big hands on either side of my head and turns it back and forth very powerfully upon my shoulders. I can feel the pressure of his calloused fingers squeezing hard against my cheeks and pressing my ears into my head and I can feel the fine, fine, coal dust which I know is covering my face and I can taste it from his thumbs which are close against my lips. It is not gritty as I had expected but is more like smoke than sand and almost like my mother's powder. And now he presses my face into his waist and holds me there for a long, long time with my nose bent over against the blackened buckle of his belt. Unable to see or hear or feel or taste or smell anything that is not black; holding me there engulfed and drowning in blackness until I am unable to breathe.

And my father is saying from a great distance: "What are you doing? Let him go! He'll suffocate." And then the big hands come away from my ears and my father's voice is louder and he sounds like my mother.

Now I am so black that I am almost afraid to move and the two men are standing over me looking into one another's eyes. "Oh, well," says my grandfather turning reluctantly toward his locker and beginning to open his shirt.

"I guess there is only one thing to do now," says my father quietly and he bends down slowly and pulls loose the laces of my shoes. Soon I am standing naked upon the wooden slats and my grandfather is the same beside me and then he guides and follows me along the wooden path that leads us to the showers and away from where my father sits. I look back once and see him sitting all alone on the bench which he has covered with his newspaper so that his suit will not be soiled.

When I come to the door of the vast shower room I hesitate because for a moment I feel afraid but I feel my grandfather strong and hairy behind me and we venture out into the pouring water and the lathered, shouting bodies and the cakes of skidding yellow soap. We cannot find a shower at first until one of my uncles shouts to us and a soap-covered man points us in the right direction. We are already wet and the blackness of my grandfather's face is running down in two grey rivulets from the corners of his moustache.

My uncle at first steps out of the main stream but then the three of us stand and move and wash beneath the torrent that spills upon us.

The soap is very yellow and strong. It smells like the men's washroom in the Montreal Forum and my grandfather tells me not to get it in my eyes. Before we leave he gradually turns off the hot water and increases the cold. He says this is so we will not catch cold when we leave. It gets colder and colder but he tells me to stay under it as long as I can and I am covered with goose pimples and my teeth are chattering when I jump out for the last time. We walk back through the washing men who are not so numerous now. Then along the wooden path and I look at the tracks our bare feet leave behind.

My father is still sitting on the bench by himself as we had left him. He is glad to see us return, and smiles. My grandfather takes two heavy towels out of his locker and after we are dry he puts on his clean clothes and I put on the only ones I have except the bedraggled tie which my father stuffs into his pocket. So we go out into the sun and walk up the long, long hill and I am allowed to carry the lunch pail with the thermos bottle rattling inside. We walk very slowly and say very little. Every once in a while my grandfather stops and turns to look back the way we have come. It is very beautiful. The sun is moving into the sea as if it is tired and the sea is very blue and very wide— wide enough it seems for a hundred suns. It touches the sand of the beach which is a slender boundary of gold separating the blue from the greenness of the grass which comes rolling down upon it. Then there is the mine silhouetted against it all, looking like a toy from a meccano set; yet its bells ring as the coal-laden cars fly up out of the deep, grumble as they are unloaded, and flee with thundering power down the slopes they leave behind. Then the blackened houses begin and march row and row up the hill to where we stand and beyond to where we go. Overhead the gulls are flying inland, slowly but steadily as if they are somehow very sure of everything. My grandfather says they always fly inland in the evening. They have done so as long as he can remember.

And now we are entering the yard and my mother is rushing toward me and pressing me to her and saying to everyone and no one, "Where has this child been all day? He has not been here since morning and has eaten nothing. I have been almost out of my mind." She buries her fingers in my hair and I feel very sorry for my mother because I think she loves me very much. "Playing," I say.

At supper I am so tired that I can hardly sit up at the table and my father takes me to bed before it is yet completely dark. I wake up once when I hear my parents talking softly at my door. "I am trying very hard. I really am," says my mother. "Yes, yes I know you are," says my father gently and they move off down the hall.

And now it is in the morning two weeks later and the train that takes us back will be leaving very soon. All our suitcases are in the taxi and the good-byes are almost all completed. I am the last to leave my grandmother as she stands beside her stove. She lifts me up as she did the first night and says, "Good-bye Alex, you are the only grandchild I will never know," and presses into my hand the crinkled dollar that is never spent.

My grandfather is not in although he has not gone to work and they say he has walked on ahead of us to the station. We bump down the hill to where the train is waiting beside the small brown building and he is on the platform talking with some other men and spitting tobacco over the side.

He walks over to us and everyone says good-bye at once. I am again the last and he shakes hands very formally this time. "Good-bye Alex," he said, "it was ten years before you saw me. In another ten I will not be here to see." And then I get on the train and none too soon for already it is beginning to move. Everyone waves but the train goes on because it must and it does not care for waving. From very far away I see my grandfather turn and begin walking back up his hill. And then there is nothing but the creak and sway of the coach and the blue sea with its gulls and the green hills with the gashes of their coal imbedded deeply in their sides. And we do not say anything but sit silent and alone. We have come from a great distance and have a long way now to go.

# Why You Travel

BY

GAIL

MAZUR

~

You don't want the children to know how afraid
you are. You want to be sure their hold on life

is steady, sturdy. Were mothers and fathers
always this anxious, holding the ringing

receiver close to the ear: *Why don't they answer,
where could they be?* There's a conspiracy

to protect the young, so they'll be fearless,
it's why you travel—it's a way of trying

to let go, of lying. You don't sit
in a stiff chair and worry, you keep moving.

Postcards from the Alamo, the Alhambra.
Photos of you in Barcelona, Gaudi's park

swirling behind you. There you are in the Garden
of the Master of the Fishing Nets, one red

tree against a white wall, koi swarming
over each other in the thick demoralized pond.

You, fainting at the Buddhist caves.
Climbing with thousands on the Great Wall,

wearing a straw cap, a backpack, a year
before the students at Tiananmen Square.

Having the time of your life, blistered and smiling.
The acid of your fear could eat the world.

# The Returning

### BY GAIL TREMBLAY

It is these long journeys to the heart
of the continent, moving too fast
thirty thousand feet above the planet
that leave me longing to whisper
to medicine roots that send shoots
as fine as hair for miles to anchor
themselves to ground. The body feels
strangely out of context. I desire
to see agates sparkle among cirrus clouds
stretched out like endless waves
washing no shore. I grow lonely
for the dirt, lonely for the horizon
that marks time in relation to sun
and stars as it spins across the sky.
Up here, there are momentary miracles:
outside Denver, a lake turns golden
as it mirrors sun; clouds and mountains
move together creating atmosphere
for one another as Earth arcs through space.
But this journey is a pause in normal
breathing; a movement through thin air
kept away by delicate walls and will,
this distant place is not meant to sustain
the flesh. Even birds fly miles
below knowing the plants creating
air can only send their life giving
gift so far. It is the returning to Earth
that lets the skin contain the pulse,
the returning to Earth that feeds the muscle
of the heart and makes love possible.

# An Interview with Alison Tilley

## BY
## GILLDA
## LEITENBERG

. . . . . . . . . . . . . . . . . . . . . . . . . . . . . . . . . . . .

*Alison Tilley, 25, is a world-wide traveller and the author of* Tilley Travel Tips for Easy Worry-Free Travelling. *For her, travel is "inspiring, empowering, fascinating...definitely the best thing I've ever done for myself." The following is an excerpt from the transcript of an interview with Alison, as well as an excerpt from her book.*

**Alison, maybe we should start by having you talk a bit about your beginnings. How did you start travelling?**
The beginnings. Well, I did a lot of travelling with my family when I was a kid growing up. We used to go to places like Guatemala and Belize while other families went to Florida and other places that were a little bit more common. Although my family used to bring us to places that were quite off the beaten path, I still didn't learn how to travel independently with them. We'd normally stay with friends who were living in Guatemala, or we'd go on two-week long package tours, or charter a yacht for a couple of weeks. But I wasn't in charge of getting things organized or choosing the location or having to pay for it, or any of that kind of stuff.

When I was sixteen, my father and I went off to Sault St. Marie for a bit of a bonding week together and to take a look at the changing of

Alison in Tonga

the leaves. Unfortunately we were a week early, so all the leaves were still green. I remember seeing a young man from Germany who had a backpack on his back covered with patches from different countries. I remember thinking that there must have been over fifty of these little patches. So I went up to him and I said, "Have you been to all of these countries?" And he said, "Yes." And I said, "How do you do it? Do you fly to one country and then fly home? How do you do it?" And he said, "No, no. I've been travelling around the world non-stop for five years." I said, "Five years!!" It was at that moment I realized that there was a possibility for me to do something like that. The seed was planted.

**What's your favourite spot in the whole world?**
I would say Indonesia although I've seen so little of it. There are over 13 000 islands, and I've seen only three of them. It's really, really beautiful, and has incredible culture. There's so much going on. And it's very cheap. There's incredible surfing if you want to learn how to body surf, electric blue butterflies, beaches, and batiks and fabrics and stunning jewellery and great food and super friendly people. They are so in touch with their spirituality. They place flower offerings outside of their homes to bless them. They put flowers on the roads to encourage good spirits to come so there are no accidents. I find Hindu and Buddhist countries very peaceful and the people very honouring and respectful.

**Do you prefer to travel alone?**

Yes, most of the time. Actually, I started travelling alone because I couldn't find anybody to go with. Most of my friends wanted to go right into university. Some didn't have enough money. Also, it's hard to find somebody who wants to go to the same country, leave at the same time, stay for the same length of time, on the same budget, and who has similar interests.

Sometimes you'll feel lonely, but remember, there are very few places in the world where you can be totally alone. I remember thinking, oh my God, I'm leaving alone, I'm going to be totally alone. At the North Pole and the South Pole, you will be alone. Other than that, just know that there are hundreds of solo travellers who you'll meet along the way. I was amazed at how many young women I met who travelled alone. There's a network of women from all over the world—women from Zimbabwe, Israel, Germany, Canada, and England.

**Are there advantages to travelling alone?**

Yes it's very liberating. You can follow your own agenda, and your only commitment is to yourself. Travelling has made me more self-reliant, aware, and adaptable, which is very important with the way the world is turning now. If new situations come up, I'm able to adapt and survive and get through them. I recognize that change is the only constant in this world. And I'm amazed at how much more confident I am.  A lot of people say, "You're so mature" and I think travelling has helped a lot. Being self-reliant has made me realize that I can fly anywhere in the world now and feel fairly safe, and know that I can get accommodation and look after myself.

**Alison, can you talk about one of your most difficult moments travelling?**

I remember I'd been alone in Bali, Indonesia, for about ten days, and I was sitting in a restaurant one evening contemplating flying back to Canada because for that full day and the day before, I'd been feeling really lonely. I'd isolated myself, didn't go out, and didn't try to meet people at dinner.  I just didn't make an effort. So I was feeling a bit lonely, and I saw this young woman sitting across the restaurant, sitting alone as well. I ended up going over to her table and talking to her. She said that she, too, was really lonely and thinking about England where she was from. The two of us sat together that night talking about how lonely we were when all of a sudden she said that she'd heard about this trip climbing an active volcano that was about a four-hour drive from where we were. She suggested renting a jeep for a couple of days and climbing the volcano before we both went home. I agreed, thinking this trip would not be complete unless we climbed to the top of an active volcano.

We had planned on being together for two or three days but we really connected with each other and ended up spending two and a half weeks together. And I still keep in contact with Emily now, five years later.

Emily and I drove to an area close to the volcano that had cheap accommodation and spoke to other travellers who recommended a friendly guide, and he came to pick us up in our guest house around 3 a.m. The whole plan was that he would pick us up bright and early and we'd get to the top of the volcano to catch the sunrise. That was the goal. And I had expected a leisurely stroll along a well-defined path. Instead, I found myself speedwalking in the darkness to keep up with our guide. The two of us were panting the whole way. Neither of us had brought our flashlights, nor did the guide, so in almost pure darkness we trudged uphill. After about an hour, we crossed a very fertile and intensely cultivated crater that was so steep that we had to use all the strength in our hands and arms to pull ourselves up. I thought I'd just be able to walk up it and get up there. I was totally exhausted and I wanted to stop, and I said to Emily, "Listen, I've had enough. I don't want to do this any more." And she said, "Well, I do. So, either you walk back down by yourself and wait for us in the dark, or you come up with us." So I decided to do it, and asked the guide if he could just slow down the pace a little bit.

At an altitude of about 4500 feet [1350 m] I grabbed a piece of volcano to pull myself up it, and it broke off in my hand. I slid down about thirty feet [nine metres], face first, on my stomach. I just went right down. I had chunks of volcano in my nose, in my eyes, and in my ears. My lips and chin were bleeding. My knees were scraped, my nose was running, and I was bawling my eyes out. Emily looked down and started laughing her head off. She said, "You idiot!! Just get going." I said, "Oh, my God. I just can't do this any more." I was totally defeated, and I'd just totally given up hope on myself. And I said "I can't do it, I just can't do it."

And then something all of a sudden happened, and I realized that there are going to be a lot of challenging mountains in life that I'm going to have to climb and, if I don't climb this one, I'd remember the defeat for years. I realized that it's important to push myself and finish what I start—and just do it.

I really don't know what came over me, but all of a sudden, I was overwhelmed with laughter. I laughed at myself until I cried. Here I was, blood gushing out of my nose, and I was just thinking, "what am I doing here?" When I finally reached the top three hours later, I was overwhelmed by the most spectacular orangy-red sunrise that I'd ever seen. It was amazing. I'll never forget it.

About an hour later our guide suspended a little metal pail, with some soft-boiled eggs in it and suspended it way down a few hundred feet into the bottom part of the volcano where it was bubbly, and cooked us breakfast. He pulled it out five minutes later and the eggs were hard-boiled and sulphur-tasting.

I've also learned that it's easy to organize low-budget, adventurous day-trips independently, just by finding a guide and doing it that way. Another thing I've learned is not to fly home and end my trips early just because I'm feeling lonely for a day or two. I wouldn't have been able to have that experience or meet Emily had I not stayed in Indonesia. I now just accept the fact that, yes, I might feel lonely for a couple of days, but it passes. I just change locations or move somewhere else and open myself up to experiencing new things and meeting new people.

**Alison, what else have you learned from all your travels?**
First, I've learned that the world is a friendly place and that it's quite small when you think about it. Now, when I look at a map of the world, I see that there aren't that many places left where I haven't been. I do see that I'm part of the global community. I wish that more people would travel, because it's made me a lot more peaceful with myself and I think that if more people in the world, instead of doing mandatory military service, did mandatory trips around the world, we would get a real sense of global peace. Other cultures aren't going to want to blow up other cultures once they have more of an understanding. I used to think, why don't the Russians send 100 000 students to the United States to go to school, and vice-versa, do a swap of 100 000 students. There's a less likely chance that they'd want to nuke each other if they've got their future getting trained there.

Travelling has taught me that I can really feel totally alive and free and that it feels good to give myself a breather in the midst of my everyday chaos. It allows me time to clear my mind out and relax and enjoy, and get away from all the pressure. Travelling around the world alone has taught me to become much more self-sufficient and independent and aware of not only myself, but of the glorious world that's around me. Travelling feeds my inner fire, because I fill my days with things I like to do. I snorkel, I sea kayak, I dance on beaches and practise my yoga, I read, I paint, and I enjoy. It's so refreshing to get away from everything that's familiar and to recharge my batteries without any interruption from anyone, which is one of the reasons that I like going alone.

One of the main reasons that I wrote this book is that I know that there are thousands of people in the world who have always dreamed of travelling around the world, but are paralyzed with fear at the thought of going alone, or don't know where to go, or how much it's going to cost, and don't have a clear idea of how to get a trip organized. And I've made a lot of mistakes along the way in my nine years of travelling, but I now look upon these mistakes as learning lessons, and I want to pass them on to other people.

Just do it. That's the main advice, I think, is just go for it and do it. You might need more than a year off between high school and university. It might take you a year just to save the money. You might need three years off like I did, and just know that it's not that big a deal if you start university later than your friends when you'll have a better understanding of who you are. I feel so different now in university than the other students in my class. Even when I watch the news, I understand so much more, because I've been to the countries they're mentioning on the screen. I am much more aware of what's really happening in the world.

**Why should people take time off to travel?**
Because I think you owe it to yourself to live, and to live life as fully as you can. How do you know what interests you until you know what your interests are? It's so incredible living around the world, breathing new air, eating new foods. Toilet water flushes down the toilet in the opposite direction in Australia!! Everything is different around the world. In Guatemala, they wave good-bye differently. When I was in Indonesia somebody died and there was all this cheer and joy, while

this huge procession of people walked with fruit on their heads to cele-brate the fact that the person's spirit was now invited to the next land. The different customs and traditions in different cultures are remark-able.

**From all your travelling, Alison, what would you say is the biggest problem facing us in the world?**
I think the biggest problem is a lack of understanding between cultures. Some countries win and other countries lose. It doesn't have to be that way. It can be "win-win" if we start playing the game differently. I don't think the people who have the power are going to give away the power. I think the people who don't have the power need to rise up with every-one's cooperation. We need to respect that everybody's different. I didn't really have any idea what different people were like until I sat together in a room one day with a Palestinian man, and a woman from Israel, and a guy from Zimbabwe, and a woman from Siberia. And we need to respect different abilities. I was talking to a woman in a wheelchair, and she was telling me how difficult it was to travel in New Zealand because of the hills, and how scary it was to go down a hill with a wheelchair. Being able bodied myself, I'd never even thought of that.

I am very different from most of the people I went to high school with. So many now seem to be settling for this "terminal mediocrity." They're in jobs they don't like, they're in dead-end situations, and they've given up hope.

We are *not* the lost generation, the teens and the twenty-somethings. What about those of us who want to be free and help heal the Earth? We need more people who will travel around the world, take a look and suss out the situation, see what's going wrong, and help to fix it. We'll group together and we'll make a difference.

If you want to do volunteer work, but you don't want to commit yourself to a year in the Peace Corps or the like, or spend a year work-ing at one location, if you want to travel around the world and make a bit of a contribution everywhere you go, call the Peace Corps or other volunteer organizations once you get to a country and say, "Listen. I want to volunteer for two days. Do you happen to know where your people are working? I'd like to help build the school. I'd like to help plant trees with the people of the Sir Edmund Hilary Foundation." There are things you can do to make a difference without having to commit yourself to a lifetime of something.

I'm so happy that this interview is for high school kids, because I know what it's like to want to travel and do something different. You don't have to go, "Baaaaaaaaa"—and sheep your way with all the rest of the herds into the universities and do the frosh scene. If you want to do something different, you can.

**Alison, is there anything else you'd like to say to students reading this interview?**
At university, I thought, how will I know what I want to do unless I've done more things? How do you know at 18 what you want to do for the rest of your life? You don't. Or maybe you do. But at 25, I don't. Different things happen, and you keep growing and learning. It's important to challenge yourself, and keep your mind open to the possibilities, instead of filling your head with a lot of self-limiting beliefs. Look at the glass half-full instead of half-empty. It's hard when you may be going down a different stream or a different path from your other friends, but you've got to fight and do it *your* way. I hope it reassures you to know that there are other people who have done it, and want to encourage you to design a great life for yourself. And once you do the first trip, you'll meet other wanderers, and you'll realize that, yes, indeed, you can be totally different from everybody.

*from*

# Tilley Travel Tips

### PACKING TIPS

◆ Your clothes often indicate the level of respect you show for the cultures you're visiting. Jeans are often inappropriate. The more your body is covered, the better dressed you're generally thought to be.

◆ Remember that in tropical climates, most buildings are air-conditioned and you may need a sweater or shawl for indoor wear.

◆ Look for lightweight, easy-to-care-for, hand-washable clothing. Test each item for comfort by sitting, squatting and kneeling while wearing it.

◆ Consider the customs of the country you're visiting. In a Muslim country, for example, you're not allowed to enter a mosque with bare shoulders. In many places, short shorts are frowned upon. In remote villages in Nepal, it's appropriate to cover most of your body. Women often find culottes or skirts suitable attire just about everywhere, and long shorts are frequently suitable when short shorts aren't.

◆ Never take new shoes on a trip.

◆ When purchasing hiking boots, buy at least half a size too big. This prevents black-and-blue toenails when going down steep hills.

◆ Take a small sewing kit with thread that matches your travel wardrobe.

◆ A pocket calculator is handy for converting foreign currency.

◆ Outside of North America, hotels don't automatically provide toilet paper, a face cloth, a sink stopper, face soap or bath towel: so pack your own.

◆ Take a small day-pack made out of a sturdy fabric. (Thieves can slash lightweight ones).

◆ Pack 2 toothbrushes ( in case you lose one) and dental floss.

# A Trio
# Who Travel
# at the Drop
# of a Hat

~

**BY**

**JUDY**

**ROSS**

uriosity may kill the cat but it keeps the travel writer alive. "Curiosity is what drives us," says *Globe and Mail* columnist Beverly Gray, one of three Toronto journalists, all women over 70, who regularly wing off to far-flung destinations on travel writing assignments. Agreeing with her are Margaret Ness and Laddie Dennis. All of them have been just about everywhere. Ness writes a travel column in *The Toronto Star* and Dennis is a freelance writer and photographer whose work appears in a variety of newspapers and magazines—"even in youth adventure publications!" she says with a laugh.

On Beverly Gray's first trip away on her own, when she was in her 20s, she travelled by train from Calgary to New York City. When she arrived at Grand Central Station in Manhattan, the first person she saw was a neighbor from Calgary. "I was furious," she says. "This was my trip. She had no right to be there." That tale explains Gray's approach to travel. She likes to venture off alone to out-of-the-way places.

Gray moved from Calgary to Toronto in 1951 and became travel editor at *The Globe and Mail* in 1957. She's lived in Toronto and worked for *The Globe* ever since. Although she officially retired in 1982, when she turned 65, Gray still writes her "Ask Away" column and walks from her downtown apartment to *The Globe* offices two days a week.

Although Gray speaks poetically about experiences such as viewing the midnight sun in Antarctica and the special beauty of a desert, she says it is people that really give travel its flavor—especially those who live in out-of-the-way places. "Having to make their own entertainment

l–r: Margaret Ness, Laddie Dennis, Beverly Gray

and struggle for a living gives people a warmth you don't find in big cities," she says. With her fondness for people living in isolated places, it's predictable that her two favourite places in Canada are the Northwest Territories and Newfoundland. On her first visit to Newfoundland, she arrived late at night in St. John's without a hotel reservation. Every room in town was booked. "I was standing despairingly in the hotel lobby," she recounts, "when the hotel manager offered to take me to his home. He had checked with his wife and they gave me their spare room. In what other city in the world would something like that happen?"

The most interesting countries Gray has been to, she says, are Israel and Egypt. "Visiting Israel is like stepping back into the Bible." And she loves Egypt, where she feels oddly at home. On one of her many trips to the Middle East, she discovered a way to avoid being pestered to death in the marketplaces. "There are always young boys hanging around markets who can be hired as guides for a few dollars," she explains. "You then become their property and they hold everyone off. It always works."

Gray seeks out adventure,

not pampering, when she travels, so comfortable clothes and shoes are higher on her list than looking well dressed. "I always tell people to remember that nobody knows you when you're travelling," she says. One essential for her is a crushable hat that keeps the sun off. "It's made of reeds, folds to nothing and I've had it for years," says Gray as she plops it on her head. "I take it everywhere, even though it makes me look like a perambulating mushroom." Gray seems blessed not only with a sense of humor but with good health, although she does observe certain practices to ensure she stays healthy on the road. "Always get the necessary inoculations," she suggests, and in countries with untreated drinking water, "don't use tap water when brushing your teeth and avoid salads."

As a woman who has travelled alone throughout much of the world, she says, "Women shouldn't be afraid, because when you travel alone, people worry about you and look after you. You meet a lot of nice people along the way. I'm amazed by how nice people are, but I have learned to melt and run, if necessary." She advises women to be adaptable, to expect the unexpected and to take help where you get it.

When choosing a travel agent for a major trip, Gray recommends you watch the travel section in your local newspaper to see if any agency specializes in that destination. Phone, explain what you want to do and ask for an appointment with someone knowledgeable. That way, you're likely to get someone who knows the destination. A lot of travel agencies specialize in travel arrangements for singles and for older people. For single women, she thinks it's best, on a cruise for instance, to ask for a roommate rather than pay the "annoying" single supplement. "Often you'll end up with a single room anyway and you've paid far less."

Gray has learned to rely on cab drivers in small towns and on islands for help finding restaurants and hotels. "Generally, they're the best source of information about a place." And because she doesn't drive, she goes to the government tourist office when she arrives in a foreign town and asks for help finding a reliable English-speaking driver. "You can learn more about a place from a driver than from any guidebook," says Gray.

What is it that keeps Beverly Gray on the road? For one thing, a joy in seeing the world unfold. "This may sound crazy," she says, "but I try to travel during a full moon when I go somewhere spectacular. Do you have any idea how beautiful the Sphinx looks sitting in the Egyptian desert lit up by the full moon? Or the Rockies, with the snow reflected in the moonlight?" The other, she claims, is "a need to always be going somewhere." She remembers one early morning in India when she was waiting to be picked up to head off to a new destination. It was already hot and perspiration was streaming down her face, but she was elated because she was going somewhere. "Then it suddenly dawned on me," she laughs, "I *am* somewhere already."

With her enthusiasm, it's no wonder that Gray is still wide-eyed about visiting new places. In fact, she takes the earnings from her column and uses them to "fill in the gaps in my travels."

Journalist Margaret Ness has written fashion for The Canadian Press and was women's editor for *Saturday Night* magazine during the 1950s. In 1962, she took off for Europe and was bitten by the travel bug. Since then, she has been in most countries of the world except China, Japan and Russia. She began writing about her travels for *The Toronto Star* many years ago, when the travel editor asked her to do a question-and-answer column for the paper. She's been writing it ever since.

Like Gray, Ness believes that people make the place and that communication is important. She suggests preparing for a visit to foreign countries by learning beforehand, in proper pronunciation, some basic phrases such as good morning and thank you. When she doesn't know the language, she carries a card with the printed address of her destination. "Someone always takes pity on me," she says. "One time, I was standing in the wrong queue at a bus station in Romania. A person took me out of the queue, crossed the street with me, ensured I was in the right place and then had to go back to the end of the other line himself."

Ness loves to poke around in museums and to wander through historic castles or palaces. Her favorite city in the world is Vienna. "I must have a romantic streak," she muses, "because I adore the Strauss waltzes, Viennese coffee, the beautiful buildings. I have been many times."

Tipping in foreign places always presents problems, and neither Ness nor the others claim to have all the answers. Ness recommends carrying American currency in small bills, which can be used for tipping everywhere. And Laddie Dennis always likes to tip the chambermaids who, she feels, are often forgotten.

As someone who has seen almost all the rest of the world, Ness gets annoyed that Canadians aren't more proud of this country: "Once I was on a bus tour driving through the Rockies. The driver was speeding along and finally someone asked him to slow down. He looked back and said, 'Why should I? There's nothing to see but the scenery.'" Ness finds it hard to choose a favorite place in Canada because they're all so different and beautiful in their own way. "They're all a part of us," she says. "I feel like a mother with her children. I don't want to say something special about one that all the others can hear."

Winnipeg-born Laddie Dennis says she collects countries the way bird-watchers collect birds. And she has a little black book to prove it. Meticulously listed on page after page is every place she has ever been. The list is long and exotic. It all began when she went to Morocco in 1970 and, encouraged by a journalist friend, wrote an article entitled "A Woman Alone in Morocco." She sold it to the now-defunct *Toronto Telegram* and says, "If I hadn't sold that story, I'm sure I would have given up and missed out on the 22 exciting years of travel that followed."

Like the others, Dennis is whittling away at the list of places she still wants to see. She prefers to travel alone "because I am less conspicuous and more approachable. I find people in foreign places won't talk to you readily if you already have your company." Even though she's been to some scary places, she doesn't scare easily; she does, however, always rely on the advice of the locals regarding safety precautions. "When three separate people in Bogota [Colombia] told me how to carry my purse, I listened." But the warnings didn't dissuade Dennis from touring the city on her own.

Dennis, also a photographer, "lugs 11 1/2 pounds [5.1 kg] of camera equipment with her on every trip. She finds that taking photographs is a great way to meet people if you approach them gently by showing interest in what they're doing. Also a people person, Dennis says that if you do so, the person will understand why you want to take a picture. Some places, though, have strong taboos about photographs and you really have to honor that.

Dennis loves the freedom of trains, her favorite mode of transportation. Over the years, she's chugged her way around Sri Lanka, India, through the

Canadian Rockies and across parts of Europe, but one of her favorite rides was a 12-hour journey in Peru. "There were no rules about where to sit on the train, and I just sat on the stairs by the open doors looking at the llamas," as the train moved across a rugged wind-swept plateau high in the Andes mountains.

Dennis, a great advocate of advance research, says public libraries have all the latest guidebooks on a country and sometimes vertical files as well. She recommends contacting the tourist boards of the places you'll be visiting to ask them to send you all sorts of information, including maps. She also suggests relying on a travel agency (with experienced staff who travel a lot) to find legitimate travel bargains. "Cheap can be a disaster," she warns. Like her fellow travel writers, Dennis works at keeping healthy and believes in being rested and fit before travelling. "I actually train before going on a trip by doing more exercise," says Dennis, who is a regular cyclist and swimmer. "But while I'm travelling, just carrying around my camera equipment and suitcase keeps me fit."

Because Dennis likes to bring home valued souvenirs, such as delicate wood carvings from Burma and clay pottery from Ethiopia, her favorite piece of luggage is a hard-sided suitcase. While packing, she makes a list of everything (and keeps it separate from the suitcase), so if the bag is lost she has an immediate reminder of what was in it. Also in this list are travel essentials, such as a travel clock, passport and two pairs of glasses; she ticks off each item on the list every time she packs, and nothing is forgotten.

Dennis, not at all ready to pamper herself on trips, has been saving the more accessible places like Canada for "old age." "I always thought I would leave travelling in Canada until I was senile," she laughs, "hoping, I guess, that my own would take care of me." She does admit to a soft spot for Montreal, which she considers "our most vibrant and interesting city," and counts among her world-favorite hotels the Montreal Ritz-Carlton, which she calls "an elegant and welcoming embrace in the heart of the city."

Despite all her travelling, Laddie Dennis has a file folder, almost two inches thick, listing places she still wants to visit. "Before I take that final journey," she says wryly, "I must get to Timbuktu. That way my epitaph can read, 'She went everywhere from here to Timbuktu.'"

*from*

# The Accidental
# Tourist

~

**BY**

**ANNE**

**TYLER**

**M**ost of his work was done at home; otherwise he might not have cared so about the mechanics of the household. He had a little study in the spare room off the kitchen. Seated in a stenographer's chair, tapping away at a typewriter that had served him through four years of college, he wrote a series of guidebooks for people forced to travel on business. Ridiculous, when you thought about it: Macon hated travel. He careened through foreign territories on a desperate kind of blitz—squinching his eyes shut and holding his breath and hanging on for dear life, he sometimes imagined—and then settled back home with a sigh of relief to produce his chunky, passport-sized paperbacks. *Accidental Tourist in France. Accidental Tourist in Germany. In Belgium.* No author's name, just a logo: a winged armchair on the cover.

He covered only the cities in these guides, for people taking business trips flew into cities and out again and didn't see the countryside at all. They didn't see the cities, for that matter. Their concern was how to pretend they had never left home. What hotels in Madrid boasted king-sized Beautyrest mattresses? What restaurants in Tokyo offered Sweet'n' Low? Did Amsterdam have a McDonald's? Did Mexico City have a Taco Bell? Did any place in Rome serve Chef Boyardee ravioli? Other travelers hoped to discover distinctive local wines; Macon's readers searched for pasteurized and homogenized milk.

As much as he hated the travel, he loved the writing—the virtuous delights of organizing a disorganized country, stripping away the inessential and the second-rate, classifying all that remained in neat, terse paragraphs. He cribbed from other guidebooks, seizing small kernels of value and discarding the rest. He spent pleasurable hours dithering over questions of punctuation. Righteously, mercilessly, he weeded out the passive voice. The effort of typing made the corners of his mouth turn down, so that no one could have guessed how much he was enjoying himself. *I am happy to say,* he pecked out, but his face remained glum and intense. *I am happy to say that it's possible now to buy Kentucky Fried Chicken in Stockholm. Pita bread, too,* he added as an afterthought. He wasn't sure how it had happened, but lately pita had grown to seem as American as hot dogs....

For his trip to England, he dressed in his most comfortable suit. *One suit is plenty,* he counseled in his guidebooks, *if you take along some travel-size packets of spot remover.* (Macon knew every item that came in travel-size packets, from deodorant to shoe polish.) *The suit should be a medium gray. Gray not only hides the dirt; it's handy for sudden funerals and other formal events. At the same time, it isn't too somber for everyday.*

He packed a minimum of clothes and a shaving kit. A copy of his most recent guide to England. A novel to read on the plane.

*Bring only what fits in a carry-on bag. Checking your luggage is asking for trouble. Add several travel-size packets of detergent so you won't fall into the hands of foreign laundries.*

When he'd finished packing, he sat on the couch to rest. Or not to rest, exactly, but to collect himself—like a man taking several deep breaths before diving into a river.

The furniture was all straight lines and soothing curves. Dust motes hung in a slant of sunlight. What a peaceful life he led here! If this were any other day he'd be making some instant coffee. He would drop the spoon in the sink and stand sipping from his mug while the cat wove between his feet. Then maybe he'd open the mail. Those acts seemed dear and gentle now. How could he have complained of boredom? At home he had everything set up around him so he hardly needed to think. On trips, even the smallest task required effort and decisions.

When it was two hours till takeoff, he stood up. The airport was a thirty-minute drive at the most, but he hated feeling rushed. He made a final tour of the house, stopping off at the downstairs bathroom—the last *real* bathroom (was how he thought of it) that he'd see for the next week. He whistled for the dog. He picked up his bag and stepped out the front door....

On the flight to New York, he sat next to a foreign-looking man with a mustache. Clamped to the man's ears was a headset for one of those miniature tape recorders. Perfect: no danger of conversation. Macon leaned back in his seat contentedly.

He approved of planes. When the weather was calm, you couldn't even tell you were moving. You could pretend you were sitting safe at home. The view from the window was always the same—air and more air—and the interior of one plane was practically interchangeable with the interior of any other.

He accepted nothing from the beverage cart, but the man beside him took off his headset to order a Bloody Mary. A tinny, intricate, Middle Eastern melody came whispering out of the pink sponge earplugs. Macon stared down at the little machine and wondered if he should buy one. Not for the music, heaven knows—there was far too much noise in the world already—but for insulation. He could plug himself into it and no one would disturb him. He could play a blank tape: thirty full minutes of silence. Turn the tape over and play thirty minutes more.

They landed at Kennedy and he took a shuttle bus to his connecting flight, which wasn't due to leave till evening. Once settled in the terminal, he began filling out a crossword puzzle that he'd saved for this occasion from last Sunday's *New York Times*. He sat inside a kind of barricade—his bag on one chair, his suit coat on another. People milled around him but he kept his eyes on the page, progressing smoothly to the acrostic as soon as he'd finished the crossword. By the time he'd solved both puzzles, they were beginning to board the plane.

His seatmate was a gray-haired woman with glasses. She had brought her own knitted afghan. This was not a good sign, Macon felt, but he could handle it. First he bustled about, loosening his tie and taking off his shoes and removing a book from his bag. Then he opened the book and ostentatiously started reading.

The name of his book was *Miss MacIntosh, My Darling,* and it was 1198 pages long. *(Always bring a book, as protection against strangers. Magazines don't last. Newspapers from home will make you homesick, and newspapers from elsewhere will remind you you don't belong. You know how alien another paper's typeface seems.)* He'd been lugging around Miss MacIntosh for years. It had the advantage of being plotless, as far as he could tell, but invariably interesting, so he could dip into it at random. Any time he raised his eyes, he was careful to mark a paragraph with his finger and to keep a bemused expression on his face.

There was the usual mellifluous murmur from the loudspeaker about seatbelts, emergency exits, oxygen masks. He wondered why stewardesses accented such unlikely words. "*On* our flight this evening we *will* be offering..." The woman next to him asked if he wanted a Lifesaver. "No, thank you," Macon said, and he went on with his book. She rustled some little bit of paper, and shortly afterward the smell of spearmint drifted over to him.

He refused a cocktail and he refused a supper tray, although he did accept the milk that was offered with it. He ate an apple and a little box of raisins from his bag, drank the milk, and went off to the lavatory to floss and brush his teeth. When he returned the plane was darker, dotted here and there with reading lamps. Some of the passengers were already asleep. His seatmate had rolled her hair into little O's and X-ed them over with bobby pins. Macon found it amazing that people could be so unself-conscious on airplanes. He'd seen men in whole suits of pajamas; he'd seen women slathered in face cream. You would think they felt no need to be on guard.

He angled his book beneath a slender shaft of light and turned a page. The engines had a weary, dogged sound. It was the period he thought of as the long haul—the gulf between supper and breakfast when they were suspended over the ocean, waiting for that lightening of the sky that was supposed to be morning although, of course, it was nowhere near morning back home. In Macon's opinion, morning in other time zones was like something staged—a curtain painted with a rising sun, superimposed upon the real dark.

He let his head tip back against the seat and closed his eyes. A stewardess's voice, somewhere near the front of the plane, threaded in and out of the droning of the engines. "We just sat and sat and there wasn't a thing to do and all we had was the Wednesday paper and you know how news just never seems to happen on a Wednesday..."

At dawn he accepted a cup of coffee, and he swallowed a vitamin pill from his bag. The other passengers looked frowsy and pale. His seatmate dragged an entire small suitcase off to the lavatory and returned all combed, but her face was puffy. Macon believed that travel causes retention of fluids. When he put his shoes on, they felt too tight, and when he went to shave he found unfamiliar pillows of flesh beneath his eyes. He was better off than most people, though, because he hadn't touched salted food or drunk any alcohol. Alcohol was definitely retained. Drink alcohol on a plane and you'd feel befuddled for days, Macon believed.

The stewardess announced what time it was in London, and there was a stir as people reset their watches. Macon adjusted the digital alarm clock in his shaving kit. The watch on his wrist—which was not digital but real time, circular—he left as it was.

They landed abruptly. It was like being recalled to the hard facts—all that friction suddenly, the gritty runway, the roaring and braking. The loudspeaker came on, purring courteous reminders. The woman next to Macon folded her afghan. "I'm so excited," she said. "I'm going to see my grandchild for the very first time." Macon smiled and told her he hoped it went well. Now that he didn't have to fear being trapped, he found her quite pleasant. Besides, she was so American-looking.

At Heathrow, there was the usual sense of some recent disaster. People rushed about distractedly, other people stood like refugees surrounded by trunks and parcels, and uniformed authorities were trying to deal with a clamor of questions. Since he didn't have to wait for his luggage, Macon sailed through the red tape far ahead of the others. Then he exchanged his currency and boarded the Underground. *I recommend the Underground for everyone except those afraid of heights, and even for them if they will avoid the following stations, which have exceptionally steep escalators...*

While the train racketed along, he sorted his currency into envelopes that he'd brought from home—each envelope clearly marked with a different denomination. *(No fumbling with unfamiliar coins, no peering at misleading imprints, if you separate and classify foreign money ahead of time.)* Across from him a row of faces watched. People looked different here, although he couldn't say just how. He thought they were both finer and unhealthier. A woman with a fretful baby kept saying, "Hush now, love. Hush now, love," in that clear, floating, effortless English voice. It was hot, and her forehead had a pallid shine. So did Macon's, no doubt. He slid the envelopes into his breast pocket. The train stopped and more people got on. They stood above him, clinging not to straps but to bulbs attached to flexible sticks, which Macon on his first visit had taken for some kind of microphone.

He was based in London, as usual. From there he would make brief forays into other cities, never listing more than a handful of hotels, a handful of restaurants within a tiny, easily accessible radius in each place; for his guidebooks were anything but all-inclusive. ("Plenty of other books say how to see as much of a city as possible," his boss had told him. "You should say how to see as little.") The name of Macon's hotel was the Jones Terrace. He would have preferred one of the American chain hotels, but those cost too much. The Jones Terrace was all right, though—small and well kept. He swung into action at once to make his room his own, stripping off the ugly bedspread and stuffing it into a closet, unpacking his belongings and hiding his bag. He changed clothes, rinsed the ones he'd worn and hung them in the shower stall. Then, after a wistful glance at the bed, he went out for breakfast. It was nowhere near morning back home, but breakfast was the meal that businessmen most often had to manage for themselves. He made a point of researching it thoroughly wherever he went.

He walked to the Yankee Delight, where he ordered scrambled eggs and coffee. The service here was excellent. Coffee came at once, and his cup was kept constantly filled. The eggs didn't taste like eggs at home, but then, they never did. What was it about restaurant eggs? They had no character, no backbone. Still, he opened his guidebook and put a checkmark next to the Yankee Delight. By the end of the week, these pages would be barely legible. He'd have scratched out some names, inserted others, and scrawled notes across the margins. He always revisited past entries—every hotel and restaurant. It was tedious but his boss insisted. "Just think how it would look," Julian said, "if a reader walked into some café you'd recommended and found it taken over by vegetarians."

When he'd paid his bill, he went down the street to the New America, where he ordered more eggs and more coffee. "Decaffeinated," he added. (He was a jangle of nerves by now.) The waiter said they didn't have decaffeinated. "Oh, you don't," Macon said. After the waiter had left, Macon made a note in his guidebook.

His third step was a restaurant called the U.S. Open, where the sausages were so dry that they might have been baked on a rooftop. It figured: The U.S. Open had been recommended by a reader. Oh, the places that readers wrote in to suggest! Macon had once (before he'd grown wiser) reserved a motel room purely on the strength of such a suggestion—somewhere in Detroit or was it Pittsburgh, some city or other, for *Accidental Tourist in America*. He had checked out again at first sight of the linens and fled across the street to a Hilton, where the doorman had rushed to meet him and seized his bag with a cry of pity as if Macon had just staggered in from the desert. Never again, Macon had vowed. He left the sausages on his plate and called for his bill.

In the afternoon (so to speak), he visited hotels. He spoke with various managers and inspected sample rooms where he tested the beds, flushed the toilets, squinted at the showerheads. Most were maintaining their standards, more or less, but something had happened to the Royal Prince. The fact was that it seemed...well, foreign. Dark, handsome men in slim silk suits murmured in the lobby while little brown children chased each other around the spittoons. Macon had the feeling he'd got even more hopelessly lost than usual and ended up in Cairo. Cone-shaped ladies in long black veils packed the revolving doors, spinning in from the street with shopping bags full of...what? He tried to imagine their purchasing stone-washed denim shorts and thigh-high boots or pink mesh—the merchandise he'd seen in most shop windows. "Er..." he said to the manager. How to put this? He hated to sound narrow-minded, but his readers did avoid the exotic. "Has the hotel ah, changed ownership?" he asked. The manager seemed unusually sensitive. He drew himself up and said the Royal Prince was owned by a corporation, always had been and always would be, always the same corporation. "I see," Macon said. He left feeling dislocated.

At suppertime, he should have tried someplace formal. He had to list at least one formal restaurant in every city for entertaining clients. But tonight he wasn't up to it. Instead, he went to a café he liked called My American Cousin. The diners there had American accents, and so did some of the staff, and the hostess handed out tickets at the door with numbers on them. If your number was called on the loudspeaker you could win a free TV, or at least a framed color print of the restaurant.

Macon ordered a comforting supper of plain boiled vegetables and two lamb chops in white paper bobby socks, along with a glass of milk. The man at the next table was also on his own. He was eating a nice pork pie, and when the waitress offered him dessert he said, "Oh, now, let me see, maybe I will try some at that," in the slow, pleased, coax-me drawl of someone whose womenfolks have all his life encouraged him to put a little meat on his bones. Macon himself had the ginger-bread. It came with cream, just the way it used to at his grandmother's house.

By eight o'clock, according to his wristwatch, he was in bed. It was much too early, of course, but he could stretch the day only so far; the English thought it was midnight. Tomorrow he would start his whirl-wind dashes through other cities. He'd pick out a few token hotels, sample a few token breakfasts. Coffee with caffeine and coffee without caffeine. Bacon underdone and overdone. Orange juice fresh and canned and frozen. More showerheads, more mattresses. Hairdryers supplied on request? 110-volt switches for electric shavers? When he fell asleep, he thought anonymous rooms were revolving past on a merry-go-round. He thought webbed canvas suitcase stands, ceiling sprinklers, and laminated lists of fire regulations approached and slid away and approached again, over and over all the rest of his days.

# Trickster Time

**BY**

**JEANNETTE CHRISTINE ARMSTRONG**

We saw trickster
there at the airport
only he wasn't raven form
coyote nanabush napi or wasakeja
I suppose we expected he might at least be Indian
looking cool dripping braids buckskin and turquoise
after all the six of us writers on the way to Aoteroa
were Cree Okanagan Nanaimo Salish Inuit and Mohawk
we know him by whatever name
he hides under
We six saw him
sitting on the Canadian Air computer
laughing as it went down
tap tapping his cane
"Sorry" said the agent
"I can't seem to pull you up"
"Tickets to Auckland hm mm mm"
tap tap tap tap
the sound was somehow different
"No luck, computer's acting up"
flaming red hair cherubic grin
trickster spins and tap tap dances on the bag's belt
behind the counter
green vested suit dapper and toes clicking
he disappears

"Let's move to another one. We might have better luck getting
        you up from the files."
instead trickster comes popping up
on the screen this time
tap tap tap tapping across the keys
the cursor moves and trickster bounces across the screen
laughing hysterically and keeping time
from moving
"I can't believe the weird things this machine is doing."
The agent is sweating "I'm sorry you are cutting it too close.
I'm not sure I can help you at this terminal. Take your tickets
and run for it down the stairs to the International agent"
clap clap clap clap our heels click across the cement
down the escalator
tap tap tap trickster slides down the rail
legs crossed
twirling his cane
top hat askew tap tap tap
down the corridor racing time
trickster appears at the shoulder of the new agent
pant pant pant  tap tap tap tap

"I'm sorry we seem to be experiencing a system shut down. The
flight is closed. We didn't get you on before the shut down. I
could try Delta for you. They might have seats. Wait right here."
slap slap slap tap tap tap "YES!"
"Yes you are on and you still connect in L.A. Come on!"
tap tap tap tap trickster laughs and laughs
this time rolling around atop the flight monitor
tap tap tap tap
the BOARDING NOW light flashes flash flash flash
"Sorry too late for that one, let's dash back over and talk to
Canadian" pant pant pant pant
"Hey we might get you on after all. The computer won't let them
shut down. Run!" gasp gasp gasp gasp
tap tap tap tap tap

"What is going on, this is crazy. Why won't they clear you?"
The Canadian agent is getting flustered and we six laugh
breathlessly we say "trickster" in unison
the computer agent's face lights up and she nods
she knows trickster
The Canadian agent looks at us nervously and shouts
"Don't pull the tags for the Delta flight yet"
chug chug chug luggage back to the Delta counter
"Wait here!"
what else can we do
tap tap tap tap tap trickster reappears
behind the Delta counter jigging this time fast
Delta agent hurries up "They got seats at 2:30 and still can
connect in L.A." "Yes" sighs the Canadian agent
"Yes that will do" we all sigh
we smile at him he has been extraordinary
we're not worried we can wait
we know there must be a reason
we can have the time to have a bite
the time to relax that's what we needed
boarding cards in hand we all sip coffee
no sign of trickster
we search the faces of passersby
travellers of all sorts
they all look away
Indians searching faces
for any sign of trickster's familiar gestures
makes people uncomfortable
no he is gone
we six begin to slowly believe we made it okay
1 pm "Let's go down early this time just in case."
we all agree
all fine past the Delta counter
all the way up to U.S. customs
"Passports please"
and then tap tap tap tap
the immigration agent's brow furrows
"Hmm mm mmmm something coming up on the screen.
    Hummmmm you sir,
step over here please, the rest of you wait over by that counter."

tap tap tap tap he is back tapping his cane
inside the glass cage
he looks sombre
tap tap tap tap
"Sorry you can't go through sir. The U.S. classifies you as an
undesirable alien.
trickster flops over on his back and closes his eyes
red hair sticking straight up
face red and ashamed looking
we all stop breathing and look at each other
"What will we do!"
under the breath anger
"What the hell, none in this party that are aliens. YOU all are
aliens don't you remember THAT."
but nobody's face betrays the weak moment
tick tick tick tick more time passes
it's hard to stay positive
tap tap tap tap trickster reappears
behind the consulate desk
"Hmm mmm let me see now" the agent drums his finger
tap tap tap TAP TAP
trickster turns and winks at us GOT HIM
"Seeing that you are travelling with a party, if you fill in this
form to guarantee that you will continue on we will allow you a
temporary stop in L.A. on the way to New Zealand."
"I wasn't planning otherwise. It's right there on my ticket."
consulate agent looks sharply
sees only a humour filled grin
detects sarcasm
that would have cost too much time
tap tap tap tap into the computer
"Yes, here you go, just give this to the agent."
trickster bows slightly
tips his hat
spins on his heel and disappears behind the glassed wall
click click click the computers click away
we all breathe easier
things get back to normal
we six laugh running down the corridor

"So that's what we needed the time for!"
time to clear the path
in good time
Indian time
the right time
trickster comes just in the nick of it
they didn't see him again of course
good thing I guess
they wouldn't have known him anyway
he looked just like one of them
behind the computers
a good thing to remember too
Irish blood comes in handy at times

*Jeannette Armstrong recorded this on paper*
*somewhere in the air*
*between Vancouver and Aoteroa/New Zealand*
*over the international time line*

*sometime between yesterday and tomorrow*
*whichever suits you best as we seem to have lost*
*December 1, 1990, unexplainably*
*somewhere in the time zone she chooses that date*
*to set this in memory in thin air*

# Wide Horizons

~

### BY
### PETER E. TARLOW
### AND
### MITCHELL J. MUEHSAM

ravel and tourism is perhaps the world's largest industry, with some $2 trillion in annual travel-related sales around the world. The travel industry plays a major role in the spheres of business, recreation, and family life.

During the last third of this century, a number of phenomena have occurred to promote mass travel, including discount air fares, the building of superhighways, the growth of the motel industry, and the abolishment in many cases of international visas. Free-trade zones have facilitated the growth of international business and business travel and will continue to fuel greater travel.

The health revolution, which has given millions of elderly persons relatively good health well into their 80s, has also driven tourism's growth. The population of 45- to 64-year-olds will grow nearly five times faster than the total population between 2000 and 2010; between 2010 and 2030, the population over 65 will grow eight times faster than the total population. Aging populations are just one factor that will have strong impacts on travel and tourism in the twenty-first century; already, travellers over age 60 make up 32% of all room nights sold within the lodging industry, according to the American Hotel and Motel Association.

Tourism specialists are keenly aware that these and other major changes are ahead as the new century dawns. The following areas are but a partial list of sometimes conflicting factors that will influence the travel industry of the twenty-first century.

## Technology and Travel

- **Communications as "electronic travel."** Electronic communications of the twentieth century, including telephones, radios, television, and fax machines, have replaced the messenger of yesteryear. Future advances such as two-way visual telephones and improved computer networking will decrease the need to travel and will save both money and time. Business people will no longer be required to travel from one spot to another to close deals. Rather, they'll negotiate "face to face" via electronic conferencing and sign contracts despite being physically separated by thousands of miles. Similarly, families divided by great distances will remain electronically connected with each other.

    Electronic communications will also give rise to mobile offices, allowing executives to take work with them, whether they're at home, at the health club, or on "working vacations."

    To counterbalance this new age of electronic travel, consumers will see the transportation component of tomorrow's travel industry emphasize the personal touch. The theme of one recent airline ad, for instance, is that "you can telex it there, send it there, or fax it there, but there is no alternative to being there." With less *need* to travel, those who do travel in the next century will demand greater levels of fast, efficient, and courteous service from transportation companies.

    Competition from electronic mail will force the travel industry to make traveling as comfortable as possible and offer more perks and benefits. Electronic mail may even help increase business travel: As the world becomes more interconnected, corporations will want to send even their lower-level executives on international fact-finding missions. These journeys will provide the next generation of business leaders with on-site training into the mind-set of their international partners—and competitors.

- **Traveler as travel agent**. Personal computers connected into worldwide reservation systems will allow many travelers to book, ticket, and purchase all of their travel arrangements from the convenience of their home or office.

- **Robots at your service.** Personal robots will become increasingly proficient at performing a multitude of services, such as greeting guests, baby-sitting, and performing security tasks. While some guests may resent the loss of the human touch, robots will allow travel industries to offer more consistent service, working tirelessly through peak seasons and retiring uncomplainingly into storage during the off-season.

## Energy Trends and Advanced Modes of Travel

Twenty-first-century travelers will benefit from increased competition among the airline, train, and automotive travel industries, spawned by increasing motor vehicle fuel efficiency and advanced forms of transportation. By the year 2010, new cars in the United States will have an average fuel efficiency rating of 36.9 miles per gallon, [7.6 L/100 km] the U.S. Department of Energy predicts. This greater fuel economy will enhance cars' popularity, and automobiles will continue to be the major form of transportation well into the first part of the next century.

The U.S. Department of Transportation predicts that the number of international travelers will double by the year 2000, placing ever more strains on overburdened airports. Supertrain systems for middle and long distances are already on the rise around the globe as an alternative to air travel as well as automobiles.

Trains will also provide more services to travelers, including onboard personal computer and communications systems that will allow customers to book reservations at hotels, restaurants, and entertainment centers, as well as check the weather at their destination. Such advances in rail travel will allow greater regional access and facilitate short- and medium-distance vacations and meetings.

## Impact of Demographic Changes

- **Smaller households.** The trend to smaller households within the upper and middle classes will continue into the twenty-first century. Family sizes in the United States, for instance, shrank from 3.37 persons per household in 1950 to 2.67 persons in 1986. Couples without children, households with few children, and singles will make up an ever greater proportion of the traveling public.

  Couples faced with increasing work demands will have less time for long vacations. These people will seek reprieves from their hectic routines through frequent get-away weekends. Family-oriented services will increase, such as "bonded daily guardians," who will serve as counselors and "parents for a day" for traveling children. These guardians will offer daily programs of children's activities, freeing parents to seek attractions that are more adult oriented.

Singles will continue to have a greater amount of per capita income than married individuals. Those with large amounts of discretionary income will view travel as one of the fruits of their labor and a way to meet new people. Relatively more independent in spirit and in means, travelers of the twenty-first century will demand more personalized vacation options.

- **Aging populations.** The number of persons age 65 and older has grown faster than the general U.S. population. The Travel Industry Association of America estimates that by the year 2000 the elderly will comprise approximately one-fourth of the nation's population. This group will not only have the most available free time of any segment of the population, but it will also have the greatest amount of disposable income.

  Elder travelers spend more nights away from home (8.2) than do travelers under age 50 (4.8), according to the American Association of Retired Persons (AARP). The financially and physically able elderly will significantly increase the demand for leisure travel. These individuals will find new opportunities and greater access to such forms of travel as heritage tourism, educational tourism, and ecotourism.

### The Changing School Year

Calls for lengthening the school year will increase in the twenty-first century in order to improve education as well as conserve energy, leading to new schedules that include staggered vacation breaks. Such changes will inevitably alter family travel patterns dramatically.

Shortened school vacations staggered throughout the year will reduce children's overnight camp sessions, family recreational opportunities, summer vacation home usage, and the length of annual family trips. With no clear season/off-season rate changes guided by schools' traditional summer vacation patterns, the travel industry may investigate new pricing schemes to attract families at different times of the year.

## Traveling for Health

The twenty-first century will see a renaissance of health spas and wellness centers. Visitors of all age groups will seek physical-conditioning programs, places to relieve stress, and centers for spiritual renewal. Closely connected with these centers will be sports-fantasy programs, where individuals will test their physical condition and act out their athletic dreams.

The trend toward increased health consciousness will continue well into the twenty-first century. Tourists in the future will find that attractions, hotels, and restaurants will adjust their physical amenities to accommodate these health demands. Some of today's extras that will become tomorrow's standard fare include all-purpose weight and aerobic facilities, fat-free/low-calorie and cholesterol-conscious diet plans, and greater protection of the skin from the sun.

New attractions and facilities based on health motifs will appear around the world. For example, the spas along Israel's Dead Sea coast attract thousands of psoriasis sufferers from Scandinavia, with much of the vacation's costs covered by national health plans. Many of these "sanitourist" facilities will center around already existing hospitals and health centers.

Cities with large medical facilities, such as Houston's Texas Medical Center, will use these structures as a springboard for new economic vitality through "sanitourism." These hospital centers will not only cater to the ill, but will offer programs such as stress reduction to patients' loved ones. Health-conscious individuals seeking to maintain their personal well-being will turn to hospitals for fully monitored, individually tailored health programs.

## Touring Nature

Environmental issues will continue to be a concern. The twenty-first century will likely see an increase in the number of ecotourists, vacationers seeking "natural vacations" and secluded places. Officials on the Galápagos Islands project that tourism will have increased eight-fold from 1965 to 1995. The conflict between protecting the environment while promoting tourist development will intensify.

Adventurous tourists will travel all over the world to remote, ecologically interesting areas. Such sites may offer few or primitive services as a part of the trip's lure. For less-adventurous ecotourists, the twenty-first century will offer daily group trips into undeveloped areas.

These day trippers will return at night to resort areas for overnight stays and evening entertainment.

And even those who want to stay close to home will seek the beauty of nature. Urban and suburban dwellers will demand more public natural preserves built in urban centers.

Advances in cinema technology such as OMNIMAX and IMAX will allow those interested in ecology to "experience" nature from the safety of a theater.

## Shopping as Vacation

Shopping will continue to represent a sizable portion of the travel budget. Improved transportation and disappearing national trade barriers will allow the public to locally purchase items produced internationally. The diversity of available products will offer the world's tourists the opportunity to experience specialty-shop atmosphere with mall conveniences. As international travel increases, multilingual clerks—even in predominantly monolingual nations such as the United States—will make shopping easier.

To capture their segment of the market, cities and entrepreneurs will develop special themes based on non-mass-produced items unique to their culture.

In some cases, shopping will be the primary purpose of travel. Some shopping malls (such as Canada's West Edmonton Mall) are becoming tourist destinations by transforming themselves into amusement parks and cultural/entertainment centers. Future travelers will also make more day trips and weekend shopping excursions to commercial centers that successfully create popular individualized atmospheres and offer regional articles. One type of "shopping vacation" that is already seeing increased popularity, especially among the budget-conscious, is excursions to regional outlet centers, where an abundance of bargains can be found.

## Postindustrial Travel

Travelers in the twenty-first century will be the standard-bearers of the world's largest industry. Travel and tourism will reflect the social and technological changes of postindustrial society. As many trips will be of shorter durations, the industry will offer travelers better service and more personal conveniences. Travel in the postindustrial age will be easier and more comfortable, especially for the affluent, but paradoxically less necessary.

Travel will move well beyond its murky and controversial past. The English language borrowed the word *travel* from the French word travail, which originated with the Latin noun *tripalium*—an instrument of torture. For a great deal of history, the association between travel and torture was appropriate.

But the latter part of the twentieth century has seen a dramatic change in travel and tourism. Travel is no longer a torturous necessity, but an increasingly pleasurable option. With its emphasis on resource preservation, individual autonomy, comfort, convenience, affordability, and personalization, postindustrial travel will offer a broader horizon of options and opportunities.

# We Need to Limit Tourism

## while there is something left to see

**BY**

**WALLACE IMMEN**

"Take only photographs; leave only footprints" is the motto of a fast-growing branch of travel dubbed eco-tourism. Unfortunately, the concept is degenerating into a travel-brochure catch-phrase. And while some tour operators are aware of environmental concerns, large groups of tourists are still arriving in places that should be permanently off limits.

Even the most ecologically sensitive visitors can create many footprints. I learned this recently when I was part of a group of 40 who were among the first tourists to visit the site of a "mummified" ancient forest on Axel Heiberg Island in Canada's high Arctic.

In just one afternoon, we changed the look of the island's fragile environment forever as our footprints created a criss-cross of trails in the soft earth. The trails will become deeper with subsequent erosion. The forest was a stunning sight, yet I left wondering whether our seeing it was worth the cost to the pristine habitat.

Certainly, the understanding gained by seeing the world's unspoiled environments heightens the awareness of tourists to what we might lose if we don't protect the Earth. But in the process we may be destroying the very ecologies we hope to preserve.

A bit of publicity can quickly put a place on the tourist map. No matter how remote it is, tourists with the means will seek it out. Until the eighties, the Galápagos Islands were as inaccessible as the Arctic. Without the presence of humans, the plant life, tortoises and exotic birds who lived there evolved in an environment that had survived for eons.

The Galápagos, which are governed by Ecuador, are now visited by more than 32 000 a year, quadruple the number of visitors of a decade ago. These tourists have inadvertently introduced more than 100 new plant species that are choking out the local flora. The tourists who brought in the seeds on their clothes and shoes would probably be horrified to find they had changed the ecology forever.

And that's not the only effect of the tourist invasion. The fuel and oil that leaks from their boats have polluted the water around the islands. Even with careful trash collection, film containers, cigarette packs and the like have become part of the landscape.

The story is the same in Guatemala, where the Peten Mayan ruin stood undamaged for centuries because it was well off the beaten track. Before 1980, no more than a few dozen tourists a year visited the ancient temple. That all changed with the building of a road and the introduction of an air service. Last year, the ancient stone steps were trodden by at least 75 000 pairs of tourist feet, and serious wear is beginning to show.

One of the worst examples of an environment harmed by tourism is in East Africa, where game parks established to preserve animal habitats are streaked with rutted trails deepened daily by dozens of tourist vans. Because farmers have claimed ownership of prime grazing land, animals that were "born free" have become confined to marginal areas vulnerable to drought and overgrazing. The animals are constantly under surveillance, even while they are eating and mating, by ever-growing throngs of humans. And the tourists' meals, which are cooked over wood fires, are adding to air pollution and reducing often precious wood supplies in remote, deforested regions.

Setting up a book of ecological sites worth protecting is not enough. Have you ever noticed how "no hunting" signs on farm fences tend to get shot full of bullet holes? Restricting a site may just serve to give it a cachet that attracts trespassers.

Even if a national or local government puts legal restrictions on visitors, it doesn't mean the laws will be enforced. Some of the most endangered environments are to be found in underdeveloped countries that have more pressing needs than protecting virgin forests and restraining people from trampling wild flowers. Although Ecuador sets a limit on the annual number of tourists allowed to visit the Galápagos, a tour operator told me recently that the number expands according to how many tourists are willing to pay for the trip.

Ideally, an international body would be created that is as diligent at keeping tabs on environmental threats by tourists as Greenpeace is at monitoring industries that pollute. A board of experts would study fragile environments to determine their carrying capacity and set quotas for visitors. High fees could be charged to get a visitor's permit, with the proceeds going to environmental protection.

There are early signs that financial limits work. Remote Bhutan, south of Tibet, controls tourist growth by charging a visiting fee of $450 (U.S.) a day. That's one way of saying only serious applicants need apply. Venice is planning to hold a random draw for passes to limit the number of tourists allowed in the sinking city.

We should remember that travel is a privilege, not a right. This may be the final golden age of unrestricted globe trotting, but there is no reason it can't last a very long time.

Chiang Mai, Thailand

# On
# Holiday

~

**BY**

**SHAUNT**

**BASMAJIAN**

indian peasants
        lined up
one by one
  on the busy
spanish street
    begging for
        dollars/pesos
  hungry for
    an american burger
a "big mac" at the
        mexican macdonald's
  (while) ravaged
    in the ring
        bulls remain
    emaciated
      massacred
        grabbing more
  tourist money
   (with) eyes radiant
  and coiled
    too poor to glare

everywhere you look
    growing more and
more jealous
    as you drink
their beer
    imported
write poetry
    on their beaches
    get burned
    in their sun
    trying to escape
    for a fun holiday
    on an "off-season"
    package deal
    watching a group
    of local workers
    doing your job
in another country
    for less than
    the minimum

# Letters
# from
# India

~

**BY**

**JENNIFER**

**LEWIS**

hree weeks. We are in the south of India in Madurai where the main attraction is the Meenakshi Temple.

By now, Sonnika and I have had palaces, mosques, tombs and temples up to here; but whereas Sonnika can, because of her birthright, comfortably say "I refuse to look at another," I feel tourist guilt prodding me to take an obligatory whip-through.

The scooter driver drops me at the eastern entrance where I stuff the forbidden camera deep into my bag and check my shoes. Inside Meenakshi, I am grateful that guilt conquered inertia. I doubt I'll ever see such a stunning collection of south Indian art and sculpture. I wander through a huge hall, the Kilikootu Mandapam, with its rows of pillars and carved figures. On the ceiling is an enormous mural of the gods. If I knew which questions to ask about Hinduism, the answers, I am sure, would all be here. As it is though, I am simply looking at a splendid collection of carvings, the names and history of which I unfortunately know nothing.

A little farther on is an enchanted forest of sculpture, the Hall of a Thousand Pillars, each pillar a different god, goddess or divinity. My jaw hangs open as I tilt my head back to view the intricately-carved ceiling and I have to wonder: if I am awed by such devotion to the gods, how overpowering must Meenakshi be for someone with faith?

How must one feel who enters this temple not as a tourist but as a believer, a worshipper? What is the impact of the thousands upon thousands of 400-year-old statues, each one uniquely significant? The powerful aura of energy created by deposits of faith and devotion alone would make this place unforgettable.

I stand in front of a massive Ganesh, trying to remember the story of the beheaded boy-god, fervently wishing the elephant divinity could mean even one significant thing to me, that I might place a garland of flowers around its neck in an act of impassioned conviction instead of admiring it simply for its artistic beauty.

On I wander, past scores of statues, through crowds of worshippers, until I am caught up in a particularly ardent bunch and swept into a smaller room. It is very crowded in here. Most people are praying, facing the shrine at the back of the room. A forefinger jabs me in the shoulder.

"You. No Hindu. You go."

A perspiring, harried-looking man is gesturing me back the way I came.

"Sorry." I try to shove through the crowds of people still entering the room.

"You go! Get out!" the man yells at me. I am not moving fast enough to suit him. Many people are watching me, smiling and murmuring to one another. I move forward, anger beginning to heat my cheeks.

"Get out! You no Hindu!"

He is still shouting at me as I reach the entrance. I glance back and our eyes meet for a split second before I turn and leave him forever.

Now I am pounding down the main hallway, past the statues, the worshippers, the vendors, toward freedom, air, the eastern doorway. And I am caught up in a fury I have never felt before.

"You're damned right I'm not Hindu you ignorant man if it means being like you how did you know half the brown-skinned people in there weren't Christian I'll tell you how you know you wretched man you don't know that's how you looked at my skin my skin my white white cursed white skin stood out like a white thumb didn't it and what were you doing power-tripping or protecting your precious gods from my blasphemous presence let me tell you something...

And I burst through the doorway, up the walkway, onto the street, into the throng of hawkers, shoppers and beggars. I stomp up and down many streets until my anger begins to cool, replaced by the heat of the afternoon sun. A nearby stall sells soft drinks. I sit on the sidewalk under a shade tree, my back to a low stone wall, an icy bottle of limca held to my flaming cheeks. There is a view of the top of the Meenakshi Temple from where I sit.

From where I sit…from where I sit. Where do I sit? Where did I just come from? Where did those ugly, profane thoughts and feelings originate? Surely not in me. Me: humanist, anti-racist, defender of all freedoms, embracer of humankind. Not me. No absolutely. I could never, for instance, say aloud what I thought and felt as I fled the temple.

Lukewarm limca slides down my throat. My face is cool now. I touch my cheeks; they feel cool and white.

But they were my thoughts, my feelings. Silently screamed or whimpered out loud, they were…they are…mine. And because they're mine, they're real and valid. They must be if I am to be.

A young Indian man strolls by, staring at me curiously. I follow his gaze with an impatient one of my own.

Yesyesyes—my skin, my eyes, my hair, my clothes. Obviously. But what about all the other ways in which we differ? Aren't you curious about them? Wouldn't knowing the other differences…wouldn't it make a difference? For the better? And what of the thousands of ways in which we're the same? Don't they matter? The needs, the wants, the fears…all the same. Yes!

And suddenly the elusive idea came into focus; I have grasped a bit of knowledge that no amount of empathy could ever have taught me and it is, now and forever, part of me.

Because *that,* that is where my anger came from in the inner sanctum: the fact that I shared so many countless things with each person in the room and differed from them only in as many ways in which they differed from each other. With one exception. The least important of all. The color of my skin.

Our train leaves Madurai late that night and I get a last glimpse of the Meenakshi Temple. My anger and pain is in there somewhere, drifting about among the pillars and the flowers. It has as much a right to be there as joy and piety. It is my contribution toward the eternal balance inside the beautiful structure. It is my offering to the gods.

But my last thought as we leave Madurai is not of the temple but of the man who banished me from it. This man will never see me again. He has already forgotten me. He will never know that in the brief moment between laying eyes on my face for the first time and the last time, he gave me the divine gift of understanding.

I wish I could tell him.

*from*

# Walking the Line

## Travels Along the Canadian/American Border

~

**BY**

**MARIAN BOTSFORD**

**FRASER**

he border has become a part of travel as routine as packing a suitcase. Still, our hearts beat faster as we approach the Customs booth, fumbling in our wallets for some sure sign of identification, in our minds for some plausible excuse for crossing the line. From the corner of an eye we see guns and the border patrol cars. We tend not to see the video monitors and computer terminals, the technology that could in a trice replace the old-fashioned cut line by recording every single crossing, every licence plate and passport number.

The line that I followed is becoming increasingly irrelevant as a regulatory barrier. In a broad sense, the movement of ideas and commodities is becoming more abstract as electronic mail and bank transfers and simulcast events erase the boundaries of time and space, the conventions by which our cultures have grown. Traffic control is also more and more removed from the actual boundary, becoming instead the scrutiny and stamping of large numbers of people and their baggage at airports. There is a minor symbol of invasion in the fact that a traveller is processed through American Customs and Immigration at

Canadian airports, before ever leaving Canadian soil. The subtle shift from one cultural climate to another, like moving from sunlight into shade, never happens. The childish thrill of stepping on foreign turf is withheld.

Again and again as I travelled along the border, I imagined its absence. Many Americans do not even imagine its presence. Far from bearing weight, as it does for Canadians, the boundary for most Americans is a line on the television weather maps, above which there is white space and white weather—the land of cold fronts. For Canadians it is a holding line, a sea wall, sandbags resisting America. The waters slapping against the sandbags are not threatening, but when we contemplate the potential force of the body behind them, in full flood, we take silent comfort in the sandbags.

I know Canadians who would happily fold up the boundary line and become part of the United States; I did not meet these people living close to the line.

When I asked people living along the border if they would like to see it removed—what if you woke up tomorrow, I asked, and the border had been erased, ripped out?—invariably, Canadians rejected the idea. The only people who would even spontaneously consider that possibility were Americans. We have different perceptions about what threatens our respective nations. The assumption around the border crossing is that there will be illegal passage of household goods into Canada and illegal passage of aliens and drugs into the United States. Americans, therefore, who talk about erasing the border really assume that the regulatory functions of the border will simply be removed elsewhere, that we will become one nation, a considerably larger United States of America. They do not feel threatened by Canada. Canadians, who invest relatively little in the physical defense of their border with the United States, do, however, feel threatened by the idea of losing that border. In some unarticulated and mostly polite way, Canadians feel more secure with a tidy line between them and the Americans.

We think we have claimed and tamed this continent. The border is a symbol of order and mutual regulation; we think of the strip along the border as thickly populated, organized, colonized, mechanized. But you don't have to go very far to get into the bush, descend into a swamp or end up in muskeg up to your ears. And in truth we are claiming the land not by populating it but by polluting it. Colonies of people can be erased by time and fresh growth—their bones become soil; their gravestones crumble into dust; their borders are erased. But acid rain in common airspace, clearcut logging by multinational companies, industrial waste poured directly into shared rivers—by these acts we are altering the chemical balance of the landscape. The border has failed to prevent infiltration of contraband more dangerous than handguns or aliens. Somehow this conspiracy of vandalism has to be dealt with on the border, with more tangible initiatives than peace gardens and peace parks and peace arches, and anachronistic rhetoric about being undefended and unfenced.

The border is a richly annotated margin in North American history, a fine line drawn through the collusion of surveyors with the sun and the stars, a procession of monuments springing from a single, precise point near the yellow birch tree hooped with iron.

The Waterton-Glacier International Peace Park straddles the boundary as one million acres [400 000 ha] of mountainous wilderness in Alberta, Montana and British Columbia. These are, in fact, two separately administered national parks, identified as biosphere reserves by UNESCO. Razorback summits, hanging valleys, gouged-out bellies called glacial cirques and deep icy lakes—the landscape asserts an authority untouched by human treaties. But the vista is diligently cleared and maintained by the International Boundary Commission and despised by rangers and wardens as an open wound on the pristine forest. And the conventions of Customs and Immigration inspections are honoured even here.

West of Waterton-Glacier, Roosville, British Columbia, sits in the Rocky Mountain Trench, the flat plateau between two mountain ranges. It consists of a Gulf station and restaurant, a Canada Customs building and a substantial chain fence. The nearest Montana town is Eureka, nine miles [14 km] south, but there is a bar on the American side about as close to the border as it could be. U.S. Highway 93, one of the longest highways in the world ("It's still 93 way down in central America," said the U.S. Customs officer), trickles to a stop just north of here. The closest border crossings are 250 miles [400 km] by road to the east, on the other side of the Waterton Lakes parks, and 117 miles [188 km] driving westward, at Eastport, Idaho. The pull of the highways is away from and around the borderlands.

The territory on the Canadian side is the reserve of the Tobacco

Plains Band, about 10 000 acres [4000 ha], in a plot three miles wide and six miles long, [5 km wide and 10 km long] butting right up to the 49th parallel. About eighty people live here. It is clearly indifferent land, flat, dusty, edged in scrubby bush.

In the band community centre, a solid shining log building, I met Elizabeth Gravelle. She is a soft-spoken, thoughtful woman who in the early sixties was elected chief of the Tobacco Plains Band, one of the first British Columbian women to be elected chief. She is still a council member. Handsome, serious, a grandmother.

"I always say you can tell when you're coming to a reservation. No matter where I travel, when the land starts getting poor, I say to myself, that's the Indian reservation. Because look at all the good land all through the valley, and we got this here. It's just dry land. We don't even have a mountain on the reserve. And it's not really ours; it's Her Majesty the Queen's. She kindly is letting us use *her* land." Her ironic tone was softened by a small laugh.

"And they keep taking the land. They put in highways and power lines all over the reserve, but they never give us more. They say it's government to government."

Elizabeth Gravelle grew up off the reserve, coming to visit relatives when she was a child, spending the last years of her childhood in a mission school. Her parents weren't registered, because her grand-mother lost her status through marriage to a non-Indian. Elizabeth gained it back through her own marriage.

The date of the establishment of the reserve is suppressed in the communal memory; there is residual bitterness about the settlement. "I guess the chief—it was Chief David back then—he never did sign. He wanted from where he sat at the border up the mountain that way, and way back, and he wanted across the river too. So instead, they just gave this little piece here, and the people that were there to survey, with the documents and everything, they pulled out in the middle of the night, and the chiefs claim they never signed any papers with them."

"Do you think of yourselves as Canadians?"

She shrugged, and shook her head slightly. "We're natives of this country, and we should be allowed to be what we were, what our fore-fathers were. They were just one nation. And if they wanted to winter over here, okay, they were here. Or if they wanted to go south, there was nobody to say, hey, you can't do that. I think that's the way it should be.

"We shouldn't be classified as Canadian or American. We are the same people; we're all Kootenays. They come here, and we go there. There are Tobacco Plains people in Montana and some in Idaho; we're known as Tobacco Plains Number Two." There was a pause, the silence dinted faintly by the grinding gears of lumber trucks on the road as they approached the border crossing.

"They grew tobacco down in Montana, but it must have been way, way back, because even the old people I talked to down there never saw the tobacco; they just saw the old furrows in the land.

"Before they put the border in, a lot of them were really into farm-ing over there. They were homesteaders; they had cattle and every-thing. Even a little store. Then they were told if they didn't come back here, they would lose out and end up with nothing." She laughed drily. "Which they did anyways.

"One fellow sold his ranch for a couple hundred pounds of potatoes [about 90 kg]. They could have just stayed there; they didn't have to move. It was just a trick to get them on the reserve, I think, because they were promised, you know, land of their own. They didn't know it was reserve land, that they couldn't ever own.

"Anyways, they were told the border wasn't for them. That they could still go back and forth. They were trusting. They couldn't read or write. That was their understanding, that they were told that the bor-der wasn't going to be for them.

"Even when I was a child, there was no fence there. You could just go anywhere. And there was no Customs building. But then later there used to be a Customs man; he just pitched a tent right in the middle of the prairie there. There was no fence, but I guess that was when he first started stopping Indians from goin' across. I guess I was about five…"

The Tobacco Plains Band asked the Department of Indian Affairs for the right to open a duty-free shop on the reservation. The band was turned down. Proposals for other projects—a mulch plant and one for reforestation—were unsuccessful. "What we wanted to do was start all these projects, so everyone on the reserve would have jobs, and get them off the social assistance programs. There's a lot of young people wonder what they're even existing for."

And no one, she said, has ever thought to apply for a job at the Customs.

# Only in Canada, We Say!

BY

**VALERIE**

**WYATT**

Quick! Where in Canada would you find Nose Creek? What about a whooping crane's favorite nesting spot or the foggiest maritime town? Try this quiz and learn a little more about this gigantic country of ours.

**1** **Where would you look for dinosaurs in Canada?**
Nova Scotia, British Columbia, Alberta, Saskatchewan

**2** **What major Prairie city has an Elbow River and a Nose Creek?**
Winnipeg, Saskatoon, Calgary

**3** **What is the biggest all-Canadian lake?**
Lake Manitoba, Great Bear Lake, Lake Superior

**4** **What Canadian street has been called the longest street in the world?**
Blanshard Street in Victoria, Yonge Street in Toronto, Sherbrooke Street in Montreal

**5** **In what province are you never more than 30 kilometres from the sea?**
Prince Edward Island, Saskatchewan, Alberta

**6** Where in Canada could you watch enough water to fill a million bathtubs thunder past in just one second?
Montmorency Falls, Kakabeka Falls, Niagara Falls

**7** In which national park can you see whooping cranes nesting?
Wood Buffalo, Banff, Auyuittuq, Point Pelee

**8** Which city has the largest Chinatown?
Toronto, Vancouver, Montreal

**9** In what town in the Eastern provinces are you most likely to see fog when you wake up in the morning?
Argentia, Nfld.; Peggy's Cove, N.S.; Charlottetown, P.E.I.

**10** Where would you go to hear the Haida language spoken?
Labrador, the Northwest Territories, Queen Charlotte Islands

**11** What's the sunniest city in Canada?
Saskatoon, Sask.; St. John's, Nfld.; Churchill, Man.; Victoria, B.C.

**12** Where would you go to meet the snowman Bonhomme Carnaval?
St-Boniface, Man.; Quebec City, Que.; Saint John, N.B.

## ANSWERS

**1** You can find fossils of dinosaur bones and footprints in all four provinces, but the best place to look is Dinosaur Provincial Park in Alberta. More than 30 different kinds of dinosaurs lived there between 90 and 60 million years ago, including a ferocious "cousin" of tyrannosaurus, called Albertosaurus.

**2** Pat yourself on the back if you guessed Calgary. Elbow River and Nose Creek are both creeks that flow into Calgary's main river, the Bow. Not planning to visit Calgary? Why not "head" out to Eyebrow, Sask., or even Pinchgut Point, Nfld.

**3** Did you get fooled by this trick question? Lake Superior is the largest lake in Canada, but only about a third of it is Canadian;

the rest is American. The largest *entirely Canadian* lake is Great Bear Lake in the Northwest Territories.

**4** Yonge Street has often been called the longest street not only in Canada but in the world. It was the first major roadway in Upper Canada. When it was built in 1796, it stretched northward from the shores of Lake Ontario almost to Lake Simcoe, a distance of 55 kilometres. As Highway 11, it now extends 1800 kilometres to the Manitoba border.

**5** If you said Saskatchewan or Alberta, guess again. They're the only two provinces that *don't* have a sea coast. In Prince Edward Island, on the other hand, you're never more than 30 kilometres from the sea.

**6** Only at Niagara Falls could you see so much water sloshing past so fast. To see the falls at their best, make sure you're there during the summer months. At other times, some water channelled away from the falls to generate electricity means the mighty torrent is reduced.

**7** There are only about 100 whooping cranes left in North America. That's why they're considered endangered. The only place they nest is Wood Buffalo National Park. In an attempt to build up the number of whoopers, biologists kidnap some of the whooper eggs and raise the young hatchlings in captivity. One day, the young of these captive birds may be returned to the wild.

**8** Vancouver has Canada's largest Chinatown, but Toronto isn't far behind. Many Canadian cities have Chinatowns, neighborhoods where Chinese immigrants first settled. Although most Chinese Canadians no longer live in these areas, many still enjoy a visit to Chinatown to buy Chinese food, books and newspapers and to celebrate special holidays.

**9** If you feel foggy in Argentia, Nfld., there's a good reason. With an average 206 days of fog a year, it's Canada's foggiest town. Fog is just a cloud on the ground, so if you want to put your head in the clouds, go for a walk in the fog.

**10** To hear the Haida language, you'd have to go to the Queen Charlotte Islands. The Haida people have lived there for more than 8000 years. How would you say "How are you today?" to someone in Haida? *Kasino dung ēdung aiata?*

**11** Grab your sunglasses and head for Saskatoon. On average, the sun beams down there 2450 hours a year. If all that sun shone nonstop, there would be 102 straight days and nights of sun.

**12** Bonhomme Carnaval is the friendly snowman mascot of Quebec City's winter carnival. Lots of other cities throw winter bashes, too, including St-Boniface, Man., (Festival du Voyageur), Ottawa (Winterlude) and Whitehorse (Yukon Sourdough Rendezvous).

# RV's

BY

TOM

WAYMAN

In early spring
they are let out of the small barns
or yards behind houses
where they have been tethered all winter.

They feel a pull toward
the open or forested country
beyond cities or towns. So they appear on the highways
singly, then in bigger numbers
until by June they have formed their summer family
   groupings
and herds. They sway in long files
up the mountain roads
and plod through the settled valley bottoms.
Three species are readily identifiable:
self-propelled, towed
and loaded-onto-pickups. Most columns, however,
consist of a mix. But every type
is an obstacle
to the car and tractor-trailer drivers
in line behind them
who curse these creatures' apparent ignorance
of the hour and the dollar.

Yet the vast distances of our continent
cry for something this large
and ponderous. The buffalo guns' final shots
were still ringing, the last of the great shaggy beasts
were just penned in corrals and parks
when the first motorized replacement
coughed, shook itself alive
and stumbled into the fields.
The persistence here of the bulky,
the slow
instructs us
these lands are not to be swiftly passed through
and that where we are heading
is not
where we are.

# Algonquin Idyll

**BY**

**JOHN**

**BEMROSE**

y wife has a theory that bears don't like to swim. She admits they can swim; indeed, she knows they're very good swimmers. But she thinks they don't *like* to do it. This allows Cathleen to go into the woods with a high heart—for she always insists we pitch our tent on an island. This was why, on a recent holiday in Algonquin Park, we found ourselves, with our eight-year-old daughter, Alix, paddling past several campsites whose only shortcoming was that they weren't surrounded by water. The day was waning fast; rain had started to patter into our canoe. Yet we labored on, looking for an island campsite, where the bears would not find us.

Bears, of course, are afraid of humans and usually try to avoid them—information that leaves Cathleen unmoved. And, to be fair, I was holding out for an island myself. A friend had told us about the particular campsite we were headed for and it sounded ideal. Only a three-or four-hour paddle (and one portage) from the parking lot, it featured (he said) a splendid view, a sandy cove for the canoe and excellent swimming. Our plan was to settle there for the weekend. This would save us the trouble of packing up our gear each morning but also limit our explorations to day trips. Other families we had met were enjoying more itinerant holidays, following circular routes through some of Algonquin's hundreds of lakes and meandering rivers.

Either way you choose to visit Algonquin, its uniqueness soon becomes apparent. Partly because it is Ontario's oldest provincial park (founded in 1893), Algonquin has been particularly well groomed. Its main portage trails are broad, its campsites usually roomy and well situated. But it's the landscape itself that strikes the deepest chord. Rolling, richly wooded hills rise above deep pre-Cambrian lakes. There's something at once wild and stately about the place, and it's little wonder that the Group of Seven were fond of painting here. Paddling along, it's easy to imagine Tom Thomson on a rocky outcrop, with his paint box on his knees, studying the contortions of a jack pine. To him, as to generations of campers, Algonquin has been, simply and affectionately, "The Park."

Though with the sky growing gloomier and no island in sight, I was not feeling particularly affectionate about anything. Just ahead of me, Alix sat absorbed in a book, her free arm cuddling Whiskey, the family dog. Whenever Cathleen and I began to talk about which route to take, she'd put her finger to her lips and, with a wicked imitation of a schoolmarm, tell us, "Shhhh, it's nature." Had we a plank aboard, we might have made her walk it.

But just then we had other problems. Several canoes appeared up ahead, all apparently making for our arm of the lake. I urged more steam, knowing that on weekends, the best campsites get taken fast. We passed one canoe, then another. Finally we saw our island, a bit of forest floating like a dark green ship about 200 metres from shore. To our relief, it was empty.

The spot was even better than we'd hoped. It was just big enough for our family, with an airy spruce grove for our tent, and an open cooking area with a stone-circled fire pit and a big rock for a kitchen counter. The sun came out as we unpacked and the water suddenly looked inviting. Soon we were in it, swimming alongside the waves of light reflecting off the rocky shore.

In another hour we were talking supper, but first we needed a fire. Small islands are poor places to gather firewood—there isn't much. So Alix and I paddled to the mainland, where I sawed limbs off some dead pines and cedars. Alix amused herself by wading at the shore, turning her white sneakers into clogs of black muck.

That evening, as her shoes dried by the fire, we ate our supper—pasta with homemade pesto, slices of sun-warmed tomatoes and fruit—on a long slope of granite above the lake. Across the way, camp-fires of our mainland neighbors flickered in the dusk. Their voices carried across the water with extraordinary distinctness. We christened the two couples directly opposite us "Loon and Co.," after the wonderfully reckless laugh of one of the women.

Quiet didn't return to the lake till well after sunset. By then, Cathleen and Alix had retired to their sleeping bags. I lingered, sharing a seat on the rock with Whiskey and staring up at the constellations: Ursa Major, Corona Borealis, The Lynx. An owl hooted mournfully. Slowly, the tensions of the city were seeping away. Just 24 hours ago, I'd been fretting, going over our lists of food and extra clothes, checking the tent, life jackets, paddles, saw, axe, ropes, grill, first-aid kit, bug repellent—a small mountain of stuff. I'd wondered if the trip was worth the trouble. Now I was wondering why we didn't live this way all the time.

For the next three days, we enjoyed a poky existence, governed mainly by our appetites. We ate when we were hungry, swam when we were hot, went to bed with the sun. Wisely, we'd left all watches behind. There was a certain luxury in this, but it led to amusing consequences. I'll never forget Cathleen as she stared blankly at the instructions on a package of soup. After a moment, she looked at me, perfectly baffled, and said, "I wonder how long 10 minutes is?" On our island, we simply didn't know.

Hurrying less, we noticed more: little minnows darting to and fro in golden shallows; long-legged water bugs that sizzled across the water's surface, until it looked as if the water was boiling ("hotshots," Alix called them). One afternoon we discovered a small canyon at the southwest corner of the lake. Resting our paddles, we drifted into the cool, uncannily still atmosphere between its granite walls. Ferns hovered motionless. Somewhere, water was trickling. There was a sense of menace but also peace. We felt we'd found the hushed living centre of the park.

We made other discoveries as well—about each other. Cathleen and I saw Alix grow up a little as we watched her paddle solo for the first time. Dipping carefully, she sallied out from shore, while I shouted instructions and grinned with nervous pride.

And then there was the morning (our last on the island) when Cathleen swam to the mainland, 200 metres away. I'm nervous of deep water, while Cathleen takes to it like a dolphin. When I looked up from my book to see her halfway across, cutting the water with deft, rhythmic strokes, I felt I was seeing her afresh—this graceful, far-swimming stranger. I couldn't take my eyes off her.

Two hours later, she was back in her familiar spot in the bow. We were paddling away from our island for the last time. Trying to be good campers, we had left no trace of ourselves: we'd burned what was burnable, including toilet paper, and were lugging the rest of our garbage out in a plastic bag. This was all in good form, but it ran against the usual human instinct to leave some mark of passage, some "Kilroy was here."

Behind us, our island already looked small, incredibly small. It was hard to believe the three of us had spread over it so comfortably. Would other campers arrive on it today? Would they enjoy it as much as we had? I turned again for a last look, but already it had disappeared behind a point: our Algonquin island, where the bears had not found us.

# Forced
# to Have
# Fun

~

**BY**

**DAVID**

**OWEN**

W hen our daughter was not quite three, we took her to
Disneyland. We were worried she might be too young, but we
were staying in Los Angeles and we couldn't think of anything
else to do, so why not? When we asked her later what her favorite
part of Disneyland had been, she said, "The horse." It turned out that
she meant the coin-operated merry-go-round in front of the Kmart
where we had stopped briefly on our way to Anaheim.

You can never tell what's going to make an impression on a child.
One of the few things I remember about the 1964 World's Fair, to
which my parents took my sister and me when she was six and I was
nine, was getting caught in the closing doors of a Manhattan subway
train. I wasn't scared. I just had the vaguely happy feeling that I was
going to be getting a lot of attention pretty soon. It was the same feeling I had had a year or two earlier when, more or less on purpose, I
had fallen through the thin ice at the edge of a pond while skating.

Like virtually all the vacations I took as a child, that trip to the
World's Fair was a car trip. We lived in Kansas City, and getting to
New York took two full days. I have fond memories of the car. It was a

1964 Buick Skylark station wagon, and it had a little window in the roof above the back seat. My sister and I were excited about the prospect of looking at the tops of skyscrapers through that roof window. The car also had brown vinyl seats on which it was easy to make lick lines. A lick line is a saliva boundary, drawn with your finger, that shows your sister exactly how close to you she can get without being punched. (This was in the days when almost no one wore seat belts, so trespassing was a problem.) Maintaining a lick line requires contributions from both parties, as in the famous Robert Frost poem about walls.

Our car must have seemed practically empty during that trip, because we had left my one-and-a-half-year-old brother at home. The summer before, though, we had taken him with us to northern Michigan in a car that was smaller and didn't have air-conditioning. Also, a college-aged baby-sitter had come with us. How did we survive? Last year my wife and I briefly considered taking both our cars on a 250-mile [400 km] trip to Martha's Vineyard, because we didn't see how we could possibly cram ourselves, our two kids, and all our stuff into just a minivan.

The best part of traveling in a car is getting out of the car and checking into a motel. After a long day's drive nearly everything about a motel seems interesting and life-affirming. Once, when I was seven or eight, my sister and I talked our father into letting us try the vibrating bed in our motel room. He put in a quarter, and the bed began to shake. It also began to make a sound that was like the sound of a vacuum cleaner being fed slowly into a Cuisinart. The control box didn't have an off switch; it was wired directly into the wall and couldn't be unplugged. The bed either shook all night or seemed to shake all night, and my sister and I fought about who got to lie on it.

Despite the logistical difficulties, I like traveling with children. It forces you to do the things you really enjoy (buying souvenirs, going to Disneyland, eating at Wendy's) and to skip the things you really don't (going to plays, touring the wine country, looking at art). Keeping your kids from slitting each other's throats compels you to find activities that are actually interesting, as opposed to merely sounding like the kinds of activities people engage in when they are on vacation.

Traveling with children also reminds you that you can find fun almost anywhere you go. Some of my happiest vacation memories involve a trip my family took with several other families when I was ten or eleven years old. We all stayed in a nice motel, went swimming, played miniature golf, and so on. The really great thing about the trip was that the motel was only ten miles away from where we all lived. Driving there took fifteen minutes. Nobody had to throw up or go to the bathroom, and nobody asked when we would be there. The kids had an entire motel to run around in, and the parents had plenty of time for cocktails. The next day, before lunch, we went home.

# Thirsty Dreams

### BY
### SUE
### MACLEOD

You come from a background
where travel to faraway places is
not an assumption.
A few weeks of summer vacation:
your parents would load up the car, going
home to Cape Breton.
Your father at the wheel
always. Your mother
taking swigs of chalky medicine
from a thick blue bottle
to white out the pangs of an ulcer.
And you, in the backseat,
crouched down from the window
each time a motorbike
zippered toward you
on the other side of the long white line.
Mystery figures
travelling lonesome in twos or in threes
they would smash
against the wind.
Their giant buzzing hurt your ears,
made you think of monster
insects.

Every once in a while, alighting
from the Pontiac,
you would see curls of heat
rise from the parking lot
stretching from the highway
to a restaurant where the toast was always
"Golden Brown." The eggs: "Grade A."
There'd be two motel stops
before the Causeway.
You always hoped for a swimming pool, and dreamed
thirsty dreams
of an aqua that would sparkle
translucent from the inside
as it did on the postcards
and glimpses you caught from the road.

But there was never time. Just the two
double beds, spread with chenille,
the tv in the middle. And once,
after stepping from your car
into late evening breeze
while others, just like you, continued
to firefly past on the highway,
their bands of light striping
the motel room curtain,
you sat, brushed with goosebumps,
on the bed, eating Cracker Jack,
watching Neil Armstrong
step onto the moon.

# The Misfortune in Men's Eyes

### BY
### EDDY L.
### HARRIS

T homas Wolfe said that going home again is like stepping into a
river. You cannot step into the same river twice; you cannot go
home again. After a very long time away, you will not find the
same home you left behind. It will be different, and so will you. It is
quite possible that home will not be home at all, meaningless except
for its sentimental place in your heart. At best it will point the long
way back to where you started, its value lying in how it helped to
shape you and in the part of home you have carried away.

Alex Haley went to Africa in the mid-sixties. Somehow he had
managed to trace his roots back to a little village called Juffure, up-
river from Banjul in the forests of The Gambia. It was the same village
from which his ancestors had been stolen and forced into slavery. In
some way Haley must have felt he was returning home: a flood of
emotions, an awakening of the memories hidden in his genes.

Those were the two extremes between which I was trapped. I
could not go home again, yet here I was. Africa was so long ago the
land of my ancestors that it held for me only a symbolic significance.
Yet there was enough to remind me that what I carry as a human

being has come in part from Africa. I did not feel African, but was beginning to feel not wholly American anymore either. I felt like an orphan, a waif without a home.

I was not trying to find the village that had once been home to my people, nor would I stand and talk to people who could claim to be my relatives, as Haley had done. The thought of running into someone who looked like a relative terrified me, for that would have been too concrete, too much proof. My Africanism was abstract and I wanted it to remain so. I did not need to hear the names of my ancient ancestors or know what they looked like. I had seen the ways they loved their children in the love of my father. I would see their faces and their smiles one day in the eyes of my children.

Haley found what he was seeking. I hardly knew what I was looking for, except perhaps to know where home once was, to know how much of me is really me, how much of being black has been carried out of Africa.

I got on another bus and the bus took me to the river. Beside me on the bus sat a Senegalese doctor who looked grim and determined, repeatedly wiping his damp, sweaty brow with a dirty white handkerchief. This bus was a great effort for him. He had been educated in Paris and in Aix-en-Provence, a quiet college town on the southern edge of the French Alps where the weather is always mild. He had been away from home for too long and now he suffered in the heat. He didn't like the dust in his eyes. He was no longer used to it. He would rather have been in France, it seemed, than here.

The bus roared on and the road ahead disappeared around a bend into the bush. Huts, each one with a grass roof, clustered in little villages lining the road. Chickens scurried across the road to avoid being squashed by the bus. Villagers with nothing better to do sat in the shade and watched our passing. The doctor beside me lifted his upper lip in a sneer at the villagers and shook his head.

"How long have you been away?" I asked, for he seemed less acclimated to the heat than I was, and unused to the slow pace and the backwardness.

"It isn't that," he said. "It is simply that one cannot see himself until he has stopped seeing himself. Do you understand?"

I made a long, hesitant sound, encouraging him to go on.

"I shave every morning," he said. "I cannot see the changes in my face because they are so gradual they are not changes at all. I do not know if I looked different last year."

He lifted a finger to his cheek.

"But here is a dark place," he said, pointing to a blemish under his left eye. "If suddenly after two years without seeing my face I notice this thing, I will say to myself, 'That wasn't there before.' And that is how I feel coming home. I see how very little has changed. If we are moving forward at all, we are moving so slowly that in comparison with France and the rest of the world, Africa is moving backwards. Mostly, I think, we are standing still."

On the seat in front of us a mother holds her little two-year-old daughter, who is tiny, much smaller than she ought to be. She wears a dingy little dress and plastic panties. She sucks on her mother's breast only for comfort. For thirst she drinks from a bottle filled with an orange-colored juice. When the juice has run its course, the mother stands the child in the aisle and pulls off the plastic pants. She lets the baby pee on the floor of the bus. Wetness runs down the child's leg and onto the floor in a puddle. When the bus runs up a short hill, the puddle spreads and runs in a long, thin line to the back of the bus and soaks a young man's luggage. He kicks his suitcase out of the path of the little stream and says nothing.

The doctor purses his lips and shakes his head again.

"We are not very advanced," he says. "You wouldn't find this in France."

"Oh, I don't know," I tell him. "I've seen worse in Paris."

He looks at me in disbelief. In defending his native home, however slightly, I have insulted his adoptive home, and he bristles.

"Yes," I say. "I saw a woman stop her car at place de la Madeleine so her little boy could defecate on the curb. Grown men urinate on the street. And there are dogs and cats in every restaurant in Paris. France and Africa are not always so different."

Now he laughs. "Perhaps," he says, "they learned something from us after all." But his mirth doesn't last very long.

The baby, now standing in her mother's lap, peeps around her mother's shoulder at me. Her eyes are big and wide around, like the moon. She coos and grins as any happy baby would. I make faces and she stares at me with those great round eyes. The whites of her eyes are so clear and so bright they seem faintly blue, the black irises so dark I can see myself in them. She smiles and she is beautiful.

The doctor's grim seriousness returns and replaces his smile. "That baby," he says coldly, "will be dead before the year is out."

I let out a little moan.

"Malnutrition," he explains. "Poor hygiene. Dehydration. If she doesn't die this year, she will die next year, or the year after. Chances are that she will never live to be five."

The hammer strikes full force and straight on. All the statistics condense into this one moment, into this one tiny child's bright eyes.

"France and Africa are a little different," he says. "And in many ways it is France's fault."

"I thought you liked France so much."

"I do," he replies. "I love France. I feel more at home there. France is very advanced. And in France there is real freedom. Not like here. In Africa our lives are not our own. There is still slavery here, in Mauritania, in Sudan. There are no freedoms from forced labor or from torture or corporal punishment. And privacy—ha! Privacy is a foreign concept. Our phones are tapped, our mail is read, and we have to carry identity papers to go from one city to the next. This is not freedom. We are only pretending. And Senegal is better than most African countries."

His dark face frowns tightly.

"France is much better with her former colonies than Portugal was, but we are the way we are because of the Europeans. They eroded our culture and left nothing in its place but an envy for theirs. They divided us into countries that make no sense. Some man with a pencil and a map drew our borders according to some European scheme and ignored tribal divisions. We call ourselves Senegalese as if we were one nation, but we are many. We are Mandigo and Fulani and we do not trust one another. We are poor and our leaders are corrupt and we do not fight back. We don't know how. Instead, we turn them into gods because after so many years of white rulers, any black ruler is better. Or so we think."...

The bus stopped at Kaolack, a town halfway between Dakar and the river, and the doctor climbed off. There was time enough to get off the bus and stretch, grab a cold drink, and get something to eat from the crowd of vendors gathered around the bus. I helped the doctor with his bags, and before he left, I asked him why, if he hated this place so much, he had come back.

"I came back because this is my country," he said. "This is where I belong. This is my home and I can help here in ways I never could anywhere else."

He looked at the vendors crowding against the travelers. He looked down the long, dusty road. He looked at the dilapidated bus and he shook his head once more. A broad grin broke out across his face and completely consumed it.

"Hate this place?" he said. "What makes you think I hate this place?" He started to laugh. "This is life. As long as one is living, one is truly alive here." He shook his head again. "I could live in Paris the rest of my days, but always a part of me would be here, in this heat, eating this dust, among these poor people. I love this place."

He took my hand and squeezed it.

"I am of two hearts," he said. "I love Paris, but I don't like to see babies die. One day we will develop and modernize, but I will be sad to see such simple ways of living disappear. If you are not careful, the same thing will happen to you."

"What same thing?"

He grinned even more broadly.

"You will not be the same when you leave. If you leave America behind and get into Africa truly, you will understand my complaints— the suffering and the starvation, the traditions that weigh us down— and you will have a crisis of the heart. When you talk about Africa, people will think you hate this place. That's when you will remember me and you will know then just how much you love this place and these people."

He laughed a hearty, welcoming laugh and finally let go of my hand.

"Be well, my friend," he said. "And have a good journey."

As he walked away, a little pack of children followed like puppies at his heels, trying to sell him a cold drink. He brushed them aside.

Pirang Primary School, The Gambia

# African
# Journey

～

**BY**

**NAWAL**

**EL SAADAWI**

My journey to Africa was belated. I saw Europe, America and Asia before I saw Africa, even though Africa is the continent in which I live, and our roots and the sources of our Nile grow from its heart.

But our eyes and our faces were always turned towards the Mediterranean, Europe and America, our backs towards Africa, away from ourselves. When one turns one's back on oneself, when one is ashamed of one's brown or black skin and tries to hide it with white make-up, how can one know oneself? The evil of European colonialism was to bleed Africa of her resources and wealth, but the greater evil was that arrow with which the white man wounded the African identity, so that being African became a shameful blemish and a black skin a contract of slavery. My journey to Africa lasted three months, in the summer of 1977; not long enough to enter into the heart of the African, but enough at least to enter into my own heart and learn about myself and about my being African.

The first aspect of my Africanness is the brown colour of my skin which turns black after some days in the sun, so that walking in the streets of Ethiopia or Uganda, hardly anyone notices that I'm a foreigner. I must admit that this does not always please me, for deep inside me, stemming from childhood, is a longing to be as white as cream. I still remember, despite the passing of the years, that ever since I was born, as a child I was certain of two things: firstly that I was a girl and not a boy like my brother and secondly that my skin was brown and not white like my mother's. With these two facts, I realised something even more important: that each of these two characteristics was enough to doom my future to failure. The only quality which prepared a girl (at that time) for a secure future was being beautiful, or at least as white-skinned as the Turks.

My maternal grandmother, who was of Turkish origin, used to tease me by calling me "Slavegirl Warwar".... From then on, it was fixed in my mind that slavegirls and slaves had skin the colour of mine and I began to hide it with white make-up, imagining that the action of hiding my skin was a move towards something better. And yet, another side of me realised that the colour of my skin was as real as my being a girl. And I love the truth. The one true love of my life is the love of my real self. In spite of that, I only gave up make-up completely after I understood the worth of my mind, and then had the courage to face the world with a clean and washed face.

I would sit with African women and men in Dar es Salaam, their skin as black as burned milk or cocoa, tall and erect in stature, the natural movement of their walk like dancing, their eyes when they talked like singing, their songs of love like their songs of revolution, the word "freedom" in the Swahili of East Africa like our Arabic word *al-huriyya* with a slight change of pronunciation. I loved their accent and sang *al-huriyya* with them. They told me I was African like them, but Africa had been divided into north and south; this was black Africa, as though North Africa were not Africa, as though there were a black Africa and a white Africa.

I felt relaxed with them and at ease with myself, with my brown skin. The real parts of myself had emerged, filling me with confidence and pride, feelings I had not had on my trips to Europe and America and Asia, feelings which after I experienced them, made me regret that my journey to Africa came so late.

I now had a comfortable feeling of familiarity with myself and with the brown colour of my skin, a familiarity I had never known so clearly before. I have not forgotten that on my first journey to America in 1965 I stood in front of a mirror in North Carolina before entering the toilet, for I had read the sign "Whites Only" on one door and "Blacks

Only" on another. That day, I stood in front of the mirror confused as to which door to enter. My skin was neither white nor black but somewhere in between and I did not know to which world I belonged.

My Tanzanian friend, Paris, laughed. She is a professor of economics at the University of Dar es Salaam and told me:

—I studied in England in 1959 and they made me feel so inferior for being black and a woman that I became ashamed of myself. But I changed a lot after I studied economics and learned how they had colonised us and destroyed our economy and our souls. In my lifetime I am seeing socialism being gradually realised in my country Tanzania and with the passing of the years I understand the strong links between economic justice and the freedom of men and women. In our authentic African heritage there is no discrimination between men and women. Do you know that our minister of justice is a woman?

She gave me the phone numbers of the justice minister both at home and in her office. I said it might be better to call her in the office rather than at home. Paris was surprised and said there was no difference. I soon realised that people in Africa treat ministers and rulers as ordinary people: there are no doors or barriers or conventions. I spoke with the minister of justice in her house and asked her:

—Are you really minister of justice?

She laughed and told me there were women in all fields, ministers and other. I told her we had one woman minister for social affairs but justice in our country was still the sole domain of men. Talking to the minister of justice, I remembered an article I had read in an Egyptian newspaper last year in which a woman writer had said that there were certain preconditions qualifying a person to take up the position of judge, the first of which was masculinity.

I looked around, walking along the shores of the Indian Ocean in Kenya, Tanzania, Zanzibar, the Seychelles and Madagascar and wondered at the magic I had never seen before. The mountains of Kenya and the towering peak of Kilimanjaro in Tanzania are no less wonderful than the mountains of the Himalayas which I saw in Nepal. The dense green mountains of Ethiopia and Uganda resemble the green paradise around Lake Victoria. The beauty I saw in East Africa I had not seen in Switzerland whose beauty I had often heard praised. The shores and mountains of East Africa were more exotic and green, a combination of mountains, water and dark equatorial vegetation;

mango and coconut trees, the strong smell of equatorial flowers, that refreshing coolness in the air—more refreshing than the cold of a European summer.

I used to think that I would fry, travelling in sub-equatorial Africa in August but I found that, being thousands of feet above sea-level, most of these countries were protected from the heat. The weather was temperate, like springtime in our country, and cooler the higher one got.

The heat in East Africa is in the political climate, and it is a natural heat. Long years of slavery led in the end to a hot revolution which had its advantages and also its dangers. When I said in Cairo that I was going to Uganda and Ethiopia and East Africa, eyes widened in surprise and everyone cautioned me, for revolution was breaking out everywhere. But I was determined to go, for I love to be where people are in revolt and angry. Anger, in my view, is a psychological state suitable to this age. Since primary school, when I first heard about Lake Victoria and the sources of the Nile, I have been determined to go in search of my own sources and roots. My paternal grandfather was called *Habashi* (Ethiopian) and I was told that he was dark-skinned and had Ethiopian blood. When my mother got angry, she would say that I had inherited the skin of my father's family. Was it not my right, after all that, to find out about my roots and sources? As for the sources of the Nile, in Uganda I stood perplexed before the splendour of its high green banks near Kampala, the point of contact between the White Nile and Lake Victoria.

I stood and contemplated the narrow neck of the river at the point of contact with its source. Unconsciously, I raised my hand to my neck and felt in it a strange terror and tremor, for that small narrow neck was an artery in the earth of my body. It was my neck, yet it was not in my body but in another body, Uganda, surging with the violence of the political upheavals of Idi Amin.

On the heights of Ethiopia and in Addis Ababa, about seven thousand feet [2100 m] above sea level, the rains poured down day and night. I understood that these rains carried irrigation and silt to us and I rejoiced at the sound of thunder, saying to myself: these gushing waters will flow into the land of my peasant people.

When my husband, children and I got out of the plane at Entebbe Airport, we realised we were the only visitors to Uganda and the airport staff looked at us in surprise and wonder. Who were these adventurers coming to Uganda at such a tense time? The management of the Lake Victoria Hotel in Entebbe advised us not to leave the hotel after sunset.

In Dar es Salaam and Nairobi they gave us the same advice: don't walk in the streets after sunset. As the days were noisy, full of sun, movement and vitality, so the nights were dark, silent and full of danger. The city of Nairobi in Kenya, built in ultra-modern style, plunged into all the activity of a modern city, but as soon as night fell, the streets were empty of all but thieves. In Dar es Salaam, before the sun set, you saw Tanzanian boys and girls strolling along the shores of the Indian Ocean, the barefoot girls selling boiled eggs or green mangoes, the boys sitting in front of the buyer peeling the egg for him, then splitting it with a small spoon and filling it with hot pepper. Green mangoes were also cut with a knife and filled with pepper. In the cafés sat women as well as men, alone or in groups, drinking beer, smoking and talking politics. But as soon as the sun set, the streets emptied of people and darkness and silence fell, apart from the small lights that came from the ships anchored in the port.

They say that Nairobi, the capital of Kenya, is the bridegroom of Africa. It is a modern city, although it seemed to me like a groom who has put on a beautiful robe on the outside, but whose undergarments are ugly. I have seen this duality in the capitals of countries which are not liberated or which are only liberated in appearance. Many capitals in our Third World are like Nairobi. I remembered Bangkok when I walked in the streets of Nairobi: the same modern buildings, the same American cars, the same broad tarmaced streets, the same corners on which prostitutes stood, same American crime and sex films in the cinema, the same advertisements for Kent cigarettes, Cadillacs, Seven Up and Coca Cola.

I stopped for a moment in front of one of the cinemas, looking at the queues of young Africans, youth completely defenceless against this creeping danger, this flood of cheap art, this evil brainwashing that is perpetrated every day not only in the countries of Africa and Asia, but in America and Europe too: but western youth has acquired a sort of immunity to such danger, due perhaps to the relatively higher economic and educational standards of living. Our African young have no weapons with which to protect themselves from this epidemic.

A tall African youth, wearing a chain around his neck and a coloured shirt on which was drawn a heart and the words, "I love New York" in English, smoked a Kent cigarette and chewed gum. I saw him as ugly, the city of Nairobi uglier still. I realised the real insult behind what we call ugliness: it is the contradiction between external elegance and the internal corruption, whether in a person or in a city.

I flew in a small plane, a German Volker that was like an old bus with torn seats and propellers that sounded like an antique motorcar. I thought it would fall from the sky as the lights of Dar es Salaam shone under me, the ships in the port glistened like dolls. The plane landed twenty-five minutes later on the island of Zanzibar, a dark and silent island that seemed to hold a closed undiscovered secret. In the airport they gave me four quinine tablets against malaria. They told me that the island was infested with malaria and filaria and tuberculosis. Those suffering from leprosy were quarantined on another nearby island known as the Island of Death.

I stared into the darkness, sitting in the taxi from the airport to the Bwana Hotel. The air was heavy with death. I considered going back to the airport, but the desire to know was strong. I had stepped onto the soil of Zanzibar, the island of slavery, and breathed the smell of enslavement. In the huge hotel on the shore, the bellboy bowed and took my case from me.

In the morning, I lay beside the swimming pool, not daring to go into the water. A smell like death emanated from the depths of the pool and from all over the garden. The bellboy whispered in my ear:

—When we dug up the earth to lay the swimming pool, we found thousands of bodies and human skeletons. They killed the revolutionaries and buried their corpses here before the hotel was built.

I jumped up and went to pack my case, deciding to move to another hotel.

—This is the only hotel on the island, the bellboy said. The others are old and third class. Nobody goes to them because of the malaria and filaria mosquitoes.

—Malaria and filaria are better than staying in this hotel, I said.

I moved to a small hotel in a narrow alleyway, called Africa House, overlooking the ocean. The building was African Muslim in style, with strong and massive pillars like African forearms. The room was clean, the bed was covered by a white sheet and the smell of cloves emanated all around and revived me. The sound of singing and drums filled the air with joyfulness. Children carrying small lanterns walked in the streets singing to the month of Ramadan. It reminded me of the children of my village on the banks of the Nile. The small roadside shops were like those of Moski in Cairo. A child gave me a branch of clover and shook my hand saying:

—*Qaribou wajini yanju*

I did not understand. A small girl who knew Arabic told me:

—He's welcoming you.

The girl's name was Hoda and she was the daughter of an Egyptian working at the Egyptian Consulate. Her mother came out of a clover shop and shook my hand. Her name was Um 'Ala. She did not have a son called 'Ala, but the whole island was Muslim and they had old customs. They did not call a mother by her name but by her son's name. If she had no son, they invented one for her, simply so that she could carry his name.

She drove me in her small yellow car to her house. On the wall was a picture of the Pyramids of Giza and the Sphinx, and a prayer mat with the picture of the Ka'aba in Mecca. Her features were thoroughly Egyptian, her head like Cleopatra, and the expression in her large black eyes was a combination of strength and sadness. She brought me a tray of tea and small festive cakes and said:

—I have read your books and wanted to come to your clinic in Cairo.

—I closed my clinic years ago, I said.

—Why? she exclaimed.

—I was not happy with the idea of giving people health at a price, I said.

—I spent everything I had on psychologists in Cairo. I suffer from depression, doctor. My drawers are filled with sedatives and tranquillisers. I left my job in Cairo to accompany my husband on his diplomatic life. Twenty years we've been travelling all over the world, from New York to Zanzibar. Hoda, my daughter, lives alone in Cairo throughout the year and we only see her in the summer holidays. My father died when I was in New York and I did not see him. My mother died last year when I was here in Zanzibar. My husband also suffers from depression because he hates Sadat and knows that he does not work for the good of Egypt, but every day he has to say the opposite because of his diplomatic post.

Her daughter Hoda came in at that moment and Um 'Ala stopped talking. Then she changed the subject and said:

—What have you seen in Zanzibar?

—Nothing, I said. Until now I was in the Bwana Hotel under which are buried human skulls.

Um 'Ala laughed.

—I'll take you by car to see Zanzibar museum, which used to be a slave house.

I sat beside her in her small car. Her delicate fingers around the steering wheel were calm and confident. I heard her say:

—Driving gives me self-confidence and makes me feel independent. My whole life I've lived in the shadow of a man, my husband, even in the shadow of an illusory son. I have created for myself another world in which I dream of freedom, as a slave does.

Some children gathered around the car and ran behind us like the village children of Egypt do. Their faces were as pale and thin as those of the children in my village, and covered with flies. Um 'Ala said:

—The island of Zanzibar has many resources and much clover, but the people here do not have meat or vegetables or even water. Everything is imported from Dar es Salaam. The necessities of life are not here on the island, but there are colour televisions and other luxuries imported from Europe and America.

The girls wore long dresses and covered their heads. A girl who wore a short dress in the street, even if she was ten years old, was liable to be imprisoned for anything from three days to six months. The voice of the *muezzin* from the minarets was louder than the sound of the radios and colour televisions.

We reached a small square called Slave Square, in the middle of which was an enormous church like those of the Middle Ages. Its windows had bars and reminded me of the inquisition courts. Behind the church was another building as huge as a palace, built on pillars and surrounded by trees. The walls of the palace were blackened as though from an old fire. The sultan had lived in this palace in 1899 with his *harem* of hundreds of women. The women conspired against the sultan and burned down the castle, then escaped to the ocean in boats. Beside the palace was a tower called the House of Wonders. The aroma of cloves filled the air and the coastline stretched onto the horizon. Tall slender coconut trees reached up to the sky, the dense green leaves of the mango trees waved in the ocean breeze, and waves broke over the rocks that rose from the water as black as the heads of slaves. The slaves' house itself, like the rocks, was a memorial to the time of slavery. The rock dungeon deep inside the building had been a storeroom, where slaves were stored like goods and where they lived with snakes for months.

In the square, the men, women and children were sold in chains in the market. In the small museum we saw the iron chains behind glass. On one piece of iron was a dark spot, like old blood.

We returned to the car with heavy hearts. In Um 'Ala's home at the lunch table, I met her Egyptian husband and two other men, one of them a civil servant named Mahmoud who worked in the Egyptian Embassy in Dar es Salaam, and the second a leader of the nationalists in Zanzibar named Sheikh Ali Muhassan. His face was as strong and sad as an imprisoned lion, a combination of Arab and African features. Arabs and Africans have intermixed in Zanzibar for hundreds of years so that you can hardly tell them apart.

Sheikh Ali Muhassan had fought with his comrades against English colonialism until Zanzibar won its political independence and began to aim for economic independence. Colonialism did not see much harm in African countries becoming politically independent as long as economically they remained attached to the capitalist market; no country was allowed to escape from its economic grasp. Ali Muhassan and his colleagues were imprisoned in Dar es Salaam. Most of them died in prison, but Ali Muhassan managed to escape and get away with his life.

He said: The English are scared of Zanzibar because the revolution is underground and may spread to Tanzania and other African countries. English colonialism continues to work in secret in Africa, together with America.

A heavy and apprehensive silence fell. The air, too, had grown still. I went to a window overlooking the ocean. The Island of Death, where they abandoned leprosy sufferers to the hyenas and snakes, signalled from afar. Between the dense trees I saw the pillars of the burned palace and the Bwana Hotel where thousands of revolutionaries had been buried under the swimming pool; the Slave Square where the chains and the rock dungeons were.

From the island of sadness and slaves, I flew to Dar es Salaam and from there to the island of Madagascar, which they call the Island of Smiles. The plane landed in the middle of the road, on an island in the middle of the ocean called the Seychelle Island, a strip of green land set in the midst of the water, waves and rocks. The features of the people were a mix of Arab and African blood, their unintelligible dialect a mix of Swahili and Arabic. White moonlight reflected on white robes, the whole island was enveloped in a sort of magic and behind the beauty was the smell of intrigue and smuggling.

From the Seychelles, the plane took me to Tananarive, the capital of Madagascar, known as the city of a thousand fighters and a thousand houses. Its small white houses with sloping red roofs were built on the hills and were gradually covering upper and lower slopes. Its people had fought the Portuguese, the Arabs, the English and the French and finally gained independence in June 1960. The women fought alongside the men, worked in all fields and had the same rights as the men.

Young men and women walked arm in arm on the shore that led to the main street, Independence Street, in the centre of town. At the end of the street was a market called *al-Zouma*, the word taken from the Arabic *al-Joum'a* (Friday market), with small shops and white sunshades. I saw flowers, fruits, a festival of colours, people wearing large hats of palm leaves and straw, smiling and exchanging greetings, beautiful and perfect handicrafts; a hybrid of Arab, Asian and European cultures.

The people on the island of Zanzibar lived in poverty and sadness whereas here the people seemed more joyful and nature more beautiful. Girls danced the flower dance around the lake, smiling, their dresses fantastic colours. If Zanzibar was the Island of Sadness and Slavery, Madagascar was the Island of Smiles and Joy.

# Provincial

~

**BY**

**MIRIAM**

**WADDINGTON**

My childhood
was full of people
with Russian accents
who came from
Humble Saskatchewan
or who lived in Regina
and sometimes
visited Winnipeg
to bring regards
from their frozen
snowqueen city.

In those days
all the streetcars
in the world slept
in the Elmwood
car-barns and the
Indian moundbuilders
were still wigwammed
across the river
with the birds
who sang in the bushes
of St Vital.

Since then I have
visited Paris
Moscow London
and Mexico City
I saw golden roofs
onion domes and the
most marvellous
canals, I saw people
sunning themselves
in Luxembourg Gardens
and on a London parkbench
I sat beside a man
who wore navy blue socks
and navy blue shoes
to match.

All kinds of miracles:
but I would not trade
any of them for the
empty spaces, the
snowblurred geography
of my childhood.

# Pilgrimage to Sighet, a Haunted City

### BY

### ELIE

### WIESEL

or most of you, the name Transylvania naturally evokes a country haunted by Dracula. For me, who was born there, it means something entirely different. In fact, I never learned of the existence, or rather the legend, of that malevolent count, one whose bizarre habits could not help but make him a star of Broadway and Hollywood, until after my arrival in the United States. When asked about my birthplace, I would naïvely reply that I came from a little city deep in a forgotten province called Transylvania, and no one would let me say more before the laughter started. The laughter would grow all the heartier because I understood nothing of it: "Ah, Dracula," they would say, with many a wink. All right: now I know.

Yet you should not think that the Jewish children of Transylvania lived happily and without fear. They lived happily, but not without fear. We were always worried, anxious, threatened from all sides. Bandits, we were told, were spying on us from high in the mountains. And there were the louts and cowards, steeped in some ancestral, hereditary hatred, who would attack us and beat us; like Dracula, they apparently needed to draw some blood—Jewish blood—to feel proud of themselves.

I am no longer a child, but even today Transylvania still chills me, or rather, a little corner of Transylvania does: Sighet, my native city. I live there no longer, yet it lives within me. It has been 40 years since I left there for good, and I am still a little fearful each time I see the place again.

If I were a tourist seeking that perfect place to spend a holiday, to learn a little and to relax as well, I would go there without hesitation.

Why not, after all? Easily reachable, picturesque and inexpensive, Sighet has everything you could want: mountains, rivers, hotels and memories.

You would take the plane or a train from Bucharest to Baia-Mare, in Crisana-Maramures, and from there a bus or a cab would take you to the other side of the mountain, into a valley. Yet another twisting road climbs over Satu-Mare, wandering through villages, small towns and hamlets so bright in colors and yet so apparently untouched by time, so nearly primitive, that they seem to belong to an earlier age.

Here, peasants match your mental image of a peasant, dressed as they have been through ages, representing today as always that durable connection with their livelihood: the earth, trees, animals, flowers, the sky. For them, the land's official Communism is but an abstraction, and like their parents they feel most at home in church. To what extent are they touched by the crises and conflicts which agitate distant societies? Nothing is more timeless than the arms of the shepherd bringing home his flock in the gloaming, or the slow steps of a laborer as he follows his wagon. Their presence will make you feel rootless, shorn of your nationhood, and so much the better for it, for isn't that why you took the trip in the first place?

Sighet, my birthplace, is a little city, so much like the rest and so little like any other. Except for a few new apartment buildings, the houses are the same ones I used to skirt on my way to school, or on my way to my grandmother's.

Back then, before the torment, it was a little Jewish city, a typical shtetl, rambunctious and vibrant with beauty and faith, with its yeshivas and its workshops, it madmen and its princes, its silent beggars and noisy big shots. We spoke Yiddish, protected ourselves in Rumanian or Hungarian or Ruthenian, and we prayed in Hebrew. In the Jewish streets the businessmen argued in the mornings and made up by evening; in the shtiblech the Hasidim said their prayers, studied the Talmud, told those wonderful stories about their miracle-working rabbis.

Immersed in Jewish life, following the rhythms of the Hebrew calendar, the city rested on the Sabbath, blossomed on the Day of Atonement, danced on the eve of Simhath Torah. Even the Christians knew there was no point in asking for bread in a Jewish bakery during Easter week, that you should never offer to buy a glass of Tzuica for a Jewish bartender on the ninth day of the month of Av, for that day, marked by mourning, recalls the destruction of the Temple at Jerusalem.

All that is now gone. The Jews of my city are now forgotten, erased from its memory. Before, there were some 30 synagogues in Sighet; today, only one survives. The Jewish tailors, the Jewish cordwainers, the Jewish watchmakers are vanished without a trace, and strangers have taken their places.

It has been 20 years since I first returned like this. Maybe it was just out of simple curiosity. Others like me have done it. The young and the no longer young return to the scenes of their youths, to the ruins of their past. Some want to perform the ancient ritual of praying at the graves of their ancestors. Others just want to see their own homes, their yards, their neighbors. There was a time when they were the only tourists here.

So it was 20 years ago that I first revisited these streets, walking for hours on end. I still remember: Passers-by saw me without seeing, and I saw them while beholding only the ghosts that surrounded them, and the ghosts were more real, more living than they! I saw friends long dead, comrades long dead, dead rabbis, dead disciples, and they were alive. I had planned on staying a few days and, gripped by panic, I fled after only a few hours.

The second time I returned with a television crew working on a documentary. It was impossible to go anywhere alone and, always accompanied, always under surveillance, I felt like an actor in an unsettling role. As soon as the filming was done, I turned my back once again on my city.

Now I am here on my third visit. I was invited by the Rumanian Jewish community and joined its chief rabbi, Dr. David-Moses Rosen, in a melancholy pilgrimage to commemorate the deportation of Transylvania's Jews 40 years ago.

For four days, all of them superbly and efficiently organized by the authorities, we went from one city to the next, from one ceremony to the next: Dej, Satu-Mare, Oradea, Sarmas: how many candles does it take to mark the deaths of thousands and thousands of men, women and children? How many times must one say Kaddish? From everywhere, it seemed, moved by a mysterious call, Jews came out of their towns near and far, came to weep together, to plumb that collective memory from which their brothers and parents, beyond a desert of ashes, spoke to them, speak to them.

At Sighet I visited the Jewish cemetery where lies the grave of the grandfather whose name I bear. It was strange: I felt more at home among the graves than among the living beyond the gate. An extraordinary serenity dwelt in the graveyard, and I spoke quietly to my grandfather, and told him what I have done with his name.

Then, with a childhood friend, a fellow pilgrim, we ambled through the streets and alleys in silence, not daring to glance at one another. I recognized each window, each tree. Names and faces spring before me as if from nowhere, as if preparing to reoccupy their former homes. I stopped before my old house and with a beating heart, nearly beside myself, I waited for a youth to come out, to beckon me nearer, to demand to know what I was doing there, in his life. A nameless anguish overcame me: What if all that I had lived had only been a dream?

In the space of six weeks a vibrant and creative community had been condemned first to solitude, then to misery, and at last to deportation and death.

The last transport left the station on a Sunday morning. It was hot, we were thirsty, and it was less than three weeks before the Allied invasion of Normandy. Why did we go? We could have fled, hidden ourselves in the mountains or in the villages. The ghetto was not very well guarded; a mass escape would have had every chance of success. But we did not know.

Hear me well, those of you who want to spend your vacation somewhere in Transylvania: You will not meet my friends there. They were massacred because no one thought it was necessary to warn them, to tell them not to go quietly into those windowless train cars. If this tragedy of Transylvania's Judaism hurts, if it hurts so terribly, it is not only because its victims are so near to me but because it could have been prevented.

So, you understand, the beauty of the countryside, the serenity and comfort and the hospitality that awaits you, none of that is for me. But go, if it tempts you. And why wouldn't Transylvania tempt you? Despite the barely concealed police state, despite the poverty, you may be happy there. The gardens are splendid, the hotels are new, the reception that awaits you is warm.

Only, while you explore the cities and the villages, while you enjoy their special picturesqueness, try to evoke within yourself the memories of the men and women, and of the children—especially the children—who years ago were driven away from this place and who today travel endlessly through mankind's wounded memory, signaling us inevitably, and yet so needfully, for the sake of our own survival.

# Because of You, Kyushu

BY

RITA

ARIYOSHI

here is a saying in our family: *okage-sama de*. Because of you. It is meant to acknowledge our interdependence, and to deflect any honor or glory from ourselves to others. Because of you, I am what I am and I have this moment. Without you, it would not be possible.

We arrived in Yoshitomi-cho by train and were greeted by relatives we had never met. We had not expected them to come. We had planned on a taxi. But there they were, instantly recognizable—the same wide faces, the same bones—come to welcome the son of their deceased brother, who had gone to Hawaii so many years ago. We all stood on the train platform, eyes brimming with tears, bowing across the years and oceans, nobody touching, just bowing lower and bowing again, and again.

Later, in a little Kyushu village surrounded by luminous rice fields, my Japanese-American husband prayed at the shrine of his ancestors. Then, accompanied by a gaggle of nieces and nephews, we walked up the hill above the house to the graves where our name was inscribed in the ancient kanji characters in the stone. We stood for long moments. Yes, because of you. Okage-sama de.

My story of Kyushu is not just the chronicle of our family, but the story of Japan itself. Kyushu is the source of all that we think of as Japanese. Recent archaeological evidence indicates that humans have lived

on Kyushu, the most southern and western of Japan's four main islands, for about 12 000 years. The oldest pottery yet discovered was unearthed here. Legends say that when the sun goddess sent her grandson Ninigi to govern Japan, he touched down on Kyushu and wed the daughter of a local god. The date, as "calculated" by imperial historians, was February 11, 660 B.C. Ninigi's line continues to this day in the person of Emperor Akihito.

Ours is a much more modest family tree, although Jim remembers that his father, who owned a laundry business in Honolulu, was, from the minute he walked in the door of his house, accorded the deference due a god.

"Yes," Jim assured the houseful of relatives gathered on the tatami mats, "I grew up in a traditional Japanese home." They were greatly relieved, especially in view of me, his *hakujin*—Caucasian—wife.

Over a lunch prepared at great expense, including a bright red lobster on a swirled black-and-white plate, we fell easily into the universal patter of families. Aunt Tsuruye, cradling a grandson, recalled marrying into the family as a very young girl. "I was a picture bride to China. Noboru was living there during—excuse me, I'm very sorry—World War II. I didn't meet him until my wedding day. But I had seen a picture of him, and my family highly recommended him to me."

Noboru had passed away only two months ago, and clearly Aunt Tsuruye enjoyed speaking of him. We looked at photographs. Jim, the family announced, was the image of his father as they remembered him... Because of you, Kyushu.

We had boarded the bullet train in Tokyo, bound for Kyushu with great expectations. We had been to Tokyo many times, and to paraphrase the 17th-century poet Basho, "Though in Japan, we longed for Japan." From the window, as the train slashed through a corridor of factories, smokestacks, power poles, and concrete condos that could have been steel mills (except for the laundry lines), it appeared that the Japanese had entirely devoured their land.

At the end of a long dark tunnel under the sea was Kyushu. We blazed into the light and almost wailed aloud at the sight: shipyards, fuel storage tanks, and the erector-set tangle of the city of Kitakyushu. Was there nothing left of serene green hills and lyrical streams tumbling over rounded rocks? Was nature in Japan reduced to a dish holding a bonsai garden?

But in time the factories began to thin out and the rice fields grew larger. There were hills in the hazy blue distance. We changed trains and boarded a lovely old coach with wooden floors, velvet seats, lacy curtains, and shiny brass fittings. The conductor wore a snappy plaid blazer. Ice cream was served, and pizza with shredded ginger. The train chugged along the coast, past fishermen in sturdy wooden boats. It puffed and tooted around curves and up into the woods and hills of Oita prefecture to our first stop, the town of Yufuin, where streets followed canals crossed by little bridges, and some of the older homes still had high thatched roofs.

Our inn was built of fragrant cedar. The entry stones and walkway through the bamboo had been washed for our arrival. Spare and cool, our cottage had mat floors and our own *furo*, a generous wooden tub that looked out on a wild, artfully untended garden. After a good soak at what seemed like the edge of the known world, we slipped into kimonos and *geta,* wooden clogs, and clumped clumsily off to dinner.

In the early morning we walked to a lake. Mist was rising slowly from the surface. The colors were palest pastel. The lotus blossoms had not yet stretched from their buds. An old torii gate inhabited the far shore. I had found Japan.

Kyushu is where the Japanese go when their souls have had enough of Western ways. The hot springs resort area of Beppu attracts 12 million tourists a year, almost all of them Japanese. They come not only for the soothing thermal pools, but to relax and wear their *yukata*, fine cotton kimonos, in the street and walk in geta.

Every evening in the town of Hita, canopied barges festooned with pink paper lanterns floated out on the river. Those aboard wore kimonos and sat around on pillows, drinking sake and eating dinner. After more sake the singing started, and the barges rocked gently with dancing, the pink lanterns bobbing in the darkness as the happy music carried across the water.

It was summer, the season, it seemed, of traditional festivals. Throughout Kyushu people celebrated the O'bon, when Buddhists believe that departed ancestors return to earth, by dancing in the streets to the hypnotic sounds of flutes, drums, and samisen.

In the small town of Hondo we came upon a parade of floats, lanterns, troops of scouts, groups of women in traditional costumes with elaborate hats, and men dressed as fishermen and samurai. The parade had begun at sundown and would continue until sunup. We surrendered to exhaustion, returned to our inn, tumbled onto the plump futon sleeping mats, and fell asleep to the sound of distant gongs.

In Fukuoka, Kyushu's main city, we were among the 700 000 people who rose before dawn to cheer the race that culminates Hakata Gion Yamagasa, a two-week festival in July. Teams of men in loincloths and *happi* coats carried seven elaborate floats weighing a ton apiece through the streets in a contest so strenuous that no man could shoulder the burden for more than 50 seconds at a time. Each float demanded the effort of 600 men to run the three miles [4.8 km] to the finish. With the battle cry *"Oissa! Oissa!"* the race started at precisely 4:59 a.m.

The shouts of the crowd became a brawny mantra as the men surged forward. "Oissa! Oissa!" The crowd roared in one voice. They threw buckets of water on the burdened men, whose bodies gleamed with sweat. It was a tradition that has been carried on for more than 750 years, little changed with the times. The floats used to be much bigger; now they have to fit beneath power lines.

All over Kyushu we continued to encounter that fabled soul of Japan, still alive and well, perhaps with a few modern compromises. At one hostel our kimonoed attendant, kneeling as she poured our tea, was interrupted by the bleep of her beeper tucked in her silk obi. *"Gomenasai,"* she whispered, "Excuse me." Then she raced for the telephone across the room.

At Yanagawa, the former home of a feudal lord has become a hotel with both Western and tatami rooms, and Western and Japanese gardens. The Japanese garden, laid out a century ago, is a miniature landscape of sea and mountains, meticulously manicured down to the smallest pine needle. The Western garden suffers some neglect. The gardeners do not understand it, or love it. Every evening the hotel staff sets out chairs and tables on the grass. They play old recordings of "Ramblin' Rose" and "Love Potion Number Nine," and serve nuts and beers to tourists from Taiwan.

In Yanagawa a friend who lives in a house with a Western-style living room and a Japanese-style dining room took us to the home of Kitahara Hakushu, a beloved Kyushu poet who died a half century ago. The house was set in a little garden. Shoji screens opened out to small views of immense delicacy. The rooms were almost devoid of furniture, the lighting soft, the wood fragrant with age. The floor timbers creaked beneath the tatami mats. The home had the sanctity and austerity of a monastery. Our friend said, "I come here often because I feel so Japanese when I'm here." From there we dashed off to pick up her young son, who had been playing in a baseball game that afternoon.

Change, whether the Japanese like it or not, is advancing at a two-steps-forward, one-step-backward pace. When we asked about a huge new home in the middle of the rice fields near Beppu, a young secretary complained, "Even Kyushu is beginning to change. In the last five years executives from Tokyo companies are coming and buying up the land and putting up big estates. It's driving our prices up."

But, she added, "Japanese society has not changed a lot since feudal times. We just have new shoguns."

The days of the original shoguns were days of glory for the privileged and saw a great flowering of Japanese arts. The era is celebrated annually in July at Kumamoto Castle, when lords in ancient armor, maids in pastel kimonos, saffron-robed monks, and brawny young men bearing golden shrines all come streaming out of the castle walls once again to parade about the city.

More than any part of the country, Kyushu seems to me to offer this sense of old Japan, not fossilized in temples and museums, but still lived and loved. One afternoon I watched a modern mother, impeccably suited in the latest fashion, gently instructing her teenage daughter in how to hold a cup of tea, turning the vessel so the best side faces the host.

The mother's gestures had the ease of a much practiced dance. The daughter was obedient though awkward, her movements jerky. But they would do this quietly together over the years until the girl grew into grace.

As a foreigner I sometimes got instruction of my own. In a small *ryokan* in Hondo, another kimonoed attendant, assuming I was unschooled in chopsticks, apologized profusely for not having any forks, and said she had no idea where she might get one.

The foreigner in Kyushu is treated with overwhelming kindness, rather like an indulged child. Our many breaches of esoteric etiquette are corrected and pardoned with a smile. The Japanese are well aware that their ways are confounding. The streets of some old cities were deliberately laid out to confuse an advancing army, and many of their customs seem to be founded on the same philosophy.

The simple act of bathing can be a perilous ritual fraught with potential for embarrassment. I was seduced into shedding both my inhibitions and my clothing by the reputation of Kyushu's thermal waters for curing an assortment of ailments and bestowing inner tranquility. We were in Beppu, the Reno of the Japanese hot springs towns, staying at the gargantuan Suginoi hotel, where the dinner buffet is as long as a football field and the *onsen* bath areas measured by the acre. I assumed that in a crowd my bath gaffes and my naked alien body might go unnoticed.

The Suginoi's two largest onsen are the Flower Bath and the Dream Bath. One for men and one for women, on alternating days. Even though I had received elaborate instructions regarding manners, I got off on the wrong foot by wearing my hall slippers too far into the

dressing room. A woman, naked except for a shower cap, bowing and smiling, showed me, bowing and apologizing, where to leave them. I disrobed; then, with what I hoped was the dexterity of an origami artist, I folded my kimono neatly and placed it in a basket. Like the other women, I draped my oversize washcloth over strategic zones and entered the bath. It was an enormous steamy greenhouse with a high glass roof sheltering what appeared to be a slice of the Amazon rain forest. Several small pools were situated around a large pool, in the middle of which, on a revolving dais, a great gilt Buddha and a Kannon, who represents compassion and mercy, presided over the bath, looking like a very big mama with a child on her knee.

It's amazing how our survival instincts work. In a fraction of a second I sized up the situation and, following the example of other new arrivals, walked to the side of the room, sat on a little stool, and poured a bucket of warm water over my body. I then soaped myself lavishly in an exercise that seemed to be part fastidiousness and part performance. Then I sat there, fully lathered, unable to figure out how to turn on the high-tech faucets with their multiple dials, hoses, and instructions printed in kanji characters. I turned a few dials. Nothing. Panic. Just when I feared I would have to retreat to my room trailing billows of suds, I spotted a shower with two easy faucets, rinsed, and stepped into the warm, soothing mineral bath. Buddha and Kannon looked down on me impassively as they made their rounds. The other women smiled, nodded, tried to engage me in conversation, then fell to talking quietly among themselves, lapsing into contented silences.

There is something very soothing about women bathing together, the soft chatter, the quietness, the absence of all maleness. Perhaps we harbor a lingering genetic memory of bathing together in rivers long ago. There was almost a solemnity, certainly a purity. I found that for hours afterward I was very alert, but my body seemed to be breathing on its own, as if I were asleep. I became an onsen junkie.

Some of Kyushu's springs are too hot to tame. They spit out of the ground, hissing over rocks in steamy rivers. At Ibusuki even the beach is thermally heated; people come from all over the country for sand baths.

Volcanic activity is at the very heart of Kyushu. One volcanic mountain, Aso, near Kumamoto city, has the largest caldera in the world. Within its crater are several towns and villages, a rail line, and lush rolling farmland. Aso is also a national park. The cliffs of the crater fall away in green palisades amid waterfalls, crystal clear streams, and forests of cedar and bamboo.

Still, the natural world has competition. One evening from a grassy knoll we watched a high-tech sound-and-light show featuring a metal grid assaulted by colored lights and space music full of growls and squeaky voices. Afterward we promised Masako Tanaka, who had accompanied us to Aso, that we would awaken her before sunrise for a real show.

In the first light of day the hills were flooded in gold and tinged with delicate pink. Wildflowers cheered the meadows—golden lilies, Queen Anne's lace, and gentians. Masako had never before gotten up to greet the dawn. She was ecstatic; "I didn't know it could be like this." She climbed a hill and stood with the sun beaming on her and lilies at her feet and threw her hands into the air, unable to contain her joy. Then she was overcome with bashfulness. She clutched her purse to her breasts in her typical shy posture, scarcely able to believe she had been so brash....

In 1543 Portuguese sailors, blown off course by a typhoon, landed on a small island off the coast of Kyushu. That chance contact brought other ships, and in 1549 tales of an alluring heathen land inspired the famous missionary, Francis Xavier, to set out for Japan. Mixing prayer and politics was standard practice for Jesuit missionaries and as they worked to convert the Kyushu daimyo, or lords, they also established Portuguese trading posts on the island, first at Hirako and Sakai, then at the small fishing village of Nagasaki.

The port quickly grew into one of the most prosperous cities in the country. The Portuguese were called *nambanjin,* southern barbarians. In spite of their uncomplimentary name and their reputation for not bathing, *namban* dress, food, religion, art, and objects became the rage throughout Japan.

Perceiving the new religion as a threat, the ruling shogun expelled all missionaries from Japan in 1587, though little was done to enforce his edict. Ten years later, however, six foreign and twenty Japanese Christians were crucified for their faith in Nagasaki. And though it seemed for a time that that was the end of the persecutions, eventually the practice of Christianity was forced underground. By 1638 some 40 000 Christians had been massacred. A year later the Portuguese were expelled from the country, Japan was closed to foreigners, Japanese citizens living or traveling abroad were forbidden to return home, and all trade (now run exclusively by the Dutch) was confined to a small island in Nagasaki Bay. For two centuries Nagasaki was the nation's only peephole to the outside world.

The religious sanctions were finally withdrawn in 1873, but even before that thousands of hidden Christians had emerged in the Nagasaki region. For generations they had practiced their faith in secret. Even though they no longer knew the meaning of the Latin, they recited prayers in their homes in front of Kannon statues that have come to be called Maria Kannon. These statues were very Buddhist-looking but were venerated as Mary with the infant Jesus.

In the 20th century death again came to Kyushu by the thousands, this time for residents of all faiths. On August 9, 1945, three days after the first atom bomb destroyed Hiroshima, a second was detonated over Nagasaki, killing more than 70 000 people and erasing half of the city.

At Nagasaki's International Cultural Hall, which is really the atom bomb museum, we were served iced tea as film footage of the devastation unreeled. It was a landscape of horror shaped by heat that reached

7200°F [3982 C] and a blast that roared through the city at the speed of sound. Factories became twisted metal, schools instant graveyards.

One single image from the footage stayed with me; not the relentless human agony (God help us, but we have seen so many piles of mutilated corpses on television) but instead a sweep of land with nothing on it living, not a tree, not a blade of grass as far as the eye could see, to the seared and burned mountains. Nothing moved. A wind would have stirred only ashes.

I stopped taking notes. It was unbearable to watch. Asked for my reaction, I could only say, "The angels must have wept." As we did.

Today, a simple black marble slab in the Peace Park marks the epicenter of the bomb. It has no inscription.

What can be said?

Later we climbed to the top of Mount Inasa and looked down on Nagasaki, rebuilt around its bowl of a harbor and straying up the mountainsides. Resurrected, it is easily one of the prettiest cities in Japan. One evening we went to not one but two lantern festivals, to listen to the grandmothers sing favorite folk songs and watch pretty girls dance with fans. It was hot, and the din of people, gongs, and loud monotonous music was intoxicating. We stuffed ourselves with *mochi,* rice paste wrapped in seaweed, and in the heat of the night we succumbed to luridly colored shaved ice cones, crunchy, sweet, cold. Strings of lanterns, each painted with a message and the name of a donor, festooned the trees. Beneath these necklaces of light were game booths and souvenir stalls laden with wind chimes. "Win a gold fish or a Donald Duck mask," shouted the hawkers late into the night. Everyone was in a kimono or a happi coat. Tired children were draped on the shoulders of their fathers.

In the end Kyushu was the Japan we had longed for, the Japan where people still string lanterns from temple trees and dance in the streets in summer, where they care deeply about how a cup of tea is held, and where they welcome the stranger with an overwhelming hospitality that has less to do with honor and more to do with simple kindness.

Okage-sama de. Because of you, we remember who we are and what paths we have traveled.

# And I Remember

~

BY

AFUA

COOPER

And I remember
standing
in the churchyard on Wesleyan hill
standing and looking down on the plains
that stretched before me
like a wide green carpet
the plains full with sugar cane and rice
the plains that lead to the sea

And I remember
walking
as a little girl to school
on the savannas of Westmoreland
walking from our hillbound village
along steep hillsides
walking carefully so as not to trip and plunge
walking into the valley

And I remember
running
to school on the road that cuts into the green carpet
running past laughing waters
running past miles of sugar cane and paddies of rice
running to school that rose like a concrete castle
running with a golden Westmoreland breeze

And I remember
breathing
the smell of the earth plowed by rain and tractors
breathing the scent of freshly cut cane
breathing the scent of rice plants as they send
their roots into the soft mud

and I remember
thinking
this is mine    this is mine
this sweetness of mountains
valleys
rivers
and plains
is mine
mine
mine

# A Father's Journey

### BY

### PAUL

### HAWRYLUK

t's 9 a.m. when I wheel the Accord into the parking lot at the Calgary International Airport. To the east, the sun is just clearing low-level cloud prior to ascending above the high stratus that covers the city. I know from my own days as a pilot, before a heart attack grounded me, that this weather makes for the best flying conditions. I am silently pleased.

My wife, Frida, sits beside me, keeping her thoughts to herself, while Jonathan, our son, remains snuggled in a quilt in the backseat, where he's slept since we left our home in Lethbridge early this morning. Sandra isn't talkative either. All summer she chatted about her experiences teaching English in China. She's been excited about going back, but if she has any misgivings now, she isn't sharing them. Today, it's hard to read any emotion in our 26-year-old daughter's face of independence. She's dressed casually in Levi's, a faded blue work shirt from a shop for foreigners in Shanghai and a purple plastic Filipino headband from Baguio. She's a true blend of East and West, at least in dress.

All the best spots in the parking lot are taken, so we have to walk. Sandra's response to this is a Chinese *ah-yooo,* a catchall negative response. I suppose this is a good sign—she's beginning to think and react in Mandarin.

Frida wheels a luggage cart over and we begin loading the two enormous suitcases, a suitcase trolley and carry-on packs that could be suitcases in their own right. I struggle with the heaviest one, which is gorged full of clothes and "essentials" not easily attainable in China: hot chocolate, candy bars and shampoo. I am unable to handle it myself and resent this obnoxious heart condition that has left me weak and helpless. I feel like saying *ah-yooo* myself.

Frida comes to my aid, and together we hoist the suitcases onto the cart. As we begin the long trek to the departure zone of the terminal, the awful gut-wrenching sensation begins again, as it has several times over the last two days. It feels almost physical, but I know it isn't. It's a sense of loss. Frida suffered through it, this emotional pain, at Sandra's previous departure for China last year, while I was quite nonchalant about it. Now the tables are turned.

We walk together in silence. An airplane thundering overhead vibrates the walkway that is leading us to the terminal. We speculate about whether or not this will be Sandra's plane. I am glad for even this short-lived distraction. My vision is blurring. I try to keep my eyes averted, but it's noticeable to all but 12-year-old Jonathan that I am definitely crying. Frida takes my hand and gives it a squeeze of reassurance. It makes me feel worse that I need to be reassured.

It's not as though Sandra hasn't travelled alone before. She's been to Hawaii, the Philippines, South Korea and Japan as well as China. But for me, this trip is different. Perhaps it's because I understand what we're facing: a Christmas without her and anxiety about her safety if letters come too infrequently. Then there's the possibility that, this time, she may not be returning. After all, she has been dating a Filipino man in Manila, where she spends her holidays, and she has more than a passing interest in at least one Chinese man she's met in Taiyuan. Marriage is a serious possibility.

Finding the baggage counter and getting Sandra's luggage off our hands takes some effort and concentration. Then we have breakfast at Harvey's, as we always do while waiting for departure time. Our breakfasts are skimpy this morning, but we settle in for the meal, glad to occupy ourselves with something menial.

I marvel at what Sandra has chosen to do. As a child, she had seemed so fearful and timid; she'd view the smallest challenges as mighty obstacles. For years she seemed to wait for her fate rather than take life on and face it with courage and boldness. Yet here she is, doing just that, taking hold of life and facing what would make many brave souls shrink.

A young couple are sitting at a table for two in the far corner. Her eyes are very red, and she keeps clinging to the man's hand with both of hers. Every few minutes, she blows her nose in a well-used tissue, then grabs on again. I wonder if one of them is leaving for China as well. Her eyes make mine water, so I turn away.

Sandra is eating her muffin, crumb by crumb, and taking small, deliberate sips of hot chocolate. Hot chocolate and muffins are supreme luxuries in China, and I can tell that Sandra is storing up memories of these tastes and smells to sustain her until she returns, whenever that will be. In the same way, she had stored memories of China to bring back with her to Canada. She even brought back several bottles of Shanxi vinegar (famous in China) so she could share with us a bit of her experience. We had a glorious meal of Chinese dumplings (*jiaozi*) drowned in this vinegar. And now it would be a memory we could all cherish, just as we would cherish these last few moments together.

I think back to the time when I was about her age. I barely thought twice about leaving my mother and other family members behind when I joined the air force and travelled across the country, from Alberta to Quebec, for basic training. It hadn't dawned on me that this would have any kind of adverse effect on my life. Yet, my mother died from cancer shortly after I left, and I still feel guilty for not being with her when she needed me.

I wonder if Sandra realizes her leaving may have important consequences? Perhaps she will marry someone in China or some other Asian country and make her life there. I speculate about what it would be like to have grandchildren living in China, and my thoughts quickly dodge that subject. Being a grandfather has never been an ambition of mine, let alone being an absentee grandfather.

Sandra looks at me with absolute calm, which I suspect is masking some insecurity about leaving. "I think it's time to go," she says in a low voice. Her eyes hold my gaze, and I see my mother's brown eyes, exactly the same color as mine. I feel shaken, almost as if I'm seeing my mother again but, for the first time, I really see the connection from my mother to me to Sandra. I check my watch and realize

Sandra still has 15 minutes until check-in time. Maybe she's as anxious to get this farewell over with as I am.

I dawdle over clearing the table and disposing of our leftovers. When I enter the corridor, Sandra is already hugging Jonathan and extracting a promise from him to write. She gives Frida a hug and turns to me, her eyes averted. Then she does something she hasn't done since she was 10: she kisses my cheek. After a quick hug, she picks up her carry-on bags and quickly walks to the departure gate. We all smile at each other, wave briefly, then we lose sight of her through the door.

Frida, Jonathan and I hurry back to our car and depart for Lethbridge long before Sandra boards her flight for Vancouver. Jonathan snuggles back into his quilt and drifts off to sleep. Frida and I are both silent. The radio is still tuned to Sandra's favorite country station. The song that's playing breaks through my thoughts. It's Sandra's favorite from last year—"I Want to Fly." Whenever she heard this song on the radio, she took it as a sign that everything would be all right. It, too, brings tears to my eyes, but I also hope hearing the song means everything will be OK.

We drive across the hilly ranchland toward Lethbridge with only the radio and car sounds breaking the silence. Frida closes her eyes and tries to drift off to sleep. I think about the links that join my parents and me, extending to Sandra and beyond to her future children.

I've always had difficulty imagining myself as a grandfather. Perhaps it's because I'm the youngest of a family of 15 and, for me, the line ended when I was born. Now, suddenly, here I am, not only at the end of a family line, a dynasty begun by my grandparents when they emigrated to Canada, but, in a sense, on the verge of being a founding member of a dynasty myself.

I like the word *dynasty*. It has a certain grandiose, uplifting ring, but it carries certain implications as well. It means I am going the way former heads of dynasties have gone. In my family, they're now all dead. I'm of the next generation to confront mortality. But I set aside thoughts of death; there is still time to live.

Sandra's song comes to mind again and I wonder if "I Want to Fly" also speaks to her of loosening family ties, of getting away to solidify her own self-reliance. Wouldn't it be ironic if I attempted to tighten family bonds while she struggled to loosen them. But I also know that grandchildren strengthen those bonds again, and I find myself warming to the idea of seeing my children have children of their own.

As we approach Lethbridge, I note that Sandra should now be at Vancouver International Airport. She has probably cleared customs for her international flight and is biding her time before boarding. I wonder what she would say if she knew that I've been imagining her future, already having her married—with children on the way. She'd probably vent her feelings with a loud, heartfelt *"Ah-yooo!"*

I laugh at how I've gotten ahead of myself and realize how much satisfaction I can get out of existing family relationships. I know we'll stay in touch with Sandra, by the grace of God and the Chinese postal system. And I begin creating more-realistic fantasies: while I drive, I plan how I can wrangle a trip to China.

# Great Explorations

~

**BY**

**JESSE**

**BIRNBAUM**

*Yet all experience is an arch wherethro'/Gleams that untravell'd world whose margin fades/For ever and for ever when I move.*
—Tennyson, *Ulysses*

old beyond imagining, a world almost devoid of human life, a horizon without hope: this is Antarctica, the Great White South, a forbidding 14 million sq km of desolation. Yet here were two men who for more than three months had been struggling stubbornly across the vast nothingness.

Frostbitten to the bone, their bodies wasted from meager nourishment, they slogged on, sometimes 35 km a day, in temperatures of –45°C, stopping now and then for a few hours of fitful sleep and moving on. What did they think they were doing?

They thought they knew, these Englishmen. Sir Ranulph Fiennes, 48, and Dr. Michael Stroud, 37, are explorers, relics of a near extinct species that achieved its apotheosis during the palmy days of Europe's 19th century global land grab. They had set out on Nov. 9 from Gould Bay on Antarctica's Atlantic Ocean side to achieve what no one had ever done: to walk and ski unsupported the 2700 km across the Antarctic continent from sea to icy sea.

They were not alone. Some distance ahead—it was impossible to tell how far—a solitary soul on skis, dragging a supply-laden sled, trudged through the snow in the same direction. Norwegian Erling Kagge, 30, a longtime rival of Fiennes's and a dauntless competitor, had departed from Berkner Island in the Weddell Sea eight days after Fiennes and Stroud, had passed them (though not close enough to exchange greetings), and was pressing on toward the South Pole. Though he had declared earlier that "I don't see this as a race," Kagge urged himself onward, driven by zeal and adrenaline. He wanted to be the first man ever to ski alone and "unsupported" to the Pole.

In the explorer's lexicon—and thus in the record books—"unsupported" means just that. You go with what you can carry or haul. Fiennes and Stroud had two sleds, each loaded with about 220 kg of food and gear; Kagge's sled carried 120 kg. You may not cadge a cigarette or a bowl of soup from a passing expedition. You may not radio for air drops or use prepositioned caches of food. Sled dogs and—obscenity!—motorized vehicles are out. You may not call for help. If you do, you are "supported" and therefore disqualified; a purist would insist that even a two-way radio or a portable phone or a direction finder is support. True explorers, they say, have to be ready to die lost.

On Jan. 7, 50 days after he had started out, Kagge reached the Pole first. "It has been a fantastic trek," he told a newspaper nonchalantly, "and actually much less strenuous than I had expected." Fiennes and Stroud could not say the same. Early on, Fiennes developed a severe infection in his right foot, hobbling their progress. It was 68 days before they reached the Pole, where they paused briefly for tea and then pushed on past the U.S. research station there without stopping. By Feb. 2, their food supplies running perilously low, they reached the treacherous Beardmore Glacier, which tumbles down to the Ross Ice Shelf and the edge of the continent on the Pacific Ocean side. By now they were battling heavy winds that whipped their sleds out of control. Fiennes was suffering mouth ulcers and blurred vision. Stroud had lost his ski poles and fallen into a crevasse; Fiennes had dragged him out before he froze to death. Yet they had succeeded in covering 2152 km, breaking a 1909 record (1992 km) for the longest unsupported polar journey and achieving the first unsupported crossing of the landmass to the Ross Ice Shelf.

Forcing themselves onward, they struck out for Scott Base, on the northern tip of the Shelf, on McMurdo Sound. There lay a ship that would take them home, though they knew the captain would not wait beyond Feb. 27; after that, the gathering Antarctic winter ice would harden, blocking passage.

At first it appeared they would make their deadline. Then, on Feb. 11, after a torturous 95 days and just 540 km short of their destination, they gave up. Their food was all but gone; antibiotics had failed to stop Fiennes's foot infection. Fiennes dared not remove his boot for fear he would not be able to get it on again. They could no longer proceed unsupported. Radioing their base camp, they called for an airlift.

Within a few hours, the starving, lacerated men were plucked from the ice and by week's end were recovering at the Army Personnel Research Establishment in Farnborough, England. Fiennes's body weight was stripped to 64 kg (from 95 kg), Stroud's to 51 kg (from 72 kg). Both men were undergoing tests to examine the effects of starvation, extreme cold and physical stress on the human body.

That they were able to endure at all seems a miracle. "On the Beardmore Glacier," recalled Fiennes during a break from his doctors, "the cold was so intense it felt as though you were naked. Your clothes didn't seem to be there. Mike had no skin on his fingers, and one day I saw him crying. It was –84°C with the wind chill, and he was trying to force his hands into his gloves. I'm amazed we did it. God was good to us."

Added Stroud, a physiologist and veteran explorer in his own right: "It got to where I even considered how to feign illness in order to be able to stop. But you have to live with yourself afterward, and I had a partner to think of. Ran and I both have blessedly short-term memories that eliminate the bad parts, and at the end of each day you feel it was worth it."

By any common standard of behavior, what Ran Fiennes and Mike Stroud and Erling Kagge chose to accomplish was audacious, some would say incomprehensible, maybe suicidal. What was it that could drive these men willingly to the edge of disaster? Not treasure, certainly, nor a new trade route. Surely they were not staking out new territory. As many as 6000 tourists visited Antarctica's shores last year, and their place is already peppered with about 80 temporary and permanent camps, and— Who knows?—somewhere in one of its icy caverns may soon be a frolicking Club Mediterranée.

Fiennes and Stroud's announced purpose is, of all things, to raise £2 million ($2.8 million) for the Multiple Sclerosis Society through public donations and to study the effects of extreme conditions on the human body. Kagge, a lawyer in his other life, claimed no loftier objective than thrills. "Excitement has disappeared from our lives, which are secure—too secure," he said. "I don't feel guilty about spending $150 000 on living out my urge for adventure."

That's the way it is with explorers: any reason will do. They are, after all, no ordinary mortals. They are obsessed, fiercely competitive, driving themselves to reach beyond the last barrier into the untraveled world, or to go their predecessors one better, to live to tell the world what they have seen, and not incidentally, to enjoy triumph and glory.

Hardly any place on the surface of the earth remains to be discovered, let alone mapped, prodded, examined and analyzed, yet explorers persist in pushing at frontiers. Italy's Reinhold Messner, 48, the first man ever to climb all 14 of the world's 8000-plus-meter peaks—he did it without using oxygen equipment—also made the first solo oxygen-free ascent of Mount Everest and walked across Antarctica. Germany's Arved Fuchs, 39, hiked to both Poles in a single year, rounded Cape Horn in a collapsible boat, explored Greenland and the Canadian Arctic—to name only a few of his exploits.

France's Philippe Frey, 35, courted death when he traveled 9000 km across the Sahara from the Red Sea to the Atlantic Ocean in 1991. Working from outdated maps (which eventually got blown away by the wind), he plowed through the desert for nine agonizing months. One after another, the wells that were marked on the map turned out dry. He had two camels; his water supply was down to five liters. Just as he was preparing to slit a camel's throat to drink its blood and stomach juices, two nomads appeared and directed him to an unmarked well 20 km away. Last year the Club des Explorateurs et Voyageurs awarded Frey its Prix Liotard for exploration.

Among Americans, the leading explorer is Will Steger, 48, for whom happiness is "going into an area that's never been visited before, an area where the sounds and the sights are foreign to human eyes." In 1986 Steger led the first confirmed expedition to reach the North Pole by traveling across the ice, and in 1989–90 made the first dogsled crossing of Antarctica. Typically, he is almost blasé when he describes adversity. "People are sidetracked by the suffering, by the cold," he says. "It's fascinating for them—the idea of going to the bathroom outdoors at 50° below zero. They imagine the hardships of cold, but it's not really much. It's just physical, temporary. But if you make a mistake, you die."

A fellow Minnesotan, school-teacher Ann Bancroft, 37, is the first woman ever to reach the North Pole by dogsled (with Steger in 1986). Last November she set out with three other women to ski across Antarctica, reached the South Pole, then had to withdraw in mid-January when weather delays upset their schedule.

Californian Sylvia Earle, 57, prefers to study the last truly unexplored region on earth: the bottom of the sea. A marine biologist, she has clocked 6000 hours underwater ("That doesn't include time in the shower," she jokes) and holds the record for reaching the greatest depth—381 m—ever attained by an untethered diver.

She has swum in the Indian Ocean with thousands of bioluminescent fish, dived in water so clear that from 30 m below the surface she could see the moon and stars; in the Pacific she has felt her body resonate with the vibrations of communicating whales—"like being in a cathedral with otherworldly music." Most of the planet, she says, "has yet to be explored. In the deep sea, less than one-tenth of 1% has even been looked at, and much of it has been mapped only in the most general way." Earle hopes to build a high-tech underwater craft that will take her to 11 000 m, the ocean's deepest depths.

It is the British, following centuries of tradition, who hold a special place in the chronicles of spectacular explorations. In a half-serious lexicon of "Great British Things We Can Be Proud Of," London's *Evening Standard* recently listed "Outwardness...From Sloaney grannies batting through the Hindu Kush in hire cars to lone seafarers circumnavigating the globe in sherry casks, the British are famously outward-looking."

Five hundred expeditions of dazzling variety and frequently exotic destination, in fact, leave Britain's shores every year. Some are supported by public or private subscription, some by the Royal Geographical Society, others by sympathetic corporations.

They are costly investments and usually lose money. Britain's Robert Swan, who raised $3.5 million for a journey to the South Pole in 1984, retraced Robert Scott's 1911–12, 1450-km route unassisted and in 1989 walked the 750 km from Ellesmere Island to the North Pole. Swan is still more than $100 000 in debt; his only consolation is that some of his famous predecessors—notably Sir Ernest Shackleton—died penniless. "I hate living in a stinking tent with other men," says Swan. "I hate being cold, and you must be a pervert to like having ice inside your underpants. Someone said it was the cleanest and most isolated way of having a bad time ever devised. But it pumps up the ego."

For all the hard work and suffering, the achievements of most expeditions nowadays rarely fall into the realm of genuine discovery. Some explorers may bring back evidence of an undiscovered bird or bit of flora; others may cite "education" as reason enough for their proposals—even when the purpose is to educate themselves—and proceed afterward to write books and give slide lectures so that they can raise enough money to launch yet further adventures.

Fiennes and Stroud follow exploration chiefly for its own sake, testing themselves against brutish nature. They also want to be first at everything. Says Fiennes, whose full name is Ranulph Twistleton-Wykeham-Fiennes (an explorer's handle if there ever was one): "To my mind, there are only two purist challenges—to be the first person to get to a source of a river or climb a mountain, or to be first at something like crossing the Antarctic without help from the outside. When you hear that the Scandinavians or the French are after one of the main known physical challenges, then one's antennae start quivering."

A picture-book handsome son of an army officer, Fiennes seems to embody everyone's notion of an Indiana Jones or a James Bond—he was once short-listed to play 007 after actor George Lazenby misfired in the role—and that notion is not misplaced. As a student, Fiennes (pronounced fines) climbed Eton's tallest spires at night in gym shoes. After a brief stint in the Royal Scots Greys, he left to join Britain's élite commando unit, the semicovert Special Air Service. He was doing all right with that outfit until 1966, when an American movie company arrived in the Wiltshire village of Castle Combe to film *The Adventures of Doctor Dolittle*. Sympathizing with angry local residents who opposed the filming, Fiennes and a few other men dynamited the set.

That little adventure blew him out of the SAS and, after fighting Soviet-armed guerrillas for the Sultan of Oman, into a career of exploration. "I'm unemployed," he once explained, "and while people normally associate titles with money, I haven't any. And I can't think of any other way to make a living."

Living by suffering unimaginable tortures is what makes Fiennes content, though he earns hardly enough money to subsist. He devoted 10 years to organize his TransGlobe expedition (1979–82), the first circumnavigation of the world through both Poles. More than 1800 sponsors put up more than $40 million for that caper. (Prince Charles, one of the backers, called it "a mad and suitably British enterprise.") The expedition was a success, but Fiennes wound up owing almost $150 000, which took him 18 months to pay off.

Nevertheless, the debt-defying Fiennes dared more adventures. He has been trapped for 100 days on a moving ice floe, has shot 4000 km of boiling Canadian rivers, has parachuted onto Europe's highest glacier. In 1992 he sought out the legendary lost city of Ubar in Oman, buried in the desert since A.D. 500 and described by Lawrence of Arabia as the "Atlantis of the Sands."

That trip was nearly his last. He and a friend, Andy Dunsire, dangled on ropes 180 m long into stinking caverns alive with scorpions, spiders, cockroaches and big white moths, and swam blind in unexplored subterranean rivers. At length, far beneath the sands, he found Ubar—the remains of nine towers and a walled fortress—a city that would have been seen for miles in the surrounding desert, just as the legends promised.

The best parts of an expedition, says Fiennes, are the preparation and writing about his adventures (in nine books so far). "I enjoy planning and getting past the hurdles and being with the team," he explains, "but physically, the polar expeditions leave a lot to be desired. You get piles, crotch rot, ulcerated blisters on the back of the Achilles heel, eye problems, and your teeth fillings fall out in the extreme cold—all the while you are pulling a heavy sled. The only compensation is that you don't risk being mugged or catching jaundice."

Fiennes's rivalry with Kagge, meanwhile, has not abated. It began two years ago, when a party led by Kagge competed with Fiennes to make the first unsupported expedition to the North Pole. The Norwegians reached the Pole from Ellesmere Island in 58 days but had to call for a plane when one of their companions fell injured. At the same time, Fiennes was forced to turn back 143 km short of the Pole. Kagge maintains that his expedition was unsupported; Fiennes argues that the air evacuation disqualifies that claim. Nobody, not even the sober elders of the Royal Geographical Society, has been able to resolve the question.

Grudging though this spat may be, it is, after all, only a

footnote in history. In due time, both men will be busy writing their books, giving their lectures and rounding up money for yet another assault on some newly targeted bleak terrain. That's what explorers do.

# Arctic
# Storm

~

**BY**

**HELEN**

**THAYER**

**DAY 20**

. . . . . . . . . . . . . . . . . . . . . . . . . . . . . . . . . . . . .

awoke at 12:30 a.m. and the first thing I saw when I checked the weather were the lenticular clouds, some cigar-shaped and others saucerlike, floating lazily across the pale blue sky. They and polar bears were the last things I wanted to see. I nervously checked the temperature. It had risen to plus 5 degrees [-15 C] and the south wind had strengthened to ten miles per hour [16 km/h]. With sinking spirits I realized last night's weather forecast was correct after all. My quandary then was whether to try to beat the weather to the pole or stay where I was, close to the coast, and wait out the storm. I knew that at this time of the year storms can have long staying power. But there was always the possibility that the storm might dissipate before developing into anything serious.

I weighed the alternative. If I tried to race the storm to the pole and didn't make it, then I would have to camp out there and wait for it to pass. I had certainly camped in worse places and I had already weathered high winds. My tent and gear were in good shape and should be able to withstand a battering. Besides, could I really expect more shelter from the storm where I was camped than out on the sea ice further south? As soon as I asked myself the question I knew the answer was no. Therefore there was no advantage in waiting. I decided to go for it.

I hurriedly packed and with Charlie in his usual place at my right side, I set off at 1:00 a.m. for the pole. My plan was to head due south, straight down the coastline of King Christian Island, then continue to the south and reach the pole in one day. Navigation would be easy until I was out of sight of land again. Then I would switch to the methods I had used to get to King Christian Island on the way north. I skied down the coast into the head wind, taking a line farther out from the coast than I had on the way up, and again was struck by the flat moonscape of the island. It was almost as if the sea only reluctantly gave up the land and allowed it to rise gradually to form low hills. I passed the slash that was the Wallis River as quickly as my skis would take me, keeping my eye on the developing lenticular clouds. The wind was now steady from the southeast.

I reached the southern tip of King Christian and turned back for one last long look at the strangest, loneliest island I had ever seen. As a land mass it was an understatement, but I would always remember it. When I was planning for the journey, the island had taken on a romantic aura because it would be my northernmost point and important to my navigation. Now as I was about to leave it, it still was a romantic place, splendidly alone, silent, with no sign of life anywhere. I finally turned away to concentrate on the task of navigating across the same blank landless space I had traveled through on the way north. After taking careful directional checks of the sun and wind, I left King Christian Island behind and headed south. The pole was only nineteen miles [30 km] away.

By four o'clock an enormous wall of blue-black clouds stretching miles across was building up and moving in from the south. The uninterrupted horizon allowed me to see an entire storm front in one overwhelming view. The wind gusted strongly at times, swirling snow high into the air. The sun disappeared behind the mass of clouds, but before it did, I checked its direction and that, combined with various directional checks all day, told me the wind was still southeast and I was steering a straight course due south. The wind continued to increase, but not enough to stop travel. The great ugly mass of black clouds in the distance appeared to be moving closer, but sideways to my path. It looked as if I would catch only the extreme edge of the storm as it went by.

Skiing at a two-mile-per-hour [3.2 km/h] pace, I was closing in on the pole. But sometime after four o'clock, I saw to my horror that the boiling mass of thick clouds from the far distance was racing low across the ice behind a great wall of wind-driven snow straight at us. I stopped and, grabbing the bag of ice screws, I quickly anchored everything securely to the ice, starting with Charlie on his chain, then his sled, then my larger, higher sled anchored at both ends. It would be our only protection from the full blast of the wind. I shoved my arms into my down parka and stuffed my overmitts into the pockets. Then, with everything as ready and as secure as it could be, I hurriedly took the tent out. There was no time to put it up, but I knew I could wrap it around me as I sheltered with Charlie behind my sled.

Pulling the sled bag zipper closed, I was about to tighten a tie-down rope when I heard a sound like an approaching jet as the wind bore down on us with maniacal force. I raced toward the sheltered side of the sled, clutching the tent to my chest, but had only taken a stride or two when the wind plowed into my body, throwing me off my feet and down onto the ice with such a bone-jarring thud that my goggles were knocked off. As I slithered to a stop, still clutching the tent to my chest, my bare face and eyes were blasted and stung by particles of flying ice. Hardly able to see or breathe in the violence of the storm that seemed to suck the air out of my lungs, I looked across to Charlie, dreading that I might see him airborne. But I had anchored him well and he was crouched down, protected by my sled. I scrambled to my sled, half crawling in the hellish wind that was blowing gear away into the unknown. The loose tie-down rope had allowed the zipper to be blasted open and the wind was tearing at the contents of the sled bag, almost ripping it off the sled. Grabbing the zipper I yanked it shut, pulled the tie-down rope tight, then dove over the top of the sled to join Charlie on the other side.

Suddenly there was a pause. The first gust had passed by, but away in the distance I could hear more jetlike gusts coming. Then I noticed blood trickling down my face. Blinking my eyes to clear away the blood I felt my forehead and around my eyes. When my goggles were knocked off, the exposed upper half of my face had been cut by ice. I couldn't keep my right eye open. I was terrified that it was seriously hurt. I stood up to look for the first-aid kit, but immediately saw another blast of wind-driven snow and ice bearing down on us. I ducked just as it hit the sled and, in a sitting position, I pulled Charlie close to me and spread the tent tightly over and around us. A boiling mass of clouds hung over us as if trying to crush us into the ice. The sled took the full force of the blast, but the wind in its fury was not to be denied its victims as it reached over and around the sled, swirling snow and ice, pulling, tugging, and slamming at our bodies, trying to rip the tent away.

With my head on bent knees and blood trickling from my face and eye, I sat close to Charlie, hanging on to the tent. I could feel the wind slamming into the sled, jarring it into my back. The jetlike noise was deafening. I worried about the gear the wind might have carried away when the sled zipper had been torn open and I worried about my eye. I couldn't see out of it. It seemed impossible to survive the hole in hell I found myself in. A few tears mixed with blood trickled down my face. Then I suddenly realized what I was doing. I was allowing the storm to take over my life, allowing it to dictate the terms of my existence. "Damn it," I said aloud to Charlie, who couldn't possibly have heard over the din, "the Arctic has rammed everything down my throat from polar bears, to storms, to weird ice, and now this. I'll sit this storm out and beat it."

Charlie showed no sign of being impressed, but for me the whole situation changed from fateful submission to a fighting attack. I needed a plan of action. Without one my mind would only drift without positive direction. Just before I was forced to stop, I had checked my mileage at eleven miles [17 km] for the last southerly leg. That meant I now sat only two miles [3.2 km] from the pole. All I had to do after the storm was ski those two miles, then head for land and the prearranged aircraft pickup spot. I was almost there. Not even this fiendish storm was going to stop me now.

But first I had to stay warm. I couldn't stand up in the wind and inactivity was allowing the cold to sink its sharp teeth into my body. I zipped up my jacket as far as it would go. I put my overmitts on and slid the end of the tent fabric under me so that I wasn't sitting on bare ice. From an inside pocket I took the last two peanut butter cups of my day's supply, ate one, and gave Charlie the other. Then, smoothing one of the wrappers, I placed it over my right eye and tied a drawstring cord taken from the inside of my jacket around my head and over the wrapper to hold it in place, allowing my eye to remain closed more comfortably. Then, pulling the tent fabric closer around Charlie and me, I prepared to sit out the storm.

Charlie was curled up at my side. I couldn't believe he was sleeping in all that screaming chaos. The cold grew worse and I had to do something to keep hypothermia away. I worked to stay warm with isometric exercises, tensing one set of muscles for twenty seconds, then shifting to the next group. I moved fingers, toes, ankles, shoulders, arms, and legs as much as possible in the confines of my tiny, sheltered space. My face and eye stopped bleeding. The blood had frozen on my face. But now that I had a plan for survival, I felt in control in spite of my precarious position. Optimism flooded my mind, leaving no space for negative thoughts.

Time crawled by. After an hour I was still pinned down behind the sled by the howling gale. The cold marched onward throughout my body. My hands and feet were cold but not frozen, while the rest of my body was shivering trying to stay warm. I pressed close to Charlie, who remained curled with his nose hidden in his tail. I was hungry, which didn't help with the warmth problem. I did not dare try to stand up, much less look for food in my sled. Food would have to wait. Occasionally I peeked out from beneath the tent fabric and saw a still chaotic storm hurling ice and snow horizontally across my world, engulfing me and reducing visibility to a few feet. My joints were cramped and feeling stiff and sore. The cold was unbearable and began to lull my mind. I did mental arithmetic to stay alert, but nothing seemed to stop the slow progress of creeping cold. As the wind continued to scream its fury, my mental arithmetic trailed off and I had to forcefully bring myself back to it, trying to keep alert. But the cold came on and on, and I became more sluggish.

Finally, after another hour the wind slowed and the screaming howl quieted. When it dawned on me that the storm had paused at least for now, I tried to stand up, but I was so cold and stiff I could only get to my knees, then haul myself up slowly. Every joint protested. It was as if the cold had welded my joints together. There was still a strong wind but it wasn't blowing me over, and I sluggishly thought that if I could get my body moving I would put the tent up. But first of all I had to warm up. So I stuffed the tent safely into the sled, then I windmilled my arms while I walked in circles. It was a pathetic slow-motion effort, but I kept at it, feeling the warmth slowly inching back. It took some time but at last my body, although not really warm, was an immensely improved version of the cold, stiff bundle that had huddled desperately behind the sled.

Once more I took the tent out and began putting it up, at the same time noticing that the wind was gradually increasing. I tried to hurry, but my fingers were still slow and my body, which seemed burdened by an extraordinary weight, wouldn't listen to my mind urging it on.

Snow picked up by the increasing wind billowed into the air. Afraid that I wouldn't get the tent up in time, my body at last kicked in, warming as I shook the great weight off and regained strength. Now pure raw desire to survive took over. I had already anchored one end of the tent, even before beginning to erect it, to prevent a possible untimely exit. Now I shoved poles into the tent sleeves, working furiously to beat the wind. One blast almost turned the tent inside out and I was afraid a pole would break, sending its sharp end through the thin nylon fabric and destroying my only protection in this hostile world.

Finally a combination of poles, ice screws, and tie-down ropes anchored the tent to the ice. I could hear far off the approach of another screaming torrent, and as I prayed that the tent would be strong enough to withstand the full fury of the next round of wind, I ran around adding as many tie-downs as there were places to attach them, then invented more until I had no more rope. I dragged my sled into the tent and propped it against one wall to help brace against the wind, then attached Charlie's sled to an ice screw just outside.

As the high-pitched scream of the wind drew closer, I ran to Charlie, rushing him into the back of the tent. After one last check that all was secure, I dove through the doorway and took out a belay rope that I carried in my sled for emergencies, tying one end around my waist and the other to Charlie's harness. Then as fast as I could I hooked the rope to an ice screw just outside the doorway so that if the tent was swept away Charlie and I wouldn't go tumbling across the ice after it. Zipping the door closed as much as the rope allowed, I leaned against the tent wall to brace for the blast I could hear coming.

It hit with a thunderous roar, throwing me forward and snapping the tent upright. With feet braced against the sled I leaned back again, stretching my arms along the walls to take the next mad blast. The tent walls vibrated and heaved as if they would burst. The storm had engulfed us again but each blast was repelled, as I fought with all my strength to brace the windward wall. It was too wild for Charlie to lie down, so he unwittingly fought the storm as he leaned calmly against the narrower back wall, his weight helping to anchor the floor. He was unruffled by the fury that raged about us.

After struggling against the wind for about an hour or so, I detected a slight pause now and then that grew more apparent until there were lulls in which I could catch my breath. Then finally there were only stray gusts that snapped at us as if reluctant to leave. The main force of the wind had passed, but the tent still flapped in the swirling snow. I looked out to see that the clouds were still heavy overhead, blocking the light, leaving only a solid grayness. My inspection of the tent showed the only damage to be a torn-out tie-down grommet. The low profile and modern design had won through. I put the antenna up to call base camp. There were worried inquiries about the weather. After giving a description of the storm and my location, I signed off, anxious to take inventory of my sled's contents.

It was with a certain amount of dread that I unzipped the sled bag. My worse fears were realized. All my food, except one small bag of walnuts in my day food bag tucked down in the front of the sled, had been blown away, along with most of the fuel, a pair of crampons, two fuel bottles, the spare stove, a few items of clothing, and assorted odds and ends. I went outside to check Charlie's sled. It was covered with drifted snow but still tied securely to the ice screw. It had flipped upside down, jarring a rope loose and allowing several sacks of food to be blown away.

It would take seven more days to reach the pole and then get to the pickup point at Helena Island. I figured Charlie had enough food left for half rations for eight days. It was one thing for me to go hungry and thirsty, but a food shortage for Charlie was a different matter. However, he was in better shape, with more weight on him than when we left base camp. I had fed him well and he had learned to drink more water, so I reasoned he would be all right on half rations and could go back to eating ice for the seven days. Inuit dogs are used to frequent periods of starvation and have learned over many generations to survive under conditions much harsher than the ones we faced now. I hated to ask Charlie to go to half rations, but I knew that he would endure it, just as he had endured so much else on this journey.

Having assured myself that Charlie would be safe, I turned to my remaining food supply. I counted out five handfuls of walnuts. Not enough. I divided them again and came up with seven handfuls. Perfect. There was enough fuel to melt ice for one pint [.6 L] of water per day, not much compared to the two quarts [2.2 L] I had been used to, but it would have to do. The next question was could I survive with so little food and water in this cold, extremely dry climate? I knew that women, due to their physiological makeup, can live off their bodies quite well in times of starvation, so I reasoned that I would survive. I understood the realities of going from five thousand calories a day to one hundred calories, and from two quarts of water a day, which is minimal, to only one pint per day while working hard in a cold dry climate. I would be fighting hunger, thirst, and weakness, which would make it difficult to travel the remaining miles, but I knew it could be done. To help the fluid problem I could chew ice and snow. I was confident that I could finish my journey. I knew I might be in for some hard times, but they weren't enough to make me quit.

As I sat there planning, I wasn't despondent. This was the Arctic, after all, and I knew that among the many hazards I might face, there could be problems at any time that would change the entire logistical picture of the expedition. I would never have begun if I hadn't thought of these problems and if I hadn't the confidence that I could handle them. There was something else that spurred me on, something deep down that I would understand better later on when I was able to reflect upon my feelings at this moment. There was a core in me that wanted to jump out and face this new challenge, give it a good shake and win.

I took out the signal mirror and first-aid kit to inspect my face and eyes. My reflection showed numerous small cuts on the upper half of my face, above the area my face mask had covered. My right eyelid was cut and one corner of the eye was very tender. Both eyes were bloodshot, swollen, and bruised, but my left was not cut. I looked like a prizefighter who had gone too many rounds. "I'm glad I've got a few days to heal," I told Charlie, "I would hate anyone to see me like this." I then thought, "What a dumb remark." Vanity seemed out of place here. My eyesight was fuzzy in the right eye and less so in my left. I covered my right eye with an eye patch to keep it closed and hoped a good night's sleep would heal everything.

I unloaded my sleeping gear and threw it into the tent. I fed Charlie in the tent and let him sleep there. He had been all that I could have asked of him that day, calm and obedient. I was hungry, but I would have to wait until tomorrow to eat and drink. The temperature had climbed to plus 16 degrees, [-9 C] an incredible change and no doubt a large factor in the storm. The wind was calming down and it began to snow. "If there are any bears around out there," I told Charlie, "they'll have to wait until morning." He was curled up asleep alongside my sleeping bag and didn't hear me. It wasn't long before I, too, fell asleep, glad to have got through that hellish day in one piece.

*from*

# Travels

**BY**

**MICHAEL**

**CRICHTON**

or many years I traveled for myself alone. I refused to write about my trips, or even to plan them with any useful purpose. Friends would ask what research had taken me to Malaysia or New Guinea or Pakistan, since it was obvious that nobody would go to these places for recreation. But I did.

And I felt a real need for rejuvenation, for experiences that would take me away from things I usually did, the life I usually led.

In my everyday life, I often felt a stifling awareness of the purpose behind everything I did. Every book I read, every movie I saw, every lunch and dinner I attended seemed to have a reason behind it. From time to time, I felt the urge to do something for no reason at all.

I conceived these trips as vacations—as respites from my ongoing life—but that wasn't how they turned out. Eventually, I realized that many of the most important changes in my life had come about because of my travel experiences. For, however tame when compared with the excursions of real adventurers, these trips were genuine adventures for me: I struggled with my fears and limitations, and I learned whatever I was able to learn.

But as time passed, the fact that I had never written about my travels became oddly burdensome. If you're a writer, the assimilation of important experiences almost obliges you to write about them.

Writing is how you make the experience your own, how you explore what it means to you, how you come to possess it, and ultimately release it. I found I was relieved, after all these years, to write about some of the places I have been. I was fascinated to see how much I could write without reference to my notebooks....

Often I feel I go to some distant region of the world to be reminded of who I really am. There is no mystery about why this should be so. Stripped of your ordinary surroundings, your friends, your daily routines, your refrigerator full of your food, your closet full of your clothes—with all of this taken away, you are forced into direct experience. Such direct experience inevitably makes you aware of who it is that is having the experience. That's not always comfortable, but it is always invigorating.

I eventually realized that direct experience is the most valuable experience I can have. Western people are so surrounded by ideas, so bombarded with opinions, concepts, and information structures of all sorts, that it becomes difficult to experience anything without the intervening filter of these structures. And the natural world—our traditional source of direct insights—is rapidly disappearing. Modern city-dwellers cannot even see the stars at night. This humbling reminder of our place in the greater scheme of things, which human beings formerly saw once every twenty-four hours, is denied them. It's no wonder that people lose their bearings, that they lose track of who they really are, and what their lives are really about.

So travel has helped me to have direct experiences. And to know more about myself.

"I won't tell you where it is," the divemaster said, when I asked about the wreck. I had read there was an interesting wreck somewhere on the north shore of the island.

"Why not?"

"You'll die if you go there," the divemaster said.

"Have you been there?" I asked.

"Sure."

"You didn't die."

"I knew what I was doing. The wreck's deep, the shallowest part is 140 feet [42 m]. At that depth, no-decompression minutes are four minutes."

"Is it really a paddle-wheeler?"

"Yes. Iron-hull. Nobody knows when it was wrecked, maybe around the turn of the century."

I tried to get him talking about it, hoping that he would drop enough clues so I could find my way.

"The ship rolled down the incline?" I had read that, too. Bonaire is surrounded on all sides by a steep drop-off, an incline that goes from the shore almost straight down 2000 feet [600 m] in some places.

"Yeah. Apparently the ship originally crashed on the shore—at least there're some fragments from it near shore, in about 30 feet [9 m] of water—and then sank. When the ship sank, it rolled down the incline. Now it's on its side, 140 feet [[42 m] down."

"Must be something to see."

"Oh yeah. It is. Hell of a big wreck."

"So there're fragments in 30 feet [9 m] of water, near the shore?"

"Yeah."

"What kind of fragments?"

"Forget it," he said.

Finally I said, "Look, I know what I'm doing; I've been diving with you guys for over a week, so you know I'm okay. You don't have to sanction what I'm doing, but it's unfair of you not to tell me where this famous dive is."

"Yeah?" he said. "You think you're up to this dive?" He got truculent. "Okay, here's how you do it. Drive east five miles [8 km] until you find a little dock. Then load up, jump in with all your gear on, and swim north from the dock about a hundred yards [about 98 m], until you pass a green house on the shore. When the house gets to be about two o'clock to you, start looking down in the water. You'll see a spar and cables in thirty feet [9 m] of water, right below you. Swim down to the spar, and then go right over the edge and straight down the incline as fast as you can go. When you get to 90 feet [27 m], leave the incline and swim straight out into the open ocean. You think you're swimming straight, but actually you'll be dropping and you'll hit the wreck about 140 feet [42 m] down. It's huge. You can't miss it. Okay? Still want to go?"

The directions sounded difficult, but not impossible. "Yes," I said. "Sure."

"Okay. Just remember, if anything happens to you, I'll deny I told you where it is."

"Fine."

"And remember, at that depth you'll be narked, so you have to pay attention to your time; remember, your no-decompression limits only give you four minutes down there. The wreck is so huge there's no way you can see it in four minutes—don't even try. Make sure you observe all the stops on the way up. There isn't a decompression chamber within eight hours' air time of Bonaire, so you don't want to screw up. If you get the bends, there's a good chance you'll die. Got it?"

"Got it," I said.

"Another thing—if you do decide to go, remember to leave your camera. Your Nikonos is only certified to 160 feet [48 m], you'll warp the case."

"Okay," I said. "Thanks for your help."

"Take my advice," he said. "Don't go there."

I asked my sister what she thought about it.

"Why not?" she said. "Sounds interesting."

The next day we drove up to have a look at the site.

There was a sort of industrial pier that went a few yards out into the water. It looked broken-down, disused. There were several ratty houses along the shore, none green. Still farther north, there was some sort of refinery or industrial complex, with big ships tied up. The water by the dock was murky and unappealing.

I was all for giving it up. I asked my sister what she thought. She shrugged. "We're here."

"Okay," I said. "At least we can look for the mast."

We put on our gear, inflated our vests, and floated north. It was a fairly strenuous swim; I kept watching the houses on the shore. I had about decided that the divemaster had given us bad instructions when I suddenly saw, at two o'clock as I looked back, a green door. It was not visible from the dock.

I looked down at the water. Directly below us was a heavy mast and spar, some metal cables draped over the coral. It looked almost new.

"Think that's it?" I asked my sister.

She shrugged. "Looks like what he described."

I asked her what she thought we should do.

"We've come this far," she said.

"Okay, let's go," I said. We put in our mouthpieces, deflated our vests, and went down to the spar.

Up close, the spar was big—forty feet long, a foot in diameter [12 m long, 30 cm in diameter]. It had very little marine growth on it. We swam along its length, moving out from the shore. Then we ducked over the edge, and plunged down the incline.

That's always an exciting moment, to drop over an undersea ledge, but my heart was pounding now. The landscape was ugly, with heavy pollution from the nearby industrial site. The water was cloudy and visibility was poor; we were swimming in crud. There wasn't a lot of light, and it got quickly darker the farther down we went. And we had to go fast, because we had to conserve our air.

At ninety feet [27 m], I looked out at the open ocean and decided the instructions were wrong. Anyway, it was difficult to leave the scummy incline and head straight out into the cloudy murk. I decided to go deeper before heading out. At 120 feet [36 m], I headed outward. I couldn't see more than a few feet ahead of me, but once I had left the incline behind, it was difficult to know where to focus my eyes. There was nothing to look at except the milky strands of crud suspended in the ocean.

I was chiefly concerned that we would miss the wreck; at this depth, it was not going to be possible to hunt for it. We would have neither the time nor the air for that.

And then, suddenly, my entire field of vision was filled with flat rusted metal.

I was staring at a vast wall of steel.

The wreck.

The size of it astonished me: it was far bigger than I had imagined. We were at the keel line, running along the bottom of the hull. We were at 160 feet [48 m]. I started my stopwatch, and swam up to the side of the hull, at 140 feet [42 m]. The metal surface of the hull was covered with beautiful sponges and wire corals. They made a wonderful pattern, but there wasn't much color this deep; we moved through a black-and-white world. We went over the side of the hull, and onto the deck of the ship, which was almost vertical, with the masts pointing down the incline. The geography was pretty crazy, but you got used to it. I took some pictures, we had a quick look around, and then our four minutes were up. We returned slowly to the surface.

When a diver breathes compressed air, nitrogen enters the blood stream. Two things then happen. The first is that the nitrogen acts like an anesthetic, and causes an intoxication—nitrogen narcosis, the famous "rapture of the deep"—which becomes more pronounced the deeper you go. That narcosis was dangerous; intoxicated divers had died because they took out their mouthpieces to give air to the fish.

The other thing is that the nitrogen that enters the blood must be allowed to come out of the blood slowly as you return to the surface. If the diver surfaces too quickly, the nitrogen will bubble out of the blood like soda from a bottle when the cap is removed. These bubbles cause painful cramps in the joints; hence the name "bends." They also cause paralysis and death. The time needed to decompress is a function of how long the diver has been down, and how deep.

According to published dive tables, my sister and I were not required to decompress at all, but the need for decompression depends on such variables as temperature, the health of the diver that day, or whether part of the diver's wet suit binds him or her and prevents the nitrogen from coming out of solution. It's so highly variable we decided to do double decompression stops—two minutes at twenty feet [6 m], six minutes at ten feet [3 m]—just to be safe. We made our decompression stops, and swam back to the dock.

We were both exhilarated; we had dived the wreck, and hadn't died! And the wreck was remarkably beautiful.

We decided to dive there again, and explore it further. Given a four-minute limit, we felt that we would have to make a separate dive to see the stern, and another to see the bow.

A few days later, we swam around the stern of the ship, about 180 feet [54 m] deep. The dive went smoothly; we had a good look at the steel paddlewheels. We were starting to feel quite comfortable around this wreck. Our pleasure was considerable. We felt like kids who had broken the rules and were getting away with it, consistently. We were very pleased with ourselves. And we were getting used to the narcosis, too, accustomed to the way we felt drunk the minute we reached the wreck.

A few days after that, we made a third dive, and explored the bow. The bow was 210 feet [63 m] down, and as we came around it, I felt the narcosis strongly. I gripped my instruments and kept checking my gauges, to be sure my air was all right. I was aware I was having trouble concentrating. We started each dive with 2200 pounds [990 kg] of air, and I liked to head back with 1000 pounds [450 kg] remaining, since it took us nearly eleven minutes to reach the surface.

The wreck was incredibly beautiful; this was going to be our last dive on it; I had 2000 pounds [900 kg] of air remaining, and we still had a little time left, so I decided to show my sister a tiny, delicate sea fan on one of the masts, 180 feet [54 m] down. We swam out and had a look, and then it was time to go back. I checked my watch; the four minutes were gone, we were moving toward five minutes. I checked my air. I had 600 pounds [270 kg] left.

I felt panic: 600 pounds was not enough air for me to make it back. What had happened? I must have misread the gauges.

I looked again: 500 pounds [225 kg].

Now I was in trouble. I couldn't go up fast; that would only increase my risk of the bends. I couldn't hold my breath, either; an embolism would kill me for sure. Nor could I breathe less often; the whole point of blowing off the nitrogen was that you had to breathe it out.

I looked up toward the surface I could not see, 180 feet [54 m] above me. I suddenly felt all the weight of this water over me, and my precariousness. I broke into a cold sweat, even though I was underwater. I didn't know such a thing was possible.

There was no point in wasting time; the deeper you are, the faster your air is consumed. We started up quickly.

The rule is, you ascend at 60 feet [18 m] a minute, which meant it would take us three minutes to get to the surface. After one minute, at 120 feet [36 m], I had 300 pounds [135 kg] of air left. After two minutes, at 60 feet [18 m], I had 190 pounds [85 kg] of air left. But still before me were the decompression stops.

I had never known such a predicament. Of course I could easily reach the surface—but that wouldn't do me any good. I had been under too long, and the surface was dangerous, possibly deadly to me now. I had to stay away from the surface for as long as possible. But I couldn't stay down seven more minutes with only 190 pounds [85 kg] of air.

We stopped for the first decompression at 20 feet [6 m]. My sister, who never consumed much air, showed me her gauge. She had 1000 pounds [450 kg] left. I was down to 150 pounds [67 kg]. She signaled: did I want to share her air?

This is something you practice in diving class. I had practiced it many times. But now I panicked; I didn't think I could manage the procedure of taking my air out of my mouth, and passing her mouthpiece back and forth. I was much too frightened for that.

So much for diving class.

I shook my head, no.

We went up to 10 feet [3 m], and hung in the water just below the surface, holding on to arms of staghorn coral. I tried to tell myself that the decompression stops were doubled, and not really necessary anyway. True, we had exceeded the no-decompression limits, but not by much. Maybe a minute. Maybe less.

I couldn't convince myself that I was fine—all I could think was how damned stupid I had been, to cut it so close, and to put myself in this danger. I thought of all the friends who had been bent, and how it had happened. The stories were always the same. Got a little sloppy one day, got a little careless, got a little lazy. Didn't pay attention.

Exactly my story.

I stared at my air gauge, watching the needle slowly go down. In my mind, the gauge was magnified, as big as a saucer. I saw every scratch, every imperfection. I saw the tiny fluctuations, the tiny pulses in the needle with each breath I took. The gauge was down to 50 pounds [22 kg]. Then 30 pounds [13 kg]. I had never had my air supply go so low. I noticed a tiny screw in the gauge, a stop-screw to keep the needle from going below zero. I continued to breathe, wiggling my arms to make sure nothing was binding. I completed the six minutes of decompression, just barely. The needle hit the stop-screw. I had sucked the tank dry.

On the surface my sister asked me if I was all right, and I said I was. But I felt very jittery. I figured I was all right, but I wouldn't know for sure for a few hours. I went back to my room, and took a nap. In the afternoon I awoke with a crawly sensation on my skin.

*Uh-oh.*

That was one of the signs of the bends. I lay in the bed and waited.

The tingly, crawly sensation got worse. It was first on my arms and legs, then my chest as well. I felt the tingling creep up my neck, taking over...moving toward my face....

I couldn't stand it any more. I jumped out of bed and went into the bathroom. I didn't have any medicines, but I would do something, at least take an aspirin. Something.

I stared at myself in the mirror.

My body was covered with an odd pink rash. It was some sort of contact dermatitis.

I went back to bed and collapsed in a sleep. I never got the bends. As best I could tell, the dermatitis was caused by the hotel soap.

Lynn and friend in Venice

# Italy Possible? Si!

## BY
## LYNN
## ATKINSON

he hardest decision you'll have to make each day is what flavour of ice cream to have," said the flight attendant when I landed in the Rome airport for a month's vacation in the spring of 1992. "They're *all* sinfully rich and creamy."

I hated to disagree with her lighthearted remark, but as a person with multiple sclerosis who uses a wheelchair, I had just spent a year planning a trip that for others was just a few phone calls to the travel agent.

With no information on accessibility available from local travel agents, and no travel companion, at times the possibility of making the trip had seemed remote. Italy could have been as far away as Tibet! And just as expensive—I realized that anybody I found willing to accompany me could not be expected to push me around cities, lift me on and off trains and carry me up and down stairs without some form of compensation.

If I were to go, it had to be spring or fall, as Italy in summer is very hot. After a frustrating year of planning, I found Janis and Jennifer. None of us had met, but we decided to do it. Thankfully, my parents agreed to help with finances. The next day I booked our flight to Rome, with a two-week stay in Florence and a few days in Venice.

Is Italy feasible for someone using a wheelchair? It's difficult, but, yes, it's an experience not to be missed.

I found that Italians were all very helpful, considering that their cities are besieged every summer by tourist hordes. They carried me up and down stairs and on and off planes and trains, answering my *"molte grazie"* with a cheerful *"prego."* Although there is a great need for improved accessibility, there are, at least, access guides for Florence and Venice and some information on Rome; however, you must be prepared for some compromising situations.

It is important that your travel companion be energetic. Pushing a wheelchair over the rough cobblestones of Florence and Rome can be taxing. Even with good shock-absorbent seating and a seat belt, after a day spent rattling along the sixty-centimetre-wide sidewalks and narrow roads with cars and scooters hurtling by I was often glad to get back to the hotel. For a smoother ride I found that eight-inch [20 cm] pneumatic castors work better than smaller wheels that catch on everything. It is also a good idea either to install tubeless 24-inch [61 cm] wheels, or, if you have pneumatic tires, take along a spare inner tube in case of punctures. On the plus side, Florence is very compact and few sights lie out of walking range.

At Rome airport, we disembarked from the plane using an ingenious stair-climbing device and boarded the local train, which has level entrance, to the main train station. From there, a regular taxi took us to our bed and breakfast.

Rome is an eclectic mixture of great, hulking ruins set among modern buildings. Although we were there only a few days, we managed to see St. Peter's Cathedral, Michelangelo's "Pieta" and the Vatican museums. Despite all the steps in front, St. Peter's is accessible, through the side entrance. The tourist information booth in St. Peter's Square has a list of recommended accessible tours of the Vatican museums, including the location of an accessible toilet. The entrance to the museums is ramped and there is a stair lift to the Sistine Chapel.

Although the YWCA where we stayed in Rome was reasonably priced, it, unfortunately, had a tiny, typically Italian elevator big enough for only one person and accessible to a wheelchair only with footrests removed and a chair-narrowing device such as Reduce-A-Width from Everest & Jennings. As I didn't have such a device, going up to our room in Rome meant standing in the elevator, clinging to Janis and praying my legs would support me, while Jennifer ran up the stairs with my wheelchair to meet the elevator on the second floor.

Catching a train in Italy is relatively easy and vastly entertaining.

It seemed that everything the Italians did, they did together. It took five men at Rome's train station to position the *ascensore* (lift) which raises the wheelchair to train level: Two men direct, one supervises and the other two do all the work. It is advisable to book the lift at least 24 hours in advance.

Every train we took with our first-class tickets seemed to differ—some with aisles wide enough for a wheelchair, and others only with compartments which necessitated some rather undignified "manhandling" to get seated.

We arrived in Florence feeling like royalty as the scene in Rome repeated itself, everybody watching as we disembarked. On arrival at the hotel we were abruptly brought back down to earth when I found that I couldn't get my wheelchair through the bathroom door. My travel agent had failed to give me the measurements that the hotel had faxed. Remember, have your travel agent obtain measurements for *all* doorways, including the width of the elevator with the door open!

Finally, after every bathroom foot in the hotel was measured, we found a more expensive, three-room apartment. Although its bathroom was not accessible, I settled for the inconvenience because of its cooking facilities. Eating out in Florence can be expensive.

Two of the most useful guidebooks containing access information on hotels, galleries, restaurants etc. are published by Delagazione Toscana e Commune di Firenze, available from the tourist information office and "Access Guide to Rome and Florence," published by Project Phoenix Trust in England.

We spent over two weeks in Florence, and every place where we encountered stairs there were always staff willing to carry me up, although at the Pitti Palace I noticed the conversation became a little strained after the fourth flight. Women ticket takers at the Carmine Church willingly helped to carry me up to see the powerful frescoes of 15th century Renaissance artist Massacio. However, you may have to resign yourself to missing some attractions which are quite inaccessible, such as the Medici Chapel Museum, which houses some of Michelangelo's sculptures.

Florence is exciting, dirty, (Italian dogs don't worry about finding a tree because there are none) and medieval. Florence is grey stone splashed here and there with red geraniums trailing from window boxes and the occasional tree caught soaring above the stone. It is a city of enclosure, where passersby can catch only a glimpse of the pink azaleas and palm trees blooming in private courtyards behind the walls.

Winding your way through

narrow grey stone streets and coming suddenly upon the monumental sugar cake that is the Duomo, the Cathedral of Santa Maria del Fiore, is always breathtaking. Crowned by Brunelleschi's monumental red dome, the cupola is the most characteristic feature of the Florentine skyline and one that I never tired of looking at.

From Florence we went on to Venice to spend three days, wondering how we would manage with all its bridges. Getting off the train in Venice and joining the throngs of tourists in St. Mark's Square, we were met with the sounds of bird calls, water lapping in the canals, and the quiet purr of motor boats replacing the noisy *vespas.*

Much to my surprise, my fears about accessibility were largely unfounded. Tourist Information supplied us with the very detailed map guide *Veneziapertutti* ("Venice for all"), published as a project of the city of Venice, which lists accessible hotels and outlines routes whereby a person in a wheelchair can see a great deal without having to cross a single bridge! As we were there only three days, I wasn't able to get a full picture, although we certainly saw a lot without having to cross any bridges. I also found the *vaporetti,* the water buses between the islands, very accessible.

According to the map, which requires some interpretation, 42 per cent of the buildings that are of "historic-artistic" interest are accessible. Accessible islands are marked in yellow, as are hotels. The Venice University of Architecture has defined "priority islands" and is working towards building retractable ramps between them. I was also told that some bridges have lifts.

We found it best to get away from the tourist throngs in St. Mark's Square and spent two wonderful days roaming around our little island in the Dorsoduro area. Our hotel was not ideal from an access point of view, but when your room window overlooks the canal and drinks are served on the terrace, one is inclined to be forgiving. Venice is sublime, a soothing mixture of toffee- and red-ochre-coloured buildings, with tree-ringed squares and quiet canals. Best of all, the "roads" were empty of cars. However, be careful of backing up to get a better view; you could end up in the canal!

# Creating
# Your Own
# Journey

## Kathleen Saadat's Story

~

**BY**

**THALIA**

**ZEPATOS**

've always liked adventure. One of my first adventures was
when a friend and I drove in a Jeep from St. Louis, Missouri, to
Anchorage, Alaska, in 1967. We left St. Louis with $300 and a
credit card, and it was wonderful. I loved learning something new, seeing something new, meeting people who were different from me,
observing the difference in the land.

Adventure means learning, it means encountering things you could
not foresee and figuring out how to address them—finding some way to
get through it, if it's scary, or just being novel in your approach if it's a
more mundane obstacle. Adventure is a creative process. When you put
yourself in a place that's totally different, you reveal yourself to yourself.

In a single year, I've had two big adventures. Both were personally
illuminating. The first was a wilderness experience which involved
rock-climbing. I don't like heights, yet I found myself climbing up the
side of a cliff. Looking down, I thought, I can't do this, it's too hard. It
was scary and also really rewarding. When I made it to the top, I cried.

The second was a sailing trip from Hong Kong to the Philippines. There were thirty-two of us from the U.S., Hong Kong, Britain, and Singapore. There were some young people in their twenties, and the oldest person was around seventy, with a bunch of us in our fifties. The ship—a 135-foot [40 m] brigantine—had three big square sails like the old-fashioned sailing ships had. Someone had to climb up in the rigging to let them down or put them up.

The biggest sail is called the drifter. When you put it out there you look at it and say, "It's so beautiful." There's nothing else to say. The ocean was so blue, I didn't believe anything in the world could be that blue. It was bluer than the bluest sky I'd ever seen, bluer than anyone's eyes, blue like something dyed, except this was something living, vibrant. How can you tell anybody about this? They have to see it, they have to feel it. Because it's not just the sight of it, it's the feel of it.

Everyone had to take their turn on the "watch"—four hours, either on bow watch, working in the galley, navigating, or on stern watch. If you're up on the stern watch, and you see a tiny light off in the distance, once you really believe it's a light, you go back and tell the helmsperson, "There's a light off the port bow," or, "There's a light off the starboard." Then you have to keep looking out for it. For a while all we did was put up sails and take them down, to learn how to do it. "This is a halyard, this is a down-pull, this is the foresail." In the chart house, everybody on the ship learned how to navigate, and everyone learned how to manage the wheel. We all learned some sail theory and how to tie knots.

Achin and Ming, two Chinese men who had been hired to work on the ship, were sitting on the sorry seat the second night out, and I was sitting there too, wondering if I'd get seasick if I went below. These guys started singing in really lovely voices and I recognized the song, "How Great Thou Art," one of my dad's favorites. They were singing in Chinese (they didn't speak any English), and I started singing in English because I didn't speak Chinese. When I joined the singing, they just lit up and their voices took off. Then we did "Amazing Grace"—it was like touching some other part of the world to sing with those guys.

I saw whales, dolphins, flying fish, cuttlefish, sea snakes, jellyfish, all kinds of things. One of the high points of the trip for me was steering the ship—I steered it right into the little harbor town of Bolinao, on the island of Luzon. We came into Bolinao on the 4-to-8-a.m. shift, so I got up at 4 o'clock in the morning and stumbled around in the dark, but as soon as I got outside the weather felt wonderful on my skin. The captain—who never did get my name right—was saying, "320, Kathryn."

"Aye, Captain, 320." And I moved the wheel back and forth, and every time he told me to change course, I repeated his instructions back to him.

"Bring her to 300."

"Aye, captain, 300."

He got us to just the right spot, and then said, "Drop anchor." I dropped the anchor, and then he said, "Midships. Good job." I felt great—I had done it—I had just brought a large ship into harbor.

We stayed for three days before we sailed back. My brother, who had been in the Philippines when he was in the service, had told me, "It's like being at home." And that's what it was for me, as a person of color. People acknowledged me as another human being; they looked at me clearly, without trying to be coy about it.

Riding the bus was great. We were sitting in the back, and I thought it was full. And then the driver stops and waves two more people in. And I think, okay, great, and we move down the bench a bit. He stops again and waves two more people in, and here comes somebody with a basket of mangoes, and here comes somebody with a couple of kids, and everybody just moves down to make room. And then we stop again and one of the guys in the front swings up onto the hood of the bus so an older man can get into the front seat. And then somebody gets on the other side of the hood. And *then* we were full. My definition of full was way off—it was *American* full. When there's caring and connectedness, people can practically sit in each other's laps. And when there's not, everyone needs a lot of space.

On the return trip, we encountered a big storm. We were running into the wind; it was a gray day, and it felt like we were flying. That night, I was on the watch from 8 p.m. until midnight. The ship was moving fast, we had lots of sail on, and it scared me to watch the bow of the ship tip down, and wonder each time if it was going to come up or if we were going to head for the bottom. I stood there with one foot in the galley and one foot on the deck and clipped my harness into a handrail. You clip in when you're on watch, especially at night or if there's bad weather, so that if you fall off your feet, or fall overboard, you'll still be connected to the ship. I could see the whiteness of the whitecaps on the waves, and then the waves would hit the ship and wash up on the deck, and I watched the phosphorescence wash on and off the deck. It was marvelous, it was like riding a living thing, like a horse, except a horse doesn't rock you from side to side at the same time you are rocking forward and backward. I held on to the wall with one hand and let the ship take me for a ride. I stayed on bow watch an extra shift, I enjoyed the storm so much.

You never know what you can do until you try to do it. The one thing I knew I probably wouldn't do was climb the rigging, and I even questioned that once I was on the ship. I did other things, even when I was afraid. Like climbing on top of the carriage house, where the mainsail is. There were a couple of times when I literally crawled across the roof on my knees because I was afraid of being tossed off by the rocking of the ship. Then I'd clip on to the wire and stand up. I don't have any knees left at fifty-one years old, so there's no point trying to do what I could have done at twenty. But it doesn't mean I can't do it at all, I just have to figure a different way to do it. The thing I kept repeating to myself was, trust yourself, trust yourself to find a way. Trust yourself to be able to handle almost anything, and allow someone to help you when you can't handle it alone.

# A
# Winter
# June

~

BY

ELIZABETH

HAYNES

The ground gleams white. Snow? It looks like snow, like a light skiff on asphalt. But as the landing lights grow bluer and the ground grows nearer, Isobel sees it's only tarmac. Not snow at all.

~

sobel sits in the Raffles Hotel garden, in front of a glass of white wine. Somerset Maugham wrote one of his novels here. She imagines him sitting in this same garden, quaffing brandies, watching the sun set over the palms, inventing dialogue.

Isobel slips on her new sunglasses, more expensive than she would have bought on her own, but Lakshmi thought it best to get good ones. The Indian sun can be very destructive to sensitive eyes, Lakshmi said. Looking around the garden now, the white furniture has a fresh paint sheen; the hibiscus petals are lipstick red; the palm leaves gleam like polished jade. A ghost wind stirs two leaves at her feet. A fly buzzes by, its hum purring in the quiet.

How cool the stem of this wine glass, thinks Isobel. How warm the sun on my back. How weightless I feel. She takes a lazy finger and traces on her map the route from Srinagar to Leh. She imagines

Ladakhi women in blue kuntops and tinkling turquoise and silver jewellery, calling "jullay, jullay. Hello, hello." In Leh, she'll buy a cholla, earrings, some bracelets perhaps…

"Hiya."

She knocks the table. Wine sloshes over the edge of her glass. Behind her, there's a boy: a tall boy in pink and orange striped Bermuda shorts and a Tiger Beer T-shirt. A boy carrying a Tiger beer. U.S. army, Isobel decides.

"Hello." She slowly takes her glasses off. He plunks his beer down, scrapes a lawn chair very loudly across the cement and collapses into it.

"You visitin' Singapore?"

"Yes, I…."

"My ship's in fer a few days. Bin shopping. Gotta great deal on a Walkman. I'd show it to you, but it's not here." He picks up his beer and drinks for what seems like a long time to go without a breath. He slaps the empty bottle on the glass table.

"You're shopping too, huh."

No, she's tempted to say, I'm just relaxing after six months in the jungles of Borneo.

"No, I'm just here for a few days. I'm on my way to Leh, in Ladakh."

She looks to see if it registers. It doesn't. She shows him on the map. "Here. I'm volunteering at a hospital for the summer."

"Singapore ain't exactly on the way."

"I got a cheap flight here and another to Delhi. I'll fly on to Srinagar from here and take the bus to Leh." She rushes on, before he can start. "It's supposed to be a beautiful bus trip—through the mountains, over three high passes. There are small Buddhist villages and monasteries…"

"You stayin' here?"

"I'm at a guesthouse in the Indian part of town." She thinks of the lady she glimpsed through a doorway yesterday—a lady with obsidian hair, almond eyes and tinkling bracelets. A lady in a pale green sari shot through with gold. A lady who looked like Lakshmi.

"You wan' another glassa wine?"

"Timeofsin, timeofsin, timeofsin."

Isobel stops and searches for the source of this new noise, louder than the drone of the candy and postcard hawkers, the tenor of taxi horns, the falsetto of Hindi pop music, the chattering people of the Srinagar Tourist Reception Center courtyard. She fans a piece of hair out of her eyes. So hot and only eight o'clock.

"Timeofsin, timeofsin, timeofsin."

She follows the sound past two elegantly sari'ed ladies perched on the edge of a trunk; a girl in a pink crinoline; a group of children in blue school uniforms; two pheran-clad men, alternately smoking and shouting; a veiled woman on an overturned cart; a man sleeping on the ground. There, in a corner, crying "timeofsin, timeofsin, timeofsin," is a squatting man and a stack of newspapers. She smiles. Of course, the *Times of India*.

"You need a place to stay, miss? You come and look at my houseboat, no charge." She turns to a small bearded man.

"No, thank you. I'm leaving Srinagar." She moves. He follows.

"Where you stay? How much you pay? I give you better price."

"No," she says louder, thinking he didn't hear her. "I'm not staying here. I'm going to Leh."

"You stay at Zero Inn, perhaps," he softly accuses. "Very bad place, many rats. You come with me." He begins to pull at her pack.

"I'm sorry, I must get my ticket." She hurries away, zigzagging between two old men, "excuse me," trying not to jostle, a glance over her shoulder, "excuse me, pardon me."

In front of the ticket building, an old woman smiles a cracked smile. "Namaste, namaste," she croaks to no-one and everyone.

Inside it's dark and cool. Smell of dust and urine. A great knot of men crowd the ticket window, the ones behind waving money over the heads of the ones in front: a many-armed Kali, Isobel thinks.

The ticket seller is shouting. "Move up," it sounds like. She deposits her pack in a corner and walks closer.

"Queue up," the ticket seller screams. The knot surges forward, voices sputter and hiss.

Someone shouts, "I've been waiting since half seven."

Isobel joins what looks like the end of the line. A boy in a wool toque squeezes between Isobel and the man in front, people behind are pushing....

"Queue up, queue up."

A man appears at the second window: the mob surging forward, a tweed-suited gentleman treading on her foot, "pardon me," pushing in front of her. Sweat, her kameez sticking to her, pelvic bones pressing into her back, another man squeezing in front, "queue up, queue up," the crowd struggling forward, hair in her face, can't reach a hand up, sweat in her eyes, pelvic bones thrusting. Out, get out.

Isobel sits on her pack, holding her kameez away from her skin. Breathing. She watches Kali's arms multiply. She thinks of Kim, moving through the caravanserai, among horse traders, thiefs, dancing girls, sweetmeat sellers, grubby-faced urchins, dogs. How exotic Kipling made it seem.

There's a small boy beside her. He holds out one dirty hand, picks at a scab with the other.

"One rupee, Mrs."

Isobel sees a procession of black-red, pus-encrusted sores crawling like spiders up and down his legs. Up and down his legs. She fumbles in her moneybelt, a coin, some coins, there, thrusting a handful at him. Please go. Please.

"You are sick, Mrs.?" he asks softly.

Isobel just shakes her head back and forth, back and forth, then turns it away.

～

Isobel remembers: sitting with Lakshmi, sitting crosslegged with Lakshmi on her bed.

"It's amazing how easily one gets used to squalor," Lakshmi had said, then paused and looked at Isobel. "You think that's callous, don't you?"

"Yes. A little."

"It's true. Books like this." She picked up *The Jewel and the Crown* from Isobel's bedside table. "The English are great romanticizers, you know. Indians, too, some of them. Narayan, for example.... I prefer Naipaul, Desai. What else have you got?"

Lakshmi languidly stretch/walking over to Isobel's bookcase; Isobel silently repeating Naipaul and Desai, Desai and Naipaul. In India, she'll get their books in India.

"Um," Lakshmi said. *"Kim, A Passage to India, Ladakhi Fables, Freedom at Midnight*—did I tell you to read that?"

"Yes. It was good. And horrible—partition, I mean."

Lakshmi looking cat eyes at Isobel. "Well, you can thank Mountbatten and Jinnah for that." Then in a caustic, joking voice, "Well, no, actually you can't, can you. Thank them I mean."

"No."

Lakshmi indicating the books with a flick of her long-fingered hand. "Have you read them all?"

"Yes, I...." Isobel wanting to say more, about *Freedom at Midnight*, how partition, the killings wouldn't end, kept going on and on. How she tried to read fast. How she tried to skim. But remembered it all. Wanting to tell. But not understanding, not trusting Lakshmi like this. So just saying, "yes."

"You history majors are always so prepared," said her kohl-eyed friend.

~

Isobel puts her sunglasses on. This is where it really starts.

She looks out at the passing shops: *Khan Brothers. All suitings for Gentlemen, Abdul's Sweet Shop, Jewel of Kashmir Karpets, Hollywood Houseboat.* She watches white, pastel-clothed couples peering into shop windows, being led through dark doorways, into alleys by smiling Kashmiris.

The bus, wrong side of the road, horn blaring, passing two rickshaws, a taxi, bus—car hurtling toward them, the bus careening back to the left.

The road narrower, the bus bumping over a bridge, bouncing over potholes; past men, boys, women in black, their veils curtaining faces or pulled back over heads like nuns' wimples.

Stop light. A woman, all in black except gold-sandalled feet, scarlet toenails.

A white mosque, its gold dome fiery in the sun.

Smaller shops now, huddled together, their signs in Kashmiri. Eggs stacked in a dusty window, a boy leaning over a balcony, calling to a woman in the street. And the bus always passing—bullock carts; bicycles with chickens swinging upside-down from handle bars; cows; rickshaws; walking women, men, children, chickens, dogs; Kipling's whole sweating stream of humanity.

A small lake, a tiny, white mosque. Houses of sheet metal, a tall iron gate, a *no trespassing* sign.

Then farm land: brown as a Saskatchewan autumn. A young girl sitting beside the road, waving at the bus. Isobel waving back. Tiny figures in the fields, bending, rising; three young women, baskets on heads, walking solemnly, gracefully toward the road.

Outside a teastall: Isobel on a bench in the sun, slurping hot tea—

hot, sweet, milky tea. A moon-faced boy bringing dāl, rice. Isobel eating, the dāl making her face, her underarms sweat, itch. Gulping more tea, more rice, more tea to stop the fire.

"Many spice," the boy says and Isobel is laughing, giving him an extra rupee as she leaves.

On the bus again, sun trying to burn through windows. Isobel thinking of women in fields; drifting. Drifting off.

Waking. Where is she? Percolation of memory. India. The bus to Leh. Stupid, so stupid to fall asleep. Looking outside. Seeing her eight-year-old self in the car going to Banff, remembering how mountains suddenly appeared, indigo incisors, behind horizonless tongues of yellow wheat. And forgetting her anger because she is now in these gray-green mountain teeth.

"Look at that sign, Jill: to keep this bus clean is our moral duty!" The girl in front of Isobel laughs.

Her friend laughs.

Isobel looks down at the sensen and amul cheese wrappers in the dirt at her feet.

"How long do we sit here?" the first girl shouts.

Two Indian men at the front turn to stare. The driver shrugs and puts on a tape. Hindi music: a girl singing in falsetto. Even the pop music here sounds ancient—the repetitive wail like Irish women keening for drowned fathers, husbands, sons. What do they keen for here? Something lost? Something never found?

"When do we leave?"

The driver shrugs again. "When the army is telling me."

It's not been so long, Isobel thinks, and looks out the window at the gently falling snow.

> Dear Lakshmi, she composes. Sorry I haven't written yet. I really meant to, before this. I thought I'd have more time but there was so *much* to do in Singapore: Chinatown, the Raffles Hotel, the Chinese and Japanese gardens, a Chinese opera—you'd have loved the flowing costumes, the graceful, symbolic movements. And, of course, little India. The only thing I missed was having someone to tell it all to in the evenings—*you* to tell it all to. My diary's a poor substitute.
>
> Well, you won't believe this but I'm sitting in the bus en route to Leh and it's snowing. Yes, snow in June! It's been coming down

for about an hour now, and we have to wait for the army to go further up the pass and okay the road. I'm loving it here, Lakshmi. The only problem so far was trying to get a bus ticket. Luckily, a nice Hindu gentleman took pity on me...

Someone in the back of the bus is coughing: short, throat-tearing barks, a drawing up of phlegm, a spit.

"You'd think he could go outside," the first girl says.

"Perhaps he's ill," Isobel murmurs to herself.

The girl turns to her. "What?"

"I, I just thought he might be ill."

"Yeah, maybe. But it's kind of gross."

Isobel swivels her head to look at the three men in the back. They are wearing blankets. It must be cold there, with the wind pushing under the door. It's chilly where she is, in the middle.

She lifts her pack onto the seat, takes out another sweater, and her book: *A Short History of Ladakh.* She looks for her place. The raja of Jammu had just invaded Ladakh, hoping to seize control of the Pashmina route. She imagines the caravans journeying through the mountains, the pashmina wool piled high on the backs of donkeys, their harness bell tinkle echoing in the cold winter air; swaddled men trudging ahead, behind.

The man coughs again: two rough barks, then a series of stacatto bursts that end in gasps—like a drowning man sucking air.

"They spit constantly here."

Don't listen. She begins to read, turns the page, realizes she hasn't understood anything, starts again.

"You should see the buses in..."

She closes the book. I'll ignore them, concentrate on the other people in the bus: those two old ladies, they must be awfully cold in only saris; the gentleman across from her, at least he has a sweater, his paper, would it be in Kasmiri?; a boy in a baseball cap turned backwards—*Nothing runs like a Deere.*

"They eat this awful kind of..."

Don't listen! The window. It's still snowing. She can't see the mountains at all now. The ash gray mountains, the bus heeling along that thin edge of a road past buses, taxis, the valley two thousand feet below. Thinking, I should be frightened but not being, smiling at the goats on the ledges below. And the snow: falling in slow motion, a kaleidoscope of snow, twirling through the air, sparkling in the sun, covering the brown earth like a tablecloth of lace. The highway signs, funny/ominous: *If you drive like hell, you'll end up there*. Must remember to write Lakshmi about them.

Coughing behind her. Isobel looks around. A man is walking, stepping carefully over the suitcases and sacks in the aisle, making his way toward the front door. He's wrapped in a red and black blanket—all she can see are his eyes.

Does she have any medicine to give him—some cough syrup? Lakshmi forced all those medicines on her.

"But I'm going to work in a hospital. They have all kinds of medicines there."

Lakshmi had laughed. Stopped. "Why are you going, Isobel?"

"Well, uh, you know, I saw the ad on the SUB notice board."

"Yes?"

"And, well, because of India. Because it sounded like you'd really be doing something. I'm so sick of summer waitressing, Lakshmi, taking orders, listening to the morning shift complain that afternoon shift didn't fill the ketchups...." She'd stopped and looked at the stern, scrutinizing face across from her. And because of you, she thought.

"Don't you ever want to go back?"

Lakshmi gracefully stretching her long arms above her head, resting her hands on her hair. "Delhi can be lovely in the morning, Isobel. When there aren't many people about and it's cool, a little breeze, perhaps. The last time I was there, I got up early one morning and walked to the restaurant down the street from my hotel. I ordered coffee and sat on the balcony watching two women sweeping the square below: the quick strokes of their brooms, the symmetry of it. It was like a dance..."

"That's beautiful." Isobel smiling, watching Lakshmi flick a shining rope of hair from her eyes.

"Yes. That's how it struck me at the time: beautiful. Aesthetically pleasing." She made a small, guttural noise. "Exactly as a tourist would see it."

Lakshmi turned her face away. Isobel picking up a hand, resting it lightly, tentatively, on Lakshmi's shoulders. Isobel feeling like she sometimes did at the end of a sad movie, when people are shuffling up the aisles, saying things like, that was really good or I just love Meryl Streep, knowing she should be saying something to her beautiful friend. But unable to think of anything not vapid or obvious. And really not wanting to talk at all.

Isobel is looking through her medical kit: lomotil, imodium, iodine (tablets and liquid), pepto-bismol, duricef, chloroquine, neosporin cream, assorted bandages, aspirin, tylenol, 222's—but no cough medicine.

"It was amoebic dysentery. I was so sick, the runs, you wouldn't believe it, in the toilet every two minutes...."

Enough. Isobel stands up. Her book falls to the floor. Not stopping, making her way around the cases, sacks of rice, bags. In front of the door. The driver looks up from his paper.

Saying, "I'd like to go outside for a bit," surprised by the anger in her voice, not meaning it for him.

"It is very cold, Miss."

"I'll just be out for a minute." She tries to smile. He opens the door.

The snow has lightened, though the sky is still the colour of slate. To her right, to her left, as far as she can see, are buses. Buses, big orange Tata trucks, taxis. And men. Men in groups: smoking, talking, drinking from cups or flasks. Men in shirtsleeves, shiny black shoes, thongs. A few solitary men peeing over the side of the mountain. Isobel walks.

"Hello." A man at her elbow.

"Hello."

"Where do you go?"

"Just walking."

"It is too cold to be walking. You are alone?" His breath hot on her cheek. She nods, continues on, a little faster; she can always go back to the bus. She can always return to the bus.

On her right: laughter, hard-edged and rough. Men. Watching her, their circle outlined by dots of fire.

Walking. The man gone now. The snow still falling, soaking into shoes, chilling toes. Her ears are throbbing, she didn't think to bring a toque. Snow in June. Lakshmi didn't tell me about a winter June.

No men here. I'll go back now, sit away from those girls, at the back of the bus. Turning, returning.

Man leaning from a truck window. "Cigarette?" Inviting upward sliding of the *e*.

"No, thank you." Four men in army uniforms coming toward her, Isobel's eyes on the ground. A kissing noise, laughter. Must be near the bus, didn't come far. The men pass.

Isobel stopping. The bus was green, like this one, *Leh—306* it says on the front. Sighing, tapping lightly on the door. It opens. He isn't her driver.

Walking on, can't feel her toes now. A bus, green, *Leh—782*; a taxi, another bus, green, Leh; bus, green, Leh; Leh, Leh, they're all going to Leh.

Her forehead, underarms prickling sweat. Methodically, Isobel. The bus number's on your ticket. Jamming her hands into pockets, pants, coat, where is the ticket? Damn it. Damn it. In your pack, on the bus. Stupid, stupid.

Two tears ironing streaks down her cheeks. Ridiculous. She hasn't cried at all—not at the airport when she left. Not in Delhi with the two a.m. customs man pushing forms at her, refusing to help, and so tired she couldn't read.

Why are you going Isobel? Yes. Why *are* you here? You. The sight of a few sores on a boy's leg makes you sick!

Now she's really crying. Crying like a baby. In front of the men. She's fumbling for her sunglasses, pushing them roughly on her face. So everything will be dark.

Black. Obsidian sky, the groups of men like some amorphous, prehistoric animal, some fire-breathing animal...

No, Isobel. Not an animal. Men. Just men. She pulls the glasses off, carelessly, bending a temple.

There's a note. A high, flutish note splitting the still air. And another. They alternate, one, two, one, two, each one, new, sharp, replacing the quivering old.

She turns. From around the mountains, out of the shadows, comes a great tumbling mass. Of sheep. A great, tumbling mass of sheep. And one small boy. His stick legs poke from a tattered blanket. His hand holds a staff. His feet crunch the snow.

The sheep, pushing and bleating like a kindergarten line-up. The sheep descending to the road. Followed by one, small boy. He runs to catch an errant lamb, smacks this one, that one with his staff. They tumble past Isobel, all those bleating sheep smelling of dirt and wet wool. And the one small boy. Past the buses and taxis and trucks, the men hitting at strays, laughing, calling out to the boy. The boy answering. In a high voice. A falsetto voice. An ancient voice.

"Miss, miss." It's the driver, standing in the doorway of the bus in front of her. "It is very cold, Miss. Please be coming in now."

Isobel in her wet shoes. Grinning at the retreating boy. Her feet crunch snow as she walks to the open door.

# Distant Intimacies

~

**BY**

**GARY**

**ROSS**

ourism is a kind of sanctioned stupidity. You walk stupidly about, ignorant of how to get where you're going, of how to ask—ignorant of how, in an alien culture, you look and sound to others. In Venice this ignorance reaches the level of theatre, and Venetians now and then forget the inconvenience of living amid magnificent disintegration for the pleasure of witnessing, say, forty English holiday-makers parading in single file through the narrow *calli* behind a fine-arts major who holds aloft a red parasol and announces by megaphone that, on the second floor of that palazzo, Browning met his maker.

Has another city been more eloquently described? A grand canal of ink has flowed uninterrupted out of the Serenissima since the invention of the quill pen, and why not? Any place that gave us Casanova, Tiepolo, Vivaldi, and Marco Polo is worth all that print. But reading about Venice—its glorious cycles of conquest and enfeeblement, its splendid treasures of Bellini and Caravaggio, its breathtaking mosaics and statuary and bridges and churches—does little to reveal its essence. You never really know a foreign city, and you don't even begin to understand it, until you have a sense of how its citizens apprehend their own lives. Such insight is especially elusive in a city of stunning appearances, perfect reflections, and brilliant façades. Each year there are more shops that sell souvenir masks, and the false faces of Carnevale are as apt a symbol today as they were in the years when they hid political and sexual intrigue. Venice not only takes for granted the tourist's ignorance but encourages it.

First-time visitors spill out of the train station and stare in disbelief. They set off to explore the magical unreality, and get lost. Oh, the place seems straightforward enough on a map—a pair of boxing gloves, the right biting the thumb of the left, a city meanderingly halved by the flopped S of the Grand Canal. But few urban settings yield more reluctantly to the cartographer's scheme, and a trip from point A to point B becomes, for the newcomer, a stumble through much of the alphabet, point B come upon, accidentally, only when you're ready to throw up your hands in despair. Closed Wednesdays, the sign informs you. You head back, believing you're on one side of the Grand Canal; you're on the other. You're sure this is the *calle* that leads to the *campo* where you had dinner; it leads instead to a foul dead-end of milky-eyed cats, syringes, and flotsam left by the receding lagoon. You haul out your map, unfold it, try to make it square with your senses. The map is in Italian, the signage in the Venetian dialect. Campo S. Angelo, says the map. Campo S. Anzolo, says the sign. Are you where you seem to be? Is *any* of this enchanted hallucination quite as it seems?

Venetians are asked directions a hundred times a day and often provide—especially to those using a tongue other than Italian—a stock answer: *"Sempre diritto!"* Straight ahead, as if anything in this most labyrinthine of cities were straight. The reluctance to succour strangers is partly the result of there being so many of them—three or four, on the busiest days, for each of the 80 000 natives. Small wonder Venetians— like the inhabitants of any tourist mecca—have mastered the art of the cold shoulder. Besides, detailed directions are futile. "Scuola S. Rocco? Cross this bridge, bear right at the *gelateria,* duck under the first *sotoportego,* right again, cross the canal at the first bridge, walk back along the canal, left at the second *calle,* follow it into the campo, cross diagonally, exit by the opposite corner, then make the first left and the second right. Cross the iron bridge, walk around behind the basilica, and you'll find yourself at the front doors of Scuola S. Rocco."

*Sempre diritto!*

One spring morning, utterly lost—though, it turned out, not 200 metres from the place I'd rented—I stepped into a hole in the wall and asked for cappuccino. The *padrone* was a middle-aged woman, arthritic and lopsided, whose unfalteringly serene absorption in the world gave her a kind of beauty. The cappuccino she made was the best I'd ever tasted and, in my fumbling Italian, I said so. I'd made banal comments elsewhere and received a cool nod. This woman registered me; then she told me, making sure I understood, that she took pride in her coffee and appreciated my remark. When I asked directions to Campo S. Polo she did not say *"Sempre diritto!"* She wiped her hands, told the others she'd be back, and led me through a maze of *calli* to my *campo*. I pointed out where I lived. She shook my hand—one firm pump—and, to my delight, invited me to come back for another cappuccino. I did go back, of course, the following morning, and every morning thereafter.

Elena was from a village in Friuli, north of Venice, and had grown up amid odours of veal and red peppers roasting on the *focolare* of the family *trattoria*. Her husband, Francesco, was a Venetian, as lanky as Elena was squat. She wore a blue work dress, he wore baker's whites. They were always together and seemed perfectly matched, both keenly interested—she with rather startling directness, he with lively, oblique mirth—in the lives of their friends and customers, who were one and the same.

Elena loved to chat, and the bar became my refuge and my schoolroom. Francesco was shy and taciturn at first, but each morning as I was having coffee he came out from the back—up to his elbows in flour—to nod hello. One morning Elena said something I didn't catch. He disappeared and returned with a rice tart warm from the oven. Did I like it? I tasted it, finished it, pretended one tart was insufficient evidence. He gave me another. I went through the routine again: he played along.

*"Molto buono,"* I pronounced at last.

*"Sicuro?"* he asked, offering yet another. *"Assolutamente?"*

That was the beginning—and, in a way, the extent—of our friendship. My Italian was no match for his thick Venetian, and he was usually too busy to talk for long. Yet we enjoyed each other immensely. Each morning he handed me a pastry to taste and awaited my judgment. I made a show of elaborate discernment; Francesco waited in a state of agonized suspense, eyes bulging, nervous and agitated, trying to calm his fluttering heart. My scarcely perceptible nod of approval elicited a ludicrous outpouring of relief—as if, had I narrowed my eyes instead, he would have scrapped the entire batch and started again.

Francesco's baking, like Elena's coffee, was exceptional. His secret was simple enough—he baked at six each morning and used only butter. Some places baked the previous evening or mixed in margarine or lard. Elena was equally uncompromising. Poor cappuccino, she said, was usually the result of scalded milk or an improperly cleaned machine. Her massive Faema machine was spotless and, if she happened to scald either the coffee or the milk, she threw it out.

Occasionally their son or daughter helped out in the bar. Giovanni had his father's long legs and his mother's sculpted features. At twenty-one, he had served his stint in the military and worked long hours in a *tipografia*. Once he'd saved enough, he intended to travel to America and visit San Francisco, Houston, and Santa Fe, none of which he could pronounce. I sometimes watched television with him—dubbed versions of "Dynasty" and "Falcon Crest"—or listened to the local hit parade. Rock music and soap opera in Italian I found unaccountably funny, like a weather report in Arabic. You know what's being communicated, but it's such nonsense in another language you realize it's nonsense in your own.

Silvia, his sister, asked us why we were laughing at the television. We didn't really know, but soon she was laughing too. A dark, reserved, private young woman, three years older than Giovanni, she had a mathematics degree but no job. Each evening she wandered through Dorsoduro with her fiancé, stealing hugs and kisses where they could. They wanted to raise a family, but the employment and housing problems were so acute in Venice they felt they had to wait for better times or seek them elsewhere.

The bar was a tiny place, always stuffy, devilishly hot in warm weather. Everyone popped in, and soon I knew many people in the neighbourhood. Guglielmo, a distracted misfit whom Elena never failed to ask about his book—a mysterious political treatise he'd been working on for sixteen years. Ida, a shrieker whose dogs barked sympathetically every time she started in. Massimo, a handsome rake at whose seafood *osteria* I've since had several of the most memorable meals of my life.

Elena loved cut flowers. I brought her something from the market each Saturday—the only day the bar was closed—then lingered in her kitchen, telling her about my life and asking about hers. She was a marvellous cook, and I played the helpless bachelor shamelessly. She taught me how to judge the freshness of monkfish, how to clean seppie, how to prepare risotto. Many Saturdays she sent me home carrying a care package of whatever she had been cooking that day.

The weeks flew by, and suddenly it was time for me to return to Canada. The Saturday before my flight, the family had me to dinner. Silvia and her fiancé had set a date; she was sorry I wouldn't be there for the wedding. Giovanni wanted me to send him any information I could find on Houston, Santa Fe, and San Francisco. While Elena served pasta fagioli, Francesco asked me to taste the wine they had bought especially for the occasion. I sipped, then drank, deliberating; then I said that one glass was insufficient evidence. We all laughed with abandon and Francesco proposed a toast. On behalf of all the family, he said, he hoped I'd come back to see them.

I did, of course, the next year, and every year thereafter.

One September I returned to Venice and found the bar secured with corrugated sheet metal and a Yale lock. Where were Elena and Francesco? My shock was out of proportion: I felt the inexplicable certainty something terrible had happened. I hurried round the corner to their door. The brass nameplate had been removed and replaced by a silver plate bearing the name of someone else. Down the *calle*, a woman was leaning out her top-floor window, pegging laundry and talking to someone below. I asked where Francesco was.

*"E morto,"* she told me, and resumed her conversation.

How could Francesco be dead? Who had been more full of life? Shaken, disoriented, I stepped into Massimo's restaurant. He greeted me effusively and, at ten in the morning, asked what I wanted to drink. Yes, he said, very sudden, a surprise; cancer, he thought, something of that sort. I asked about Elena. As you'd expect, he said, but getting along.

And how were things at the *osteria?* Oh, he said, the fish! So polluted had the lagoon become that fishermen had to go halfway to Yugoslavia. He paid double what he used to each morning at the Rialto. But the restaurant seemed to be thriving: it had been enlarged and painted a pale peach, with linen tablecloths and an interior courtyard. Yes, he said sadly, it had been written up in *The New York Times*. So many people started coming he'd had to raise prices to discourage them. Meanwhile, a restaurant that cost fifty dollars a head had to look like one, hence the renovations and expansion. I said this sounded suspiciously like a success story. No, he protested, he'd opened the restaurant for his friends; most of them could no longer afford to eat there.

"Where can I find Elena?"

"She's staying with her sister while she looks for a place closer to the market. Her arthritis isn't getting better. Ask at the trattoria in S. Stae."

I stopped at a florist's and bought calla lilies. Usually when I gave Elena flowers she marvelled at them and savoured their bouquet. This time she set the lilies in a vase without quite noticing them. She had aged dramatically; the spark was gone from her eyes; her serenity had become a kind of shaky resignation. We sat at her sister's kitchen table.

"I'm so sorry."

"It happened not long after you left."

"You made no mention in your Christmas card."

"I knew how fond you were of him. There was nothing you could do and I didn't want to upset you."

"What happened?"

"He complained of feeling unwell. When his feet swelled up, I knew it was his heart or kidneys. He insisted it was just the heat. For weeks he wouldn't go to the hospital. When he finally agreed, we had to get a water ambulance. The doctor examined him and told him to return in October."

"Did he improve over the summer?"

"As we were leaving, the doctor took me aside and said, 'His kidneys and his liver are riddled with cancer. He won't live to see the Storica in September. If you wish to tell him....'"

"Did you tell him?"

"Of course not," said Elena.

"It's none of my business, but why not? I think I'd want to know. Wouldn't you?"

"He did know."

"How can you be certain?"

"He knew all along, and he knew when the time had come. One Saturday morning he called for me. I'd just returned from shopping. He'd been unable to eat anything for a week. He couldn't even sip water. His ankles were as big as his thighs and he was in terrible pain. I took his hands and asked if he wanted me to stay with him. He shook his head—no—and winked at me the way he did when we were young. Then he took off his watch and his wedding ring and gave them to me."

Moving the accumulated possessions of a lifetime is especially difficult in Venice. One must arrange boats and *carrelli,* the wheeled carts that, propelled by muscular youths and laden with everything from potatoes to silk, bang up and down the endless stone steps of the city. Later that fall, when Elena found a new flat, I helped the family pack and carried some of the items—china, glass, silver—she didn't want to entrust to a mover.

I was about to leave the city for another year, and we agreed to meet for dinner at a little *osteria* I like on one of the back canals. It's the kind of place where a Miles Davis tape repeats itself and the proprietor drops in when it occurs to him. It has an air of animation and friendly energy, and I hoped it might help restore Elena's spirits. She seemed calm and composed after visiting her husband's grave, and I asked about her plans.

"Are you able to look ahead at all?"

A gondola bearing Japanese was announced by an accordionist who played and sang *"Arrivederci Roma."* The gondolier turned out to be a red-nosed fellow I used to see drinking grappa at Elena's bar. He grunted at us, took the glass the proprietor had set out for him, and returned it without breaking rhythm. The gondola slipped into darkness, its bow curled like the toe of a jester's slipper.

"When I was a girl," said Elena, "I lived for the life to come. With Francesco, I lived for the life we had—our marriage, our children, our bar. Now, after thirty years in Venice, I've become a Venetian. I'm a widow with arthritis who remembers better days. I live for what used to be."

"Do you have any idea what you're going to do?"

She'd been thinking of reopening the bar, she said, but couldn't do so alone. She hoped one of the children might decide to join her, but Giovanni had saved enough for his American trip and Silvia was preparing to move to Treviso, where her husband had found work. It would be difficult to pay a baker an adequate wage. Unless one of the children had a change of heart, Elena would probably have to sell the bar. In that case, she said, perhaps she would find a young couple who reminded her of herself and Francesco three decades earlier—eager to make a life for themselves.

I walked her home, said my goodbyes for another year, and asked her to let me know how things turned out. In the morning I stepped on a plane for Toronto. Many times during the autumn I wondered about Elena, and whether she had found someone to help with the bar. We exchanged Christmas cards, but hers had no news, only *"Tanti auguri da tutta la famiglia."*

My curiosity went unsatisfied until I returned to Italy in the spring. Arriving in Venice exhilarates me; the cockeyed spires and golden domes, shimmering in the hazy air, make me feel as if a weight has been lifted from my shoulders. The familiar slap of water, the tranquil sounds of boats and church bells, the hordes of tourists intent on San Marco make me feel that Venice is now partly my own. I made my way along back canals to my apartment. Once I'd greeted my landlord, settled my ` things, and inspected the garden, I hurried across Campo S. Polo to see what had become of the bar.

Life teaches the same lessons, over and over. Why should I have been shocked that there's no longer the demand there once was for cappuccino that's never scalded and pastries baked at six each morning? There was no sign of Elena. The bar itself had been razed, the interior reconstructed in blonde wood. Papier-mâché expressions of gaiety and grief crowded the front window. Peering through the plate glass, I attracted the irritated glance of a middle-aged woman with flaming red hair and enormous hoop earrings whom I'd interrupted at her workbench and who waited sourly for me to step inside and ask directions—the artisan and proprietress of a shop that sold masks.

# Edinburgh
# or Bust

~

**BY**

**ROHINTON**

**MISTRY**

nd what would you like from Edinburgh?" I asked my friend; I was leaving shortly for the Book Festival there.

"Well," he said without stopping to think, as though the answer had been waiting a long time for the question, "a little bust of Stevenson, if it's no trouble." Like me, my friend is a writer; unlike me, he is also a collector.

"No trouble," I said. "A wee bust of RLS it is, then."

"It's closed for lunch," murmured the museum attendant apologetically, when I tried to enter the basement room marked Robert Louis Stevenson. The official purpose of my Edinburgh visit—a lunch-time reading from my novel, advertised to festival patrons as "The best value in town: the price of your ticket includes a filled roll"—was behind me. Now I was free to explore the city and search for the wee bust. It was just past two, and the attendant said downstairs could be viewed after three. So I went upstairs, to the Robert Burns and Sir Walter Scott sections, which were open. Stevenson, Burns, and Scott had separate lunch hours.

I was in Lady Stair's House. Built in 1622 by a prominent merchant burgess of the city, read my map-guide, it contained portraits, manuscripts, and relics relating to the three writers. A sign warned visitors to exercise caution when ascending the stone stairway, for in Lady Stair's house the steps did not rise equally. It was a seventeenth-century architectural feature, explained the sign, and had been preserved during restoration of the house. The function of the dissimilar steps was that of a built-in burglar alarm: to make an intruder stumble, thus warning the occupants. I went up and down the stairs several times, but could not trip, for the two deviant steps had been painted white. It was like being told the punch line before the story.

Finding the basement room still shut when I finished upstairs, I walked the Royal Mile and examined a few souvenir shops in the High Street with the bust in mind. Earlier in the day, the guide on the Award Winning Green & Cream Open-Top Double Decker Edinburgh Tour Bus had explained that the Royal Mile which extended from Edinburgh Castle to Holyrood Palace, was really more than a mile: "It's a shining example of the generosity of royalty, you know," he had said.

Almost every shop displayed pewter busts of Burns and Scott, along with miniature editions of their works. Then there were lists of surnames with corresponding clans and tartans Scotch-taped to a prominent wall, enabling visitors from the New World to locate their roots in a jiffy. Bushy-bearded Highland dolls in kilts and sporrans overran the shelves, bearing generic labels like MacGregor and Buchanan and Macleod. But I did not spot a single Stevenson among them.

There were pocket-sized versions of bagpipes, models of haggis, little glass Nessies, video cassettes of Highland Dancing Made Easy in Ten Simple Lessons, plaid scarfs, plaid socks, plaid ties, and anything else imaginable in plaid. But of the one who was the object of my friend's veneration, there was never a trace. It seemed quite an unfair state of affairs—squads of Scotts, battalions of Burnses, but not one solitary Stevenson.

It's no use going to Switzerland and grumbling about the Alps, my friend always says, the one who requested the bust. But surely a little spot could have been found for RLS, a tiny bit of shelf space, so I could be done with my friend's shopping. Although, given the choice, he (RLS, that is) would probably have preferred this benign neglect to the alternatives on sale.

In my place a man of action—someone like my much-mentioned friend, perhaps—would have fired off deliciously pungent letters to the Edinburgh Tourist Board, the Chamber of Commerce, and the Lothian Guild of Souvenir Manufacturers (with carbon copies, in the last instance, to head offices in China and Taiwan). I, instead, kept searching in silence.

Next day, I returned to Lady Stair's House, and the Stevenson room was open. Among the usual collection of dark ink pots and warped pens, a straight razor caught my eye. It had belonged to Stevenson's grandfather, who had been nicknamed Beardie, explained the label. Why Beardie? Because he had sworn not to shave ever again until Bonnie Prince Charlie was restored to the throne.

Then there were Stevenson's things that had been brought back from Samoa: riding boots, stirrups, a crop, a palm-frond fan, a hat, walking sticks, guns. None of these had an explanatory note as interesting as Beardie's razor. The attendant wandered into the room, and I asked if he knew where I might be able to buy a little souvenir bust of Stevenson.

He held his hands behind his back and swayed a little, like someone appreciating a landscape. "Hmm, I'm sorry, but I'm merely on loan here for two days from the City Art Centre, and not so well acquainted with this museum." He stroked his ginger moustache. "Might be something in the shop upstairs, though. Let me ask the fellow there."

I should have told him I had checked upstairs the day before but I wanted to see him climb the stone stairway, the one with the uneven burglar-tripping steps. He completed the ascent without mishap, and was back moments later. "They only have a Walter Scott. Have you tried the shops in High Street?"

"Yes, I looked in them yesterday."

"You should ask," he advised. "If there is no demand for Stevenson, the shopkeepers might not have him on display. But there could always be something in the back."

"Yes, that's a very good idea," I said.

He began strolling with me from exhibit to exhibit. "I could let you have that one for five thousand pounds," he joked, when we came to a two-foot bronze of Stevenson standing. We laughed and strolled on. The stern law-enforcement quality of his black uniform seemed increasingly out of place in that quiet little room.

On the walls were charts with snippets of biography, and one in particular was of a caretaker reminiscing about the little Stevenson, who would always follow him about the grounds, full of questions, never without his tiny stub of a pencil, stopping dead every now and then to scribble "goodness kens what" in his little notebook.

I asked my new friend if he could read the bits in dialect with the proper accent. "I don't know what you mean," he answered, testing me, his tone a mix of defence and challenge.

"These lines look so rich," I said. "I can hear them in my head but cannot make them sound the way they should."

His reluctance melted when he became certain that my request was spurred by genuine interest and not intended to poke fun. There was an old map of the country, and he pointed out the place in the Highlands where he came from. At my prompting, he spoke a few lines in the brogue that was native to his region, and then, to show the difference, followed it with a few words in the border accent (the one with England, that is, he clarified). Before I left he treated me to a beautiful recitation of a Burns poem that began:

Ye flowery banks o' bonie Doon,
How can ye blume sae fair?
How can ye chant, ye little birds,
An I sae fu' o' care?

His voice, the words, something about Lady Stair's House, all made me nostalgic for places I had never seen, which was a bit silly, though I did not think so then.

"Good luck with the Stevenson bust," he called as I passed through the courtyard and into the street.

A piper played at the corner, his hat at his feet. The skirl of bagpipes filled the air like a flock of lazily gliding birds. The sun was shining as I emerged from Lady Stair's House. We'll pay for it by evening, I thought. I had already assimilated the local method of weather forecasting.

Yesterday the shops between here and St Giles Cathedral had been examined. Today I decided to tackle the ones in the opposite direction, towards the Castle.

"Would you have a little bust of Robert Louis Stevenson?" I asked at the first place, "something like those, perhaps?" pointing to a glass case of where half a dozen Walter Scotts pouted in pewter.

"A bust of Stevenson?" His tone made me feel like Oliver Twist asking for more. I quickly added that it was for a friend, nothing really to do with me.

"Ah, a gift." He brightened. "Would you like to give your friend a Burns instead?"

"Do you think he might notice the difference?" I hedged, reluctant to dismiss him outright.

He pondered the possibility for a bit. "Aye, that he might. That he might."

In the next shop, the woman's suggestion was more to the point, though a trifle impractical. "You must come back next year," she said. "The shops will be full of Stevenson souvenirs then—1994 is his death centenary."

The third place had none of the cheap tourist stuff, and was more in the nature of an antique store. If I found a bust here, it would be expensive. But I asked my question of the shopkeeper, who could easily have been the model for some of the bushy-bearded Highland dolls I had seen.

"Stevenson. Robert Louis Stevenson," he said, spacing the names carefully, as though to make sure we had the right man.

I nodded, that's the one.

"A fine writer," he continued. "A very fine writer. *Treasure Island. Kidnapped. The Strange Case of Dr. Jekyll and Mr. Hyde.*" More confirmation of the man's identity. I nodded again. "And didn't he go abroad and live in a faraway foreign land?"

My hopes were rising. "In Samoa," I said. "He died there."

"Ah, yes, Samoa." His eyes grew distant now, even romantic, before he continued, "I'm sorry I don't have what you're looking for. But may I ask you something personal? May I ask why you want Stevenson's bust?"

"It's a gift for a friend who adores his writing."

"Oh, I see." He seemed disappointed. "Shall I tell you what I thought? I thought, from your skin colour, that you yourself might be Samoan, which might account for your interest in the man." He was amused by his own admission. "And where do you come from?"

"Canada. And before that, India," I volunteered, without waiting for the routine follow-up question that was forming on his lips.

"But you can always pretend to be from Samoa," he laughed. "Claim that your family were Stevenson's neighbours on the island. You could write a history of it, become a Stevenson authority." We laughed some more and then I left, too lazy to explain that Samoans and Indians were about as interchangeable as the Scots and English.

A souvenir store across the road, larger than most, was enticing shoppers inside by offering a taste of shortbread: a man stood in the doorway with a plate. I asked him my questions and got the expected answer. But this time I persevered. "Don't you have any souvenirs of Stevenson? A postcard, perhaps of the Stevenson museum? Or his childhood home in Edinburgh, or his house in Samoa? Anything?"

A shop attendant who looked like the shortbread man's brother or twin brother overheard me. "This shop is full of Stevenson souvenirs. Overflowing with them," he greeted me, flinging his arms around him to indicate the merchandise. "You're in luck, my friend."

I was willing to listen.

"This thimble, for example," he said, extricating it from a sewing kit. "It is the exact copy of the thimble that Stevenson wore while darning his socks after a day of hard writing. It was his way of relaxing."

I couldn't help laughing, but he continued solemnly, picking up a plaid-covered tea cosy. "And this is a perfect likeness of the one with which Stevenson kept his teapot warm."

Now the shortbread fellow too got into the spirit of things. "And this mug is the exact model—down to the last detail, mind you— of the one in which Stevenson poured his tea after it had steeped." In a con-fiding voice he added, "He liked his tea quite strong."

"And have you seen this? A superb copy of the sunglasses Stevenson used to wear—the sun was bright in Samoa, far too bright for someone accustomed to the cloud and fog of Scotland."

The two passed the gag between them with ease, like a seasoned vaudeville act. They covered all the items within their reach. Shoppers formed a circle to listen. Scarfs, ties, wineglasses, teaspoons, dolls, bracelets, pens, ashtrays, cigarette cases, key chains, photo-frames, all were integrated into an instant hagiography and given the Stevenson seal of approval.

Finally, the one who had begun the entertainment picked up a plaid-handled toy revolver, cocked it, and raised it above his head. "And this gun, produced in our finest workshop, is the exact replica of the one with which Stevenson, alas, shot himself in the head."

"Ah, yes," I interrupted, thinking I had him now. "But Stevenson died of a cerebral haemorrhage. I read it only this morning at the museum."

"Of course, that's what it would say in the museum, wouldn't it?" he said patiently. "For is it not the perfect euphemism for blowing out one's brains? Mind you, it's always in the souvenir shops that you get the real story, not in the museums."

My search for Stevenson had ended, I decided, and my friend

would have agreed with me. Besides, after this bravura performance, everything else was bound to be anticlimactic—good thing I had taken in the Highland Regiments and the Edinburgh Military Tattoo last night at the Castle.

People began drifting out of the shop. The shortbread man held the plate before me: "Won't you try a little piece? It is the exact recipe that Stevenson used."

"Aye, that I will, thank you," I laughed, and went to look for a cup of tea that would complement the shortbread while I pondered the questions of mortality, memory, monuments, and the manufacture and management of fame. I was grateful to my friend for having endowed me with the quest. Without it, my time in Edinburgh would have been the poorer; instead, I felt as exhilarated as though I had returned from a lengthy ocean voyage to Samoa, the sea spray still moist on my cheeks, the tang of salt upon my lips, and clutching with great care against my chest the sweet, freshly baked transubstantiation of RLS.

# The Personal Touch

## BY
## DAVID
## DALE

ig museums, with their dinosaur bones and coloured rocks and stuffed albatrosses, are all very well, but the best museums grow out of individual passion. The trouble is that when I set out to discuss the great small museums of the world, I'm instantly depressed at how many I have failed to visit in a short life span.

In America alone one is overwhelmed with possibilities. I cannot, for example, comment with authority on the Poultry Hall of Fame in Beltsville, Ohio ("to honour the scientists and entrepreneurs who prolonged the lives of feathered creatures"); or the Pet Hall of Fame in San Antonio, Texas ("to honour animals who, through unselfish and courageous accomplishments, exemplify the human-to-animal bond"); or the Wyandot Popcorn Museum in Marion, Ohio ("world's largest collection of antique corn poppers and peanut roasters"); or the Tupperware Gallery in Orlando, Florida; or the Turkey Hunters' Hall of Fame in Birmingham, Alabama. I haven't see them and the horrifying possibility is dawning on me that I probably never will.

I know that important revelations await me in Fall River, Massachussetts, which is setting up the Lizzie Borden Museum (they didn't think calling it a Hall of Fame would be quite appropriate). When I last read about it, they were planning a life-size diorama with quadrophonic sound track and computer generated light show depicting the bludgeoning to death of Ms. Borden's father and stepmother in 1893.

I really want to make time for Lee Harvey Oswald's can opener, which is the key exhibit at the Gafford Family Museum in Cromwell, Texas, and for the test tube containing Thomas Edison's last breath at the Henry Ford Hall of Fame in Dearborn,

Michigan, and for the wedding nightie of Barbara Mandrell in the Country Hall of Fame in Nashville, Tennessee.

I'm less anxious about missing the New York State Museum of Cheese in Syracuse, New York, because when I last read about it, it had no exhibits, despite receiving a grant of $75 000 from the State legislature each year since 1986. There have been dark suspicions that the grants are designed to attract votes for the local congressman, and that the cheese museum is more in the nature of a pork barrel.

No such accusation could be levelled at The Potato Museum of Washington, which has been a labour of love for a couple named Tom and Meredith Hughes for more than ten years. They've accumulated Mr. Potato Head dolls, couch potato dolls, a poster of Marilyn Monroe in an Idaho potato sack, and naturally an assortment of digging, peeling and mashing implements. The highlight of their exhibition is a 4000 year old potato found at an archaeological dig in Peru.

I must, however, take exception to a claim made by the Hugheses in their publicity: "The Potato Museum does something no other independent museum in the world does—it examines the essential role food plays in our lives."

Humbug, I say to that. Have these potato heads not heard of the Greatest Small Museum in the World: *Il Museo Storico degli Spaghetti* in Pontedassio, Italy, known to its devotees as The Pasta Museum? I'll return to this shrine in a moment, but first I must consider some important American museums which I have managed to see.

Top of my list is the Liberace Museum in Las Vegas, maintained by the entertainer's sister-in-law, Dora Liberace. In three rooms scattered round a shopping centre left to her by the Shining One, she offers a cornucopia of extravagant costumes, rhinestone-studded cars and mirror-tiled pianos. There's a $750 000 black mink coat "made of 500 top quality female skins," an oil painting of Liberace kissing a cardinal's ring, and a reconstruction of his bedroom, which has two single beds.

Dora Liberace describes the reaction of many visitors as "fainting, sobbing, too stunned to talk." That's understandable, but I'm saddened by the realisation that this museum has a limited future. Liberace fans are growing older, and it's hard to convey his fascination to any young person who hasn't seen him. Unlike Beethoven or Elvis, Liberace didn't leave a body of work that will outlast him. You had to be there. So the Liberace Museum is all the more precious for its impermanence.

I'm also inclined to think that the Museum of Marketing in Naples, New York, will be unlikely to survive its creator. Few people would match the passion with which Robert McMath collects the manifestations of American ingenuity that fill the supermarket shelves of the world. When I visited the wooden bungalow which houses his museum, there were 75 000 items on display: boxes, bottles, cans, jars, tubes and packets, everything the compulsive consumer could dream of. Robert McMath just loves to shop.

The best part of his museum is devoted to products that failed, often despite massive advertising campaigns. You can see "I Hate Peas," a green mash designed to be fried like chips so fussy children will be fooled into getting their vegetable goodness; a hair shampoo called Gimme Cucumber; a soda named Afrokola, the "soul drink" for black people; Baker Tom's Baked Cat Food; and jars labelled "Singles," which look like baby food but are designed for single people to cook in a hurry. The presence of so many failures only confirms Robert McMath's enthusiasm for capitalism: "Of course an awful lot of money is wasted," he says, "but it keeps people employed. And it keeps bankers happy every time someone with an idea, or even an imitation, borrows money to put it on the market, even if it fails in the end."

American technological innovation on a larger scale is celebrated in the Los Alamos Historical Museum, which seems likely to have a more secure future than the Liberace Museum. Even with the end of the Cold War, people will stay fascinated by a place devoted to the creation of an instrument of mass extermination.

Los Alamos used to be a private boys' school in the mountains of New Mexico. In 1942, the US army suddenly took over the school and the area disappeared off maps. Only on 6 August 1946 did the world learn that Los Alamos had become a town of 6000 scientists and support staff who had spent the past four years secretly developing the atomic bomb. The museum, in a fake log cabin that used to be a guesthouse for visiting boffins, commemorates their efforts....

Yes, you can learn a lot from little museums. I know, for example, that during the 1960s an Italian scholar named Dr. Rovetta decided to undertake a census of pasta, trying to count all the varieties available in Italy. He gave up counting when he got to 600.

English speaking nations are less fortunate in their farinaceous diversity. I'd be surprised if there were more than 50 types available even in the United States, the land of excessive choice. The Australians and the British seem boringly content to stick with the quintet of spaghetti, fettucine, ravioli, tortellini and lasagna.

This Anglo-Saxon narrowness of vision baffles Italians. They insist that it is essential for pasta to take hundreds of shapes. This is not just to make the dish look interesting. The question of whether a pasta is long or short, round or flat, curly or straight, is a key contribution to the flavour. The ingredients may stay the same— durum wheat flour, water, sometimes eggs—but Italians will swear that a pasta shaped like a tube has a different taste from a pasta shaped like a shell and of course there is nothing like a pasta shaped like a string. Shape, you see, determines how the sauce adheres to the pasta and how much air is circulating through the mouth and nose....

How do I know all this, you may well ask. I know it because I am one of the few Anglo-Saxons to have visited the pasta museum at Pontedassio. The Museo *Storico degli Spaghetti* is a large stone house in a small stone village buried inaccessibly in the mountains near Genoa. The Agnesi family started Italy's first mass production of pasta in that house in 1824. A century later, having become a multinational company with factories all over the country, the Agnesis decided to turn their first factory into a monument to all the great pasta makers and eaters of history.

The company president, Eva Agnesia, an elegant lady in her mid 50s, divides her time between running the business and expanding the museum. She loves to give guided tours.

The first fact she explains as she unlocks the museum's heavy wooden door is that the commonly held theory of pasta being introduced to Italy by Marco Polo after his voyages to China is nonsense. The museum displays evidence that the ancient Romans had pasta. They particularly liked lasagna, which they called laganum. In fact it seems to have been around before the Romans— an implement assumed to be a pasta shaper (because no-one can figure out what else it could have been for) was found in the tomb of an Etruscan who died in the sixth century BC.

And if you're still clinging to the Marco Polo myth, cop this:

- a doctor's letter from twelfth century Genoa, advising his patient to stop eating flat pasta (like fettucine) and to start eating round pasta (like spaghetti) to ease pains in his stomach;
- a will dated 4 February 1279, in which a soldier named Ponzio Bastone leaves his son "a basket full of macaroni";
- and a page from the city records of Bologna showing that in 1289 a youth was arrested for wandering round after dark without a torch. He was released when he explained that some friends had dropped in unexpectedly and he'd rushed out to buy tortellini.

That should dispose of Mr. Polo's claim, since he didn't get back from his first visit to China till 1295....

The museum has detailed instructions written over the centuries on how to eat spaghetti. Apparently you must never raise your forkful over your head and lower it into your mouth— although the museum displays a painting of the clown character Pulcinella doing exactly that— because the sauce will dribble all over your chin. Cutting it up with your fork is cheating. You must roll it around the fork and then suck it in like a vacuum cleaner.

The only problem with the pasta museum is getting there. Pontedassio is such a small town that it doesn't feature on most maps. The nearest city is Imperia, about four train stops into Italy from the French border. Imperia is a pretty mediaeval hill town whose principal industries are the making of olive oil and the making of pasta. You need to phone the Agnesi factory, ask for Eva Agnesi's office, and inquire when there's going to be a tour of the museum. You may have to wait a day or two, but in the meantime you can tour the gigantic modern factory, which produces 70 different shapes of pasta.

Finally, at the appointed time for the tour, you head for Pontedassio and prepare to worship at the shrine of Italy's greatest contribution to international cuisine. That's what I call a Museum.

*from*

# Equator:
# A Journey

~

**BY**

**THURSTON**

**CLARKE**

**M**y clothes are exhausted, thin as silk from being slapped on rocks and scorched by irons heated over charcoal. I slip them on and smell, I think, the equator: sweat, charcoal, and low tide.

Souvenirs litter my rooms. There is a paper clip from Albert Schweitzer's desk, a box with a pop-out snake, and a chunk of propeller from a plane crashed on a Pacific atoll by Amelia Earhart, or so I was told. I have a T-shirt saying Happy Trails, in Indonesian. I won it racing Baptist missionaries up a Borneo hill. I keep pencils in a soap-stone box from Somalia, as white and square as the houses of Muqdisho. I weight paper with a gold-flecked rock from a Sumatran mine. My wife says it is fool's gold.

I have become a connoisseur of heat. There is the heat that reflects off coral and scorches and softens the face like a tomato held over a fire. There is the greasy heat of a tropical city, a milky heat that steams a jungle river like a pan of nearly boiled water, a blinding heat that explodes off tin roofs like paparazzi's flashbulbs, and a heat so lazy and intoxicating that all day you feel as though you are waking from a wine-drugged nap....

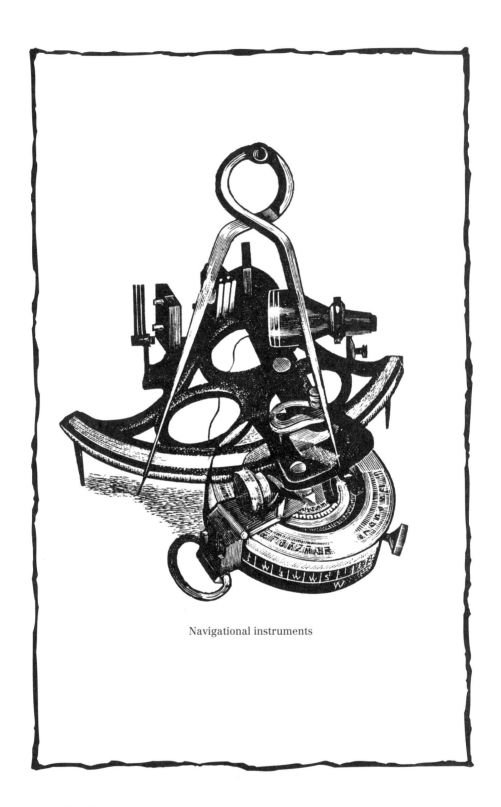

Navigational instruments

A boy kicks a ball, and I remember the soccer-crazy governor of Macapá and his plan for an equatorial stadium. The equator will be at midfield, with each team defending a hemisphere.

A satellite dish in a suburban yard reminds me of larger equatorial ones, oases of technology encircled by jungle, glowing ghost-white at night and marking the line as surely as crumbling obelisks and rusting signs.

Lazy northern sunsets bring back fast equatorial ones flashing like color slides across a screen. Click: The sun quivers above the horizon. Click: Quick as a guillotine it falls into jungle or ocean. Click: Stars glitter bright and close in a planetarium sky.

Some memory pictures flash without warning: A tornado of bats circles a French war memorial in the jungle; crabs scuttle through the collapsed blast towers of ground zero, Christmas Island; and a spider web of cracks surrounds a bullet hole in the windshield of a Ugandan taxi.

I can order these pictures by consulting my maps. Before a journey a map is an impersonal menu; afterwards, it is intimate as a diary. Before, I had stared at my maps and wondered if there was still a Jardin Botanique in the middle of Zaïre. Did passenger ships sail between Sumatra and Borneo? Tarawa and Abemama? And what should I make of the black dots signaling a "difficult or dangerous" road? Now I know, and these maps have become as comfortable as my canvas boots. I enjoy touching them, imagining I can feel, as if printed in Braille, the mountains, rivers, roads, and railways, all the familiar contours of the longest circular route on earth.

Why do maps attract the finger? Who has not—well, who nearing middle-age has not—run a finger across a page in an atlas and imagined traveling to the end of this highway or that river, sailing to every island in a chain or climbing every mountain in a range? What child has not traveled by spinning a globe? I owned an illuminated one. I switched it on and darkened the room and it became the glowing, revolving planet that introduced travelogues and newsreels. Then I closed my eyes, stabbed at it with a finger, and imagined going wherever I landed.

My journey began this way on a snowy February evening in New York when I grabbed a globe off a friend's bookshelf and spun it into a whirling bouquet of continents and oceans. Then I held it in front of a frosted window and watched places I might never see race past. It stopped and I saw a box in the South Pacific, saying W.A.R. Johnson Ltd., Edinburgh and London, 1898. On a modern globe, Africa and

Asia are a patchwork of colors, but on this Victorian model they were piebald, British red and French blue, and my eye was drawn to lines instead of colors: wavy ocean currents throwing tendrils around continents, thin isothermals swooping from Cancer and Capricorn, and a date line zigzagging down the Pacific. Longest and most prominent was a triple-thick, brown-and-yellow-checkered line coiled like a snake around the middle of the earth. The equator.

I traced it with a finger, imagining for the first time a trip along its path. It sliced Borneo and Sumatra in half. It cut across Mount Kenya and the mouth of the Amazon. It brushed Singapore, Nairobi, and Quito, and threaded through the Maldives, the Gilberts, and the Galápagos. There was desert in Somalia, a volcano in Ecuador, savanna in Kenya, and most of all, jungle.

Along the equator, I learned in the Library, you find superlatives: the largest atoll and heaviest rat, the widest river and longest snake, the highest volcanoes, heaviest mammals, biggest flower, stinkiest fruit, and greatest expanse of virgin forest ever destroyed by fire. It is a reassuring line, geometry imposed on nature's seeming anarchy, evidence of a divine intelligence at work in creation. Even the earliest flat-earth cartographers believed in the earth's symmetry and drew equators across the Danube, the Mediterranean, and the Nile. If the earth were stationary and perfectly spherical, any circle would divide it into equal halves, and by now an international conference would have chosen an artificial equator to standardize maps. This is what happened in the case of zero degrees longitude, which can theoretically be any vertical line connecting the poles. For centuries chauvinistic map-makers drew it through Rome, Paris, Washington, Stockholm, and Peking, until finally, fatigued by this chaos and bowing to British sea power, the world agreed at the Washington conference in 1884 that zero degrees longitude, the prime meridian, ran through the Royal Observatory in Greenwich, England.

But since the earth is an imperfect sphere, rotating about the poles and bulging in the middle, the equator, like a river, desert, or mountain range, can only be exactly where it is: equidistant from the poles and perpendicular to the earth's axis, at 24 901.55 miles [40 091.4 km] the longest circle that can be thrown around the earth. It divides the world into climactic and vegetative mirror images. On the equator at sea level, gravity is weakest, barometric pressure is lowest, and the earth spins fastest. To its north, winds circulate clockwise around zones of high pressure; to its south, counterclockwise. Where it crosses oceans, placid seas spin unpredictable hurricanes into the hemispheres; where it crosses land, predictable temperature and rainfall nurture life in sensational abundance and variety. The Amazon, the Congo, and the Nile rivers have been charted and explored, the Sahara and the Empty Quarter crossed in every direction, but the equator remains a virgin, known in part but not in sum, the longest but least visited, least appreciated, natural feature on earth.

When I proposed the equator as a natural feature, I heard a lot of "Bah, humbug!" It was nothing but a line on a globe, the only line on those little maps fastened to zoo cages that show the habitat of exotic animals. Because no one could "see" the equator, it was unworthy of exploration. Some people, remembering the Coriolis effect from high school physics, said it was where water changed direction as it flowed from a sink or a toilet, clockwise north of the line and counterclockwise to the south, and they saw me traveling around the world, flushing toilets to discover in which hemisphere I stood. Well, "Bah, humbug" to all that. A blind man cannot see mountains, but his ears sense the change in altitude and he becomes light-headed. In a swamp, his pores open and he senses humidity. He feels his nostrils drying in a desert and his skin catching the salt from the ocean. We can none of us see the equator, but we can sense it, and feel its effects.

Mariners consider it a dangerous line. At sea, rising warm air produces the belt of lazy winds and dull seas known as the doldrums. The history of tropical trade and exploration is full of ships becalmed for weeks near the equator, of crewmen dying from thirst under drooping sails. Because of the doldrums, a successful crossing of the equator came to be celebrated by a "crossing the line" ceremony, one with strong overtones of rebaptism and thanksgiving. And because of the doldrums, French slavers carried barrels of lime so if they were becalmed in the equatorial "middle passage," they could poison their cargo before tossing it overboard—a more humane solution, they argued, than the despicable Anglo-Saxon practice of throwing live slaves into the sea.

Underneath the oceans' surface, the powerful equatorial countercurrent forces the captains of even the supertankers to adjust their steering as they cross the line. In the Pacific, this current stirs up a feast of plankton that attracts whales, and their killers. The first American whaleboat to reach Honolulu was named *The Equator.*

Captain Ahab tracked Moby Dick into these equatorial hunting grounds, and Melville wrote of his own journey there: "…we spent several weeks chassezing across the Line, to and fro, in unavailing search for our prey. For some of the hunters believe, that whales, like the silver ore in Peru, run in veins through the ocean. So, day after day, daily; and week after week, weekly, we traversed the self-same longitudinal intersection of the self-same Line; till we were almost ready to swear that we felt the ship strike every time her keel crossed that imaginary locality."

On land and sea, the equator is characterized by a consistent absence of twilight and daybreak. Nowhere else do you have less time to adjust between day and night. Nowhere is the sun so high in the sky at midday for so many days of the year.…

You cannot feel the lessening of gravity at the equator, but you can see the results. A scale would show you weighing less at sea level in Borneo than in Belgium. A pendulum clock calibrated to mark time at a temperate latitude will slow down if moved nearer to the equator. In 1673, the French astronomer Jean Richer journeyed to Cayenne, in Equinoctial France, to observe the movements of sun and planets near the equator. By chance, he noticed that a pendulum clock he had carried from Paris lost time at the sea-level city of Cayenne. He had stumbled on proof of Sir Isaac Newton's theory that the earth bulges in the middle and flattens out at the poles. Since Cayenne was nearer the equator than Paris, it was further from the center of the earth, and thus gravity exerted less pull on the pendulum.

Like other natural features, the equator has given its name to the places it touches. Just as there is an Atlantic City and a Pacific Palisades, and just as the cities of Erie, Geneva, and Como border their namesake lakes, so too is there an Equator railway station in Africa, an Equator Town, founded by Robert Louis Stevenson, in the Pacific, and an Equatorville (since renamed) where the line crosses the Zaïre River. In South America, there is Ecuador— "equator" in Spanish—and in the Pacific, the Line Islands. Open an atlas or pick up a globe and run your finger along zero degrees longitude. What do you find named after the prime meridian? Nothing.

Nations have tried to profit from the equator, as from any natural resource. One reason the French built a space center in their Guiana colony is because the weaker gravitational pull of the earth there enables missiles to be launched with a quarter less fuel than those of identical weight shot from Cape Canaveral. For centuries, Norwegian packets bound for the southern hemisphere have carried sherry casks filled with aquavit. Connoisseurs of aquavit believe some alchemy occurs at zero latitude that improves their favorite beverage. Multiple voyages make it still more prized and expensive. I tracked down a bottle of this "Linie [or Line] Aquavit." Its label certified that on January 19 and July 15, 1985, it had crossed the equator on the M/S *Tourcoing*.

Countries touched by the equator have tried claiming national sovereignty for 22,300 miles [35 903 km] into space, from their land equators to the necklace of communications satellites hovering exactly overhead in geostationary orbit. These satellites relay telephone calls and television pictures and are positioned over the equator so they can travel at the same rotational speed as the earth. In 1977, some nations attempted to form a cartel to regulate and charge rent for the satellites sitting above their equators. The Colombian delegate to a United Nations conference on broadcast satellites argued that since "parking places" above the equator are limited, the equatorial orbit is a "natural limited resource" over which the equatorial states have "inalienable rights of sovereignty."

Evidence that the equator is a natural feature is so convincing that some people are fooled into "seeing" it. For centuries, sailors have pasted a blue thread across spyglasses offered to shipmates for "viewing" the equator. One nineteenth-century traveler reported cabin boys being "sent aloft to see the line." They came down describing a "blue streak."…

In 1974, American astronauts orbiting the earth in *Skylab* noticed fire lines flaming across the tropics. At night the fires twinkled; by day, canopies of smoke and dust swirled over eroded land, obscuring burning forests. In Africa, a fire line ran north and parallel to the equator through Cameroon and the Central African Republic; to the south, one cut through central Africa. They had been set by farmers clearing land and herders desperate for pasture, by hunters flushing game and loggers destroying "garbage" trees. Trapped between them were the tropical forests that straddle the equator.

Within this shrinking green band are African Pygmies, Amazonian Indians, and Asian aborigines, the last survivors of a centuries-old war waged against tribal peoples. Trapped as well is an irreplaceable library of genes: two thirds of all living species and several hundred thousand plants, animals, and insects as yet undiscovered and unidentified. Consider that the British Isles contain fifteen thousand species of trees and shrubs, while in a single square mile of Colombian rain forest botanists have identified a thousand, some unique to this square mile. When it is burned, they will be lost forever.

Since 1974, the tropical fire lines have advanced on the equator, consuming every year forests half the size of California. So where astronauts once saw fires, they would now see dust spiraling upward from eroded fields. Where they saw rain forest, they would see fire lines. Even the most optimistic scientists predict that during the next century the jungle fires of the northern and southern hemispheres will meet almost everywhere, and then anyone looking down at the equator will see a continuous band of smoke and flames....

I decided to move from west to east, following the prevailing winds and the earth's rotation. To find a starting point I traced my New York latitude south to the equator. I was in the middle of the Colombian jungle, surrounded by those one thousand species per square mile but far from any road or village. I was looking for an adopted home, somewhere I might be remembered when I returned. I followed the equator across South America until, at the mouth of the Amazon, it hit the port of Macapá. My South American map letters towns in five sizes of print. Macapá was third darkest, neither an overwhelming city nor an obscure backwater, a good place to begin....

In the days before my departure, the equator began appearing in overexposed daydreams, not a blue streak shimmering across the doldrums but a hairy rope, woven from sisal and thick as a tugboat's line. I saw it draped over volcanoes, bleached white in the desert, and smothered by orchids in sun-flecked forests. Plankton and well-fed whales choked equatorial currents. Norwegian packets with barrels of aquavit lashed to their decks pitched through typhoons. A wreath of satellites hummed and clicked in equatorial skies, and water paused over sink drains, uncertain which way to flow. Aborigines crouched in smoldering forests, their eyes pinwheeling as bulldozers carved roads to Macapá. Then I saw snakes as thick as a wrestler's thighs and jerked awake, wondering how any journey can match the daydreams that precede it, or the extravagant memories that follow.

# The
# Soul of an
# Intercontinental
# Wanderer

~

**B Y**

**P I C O**

**I Y E R**

y the time I was nine, I was already used to going to school by
transatlantic plane, to sleeping in airports, to shuttling back and
forth, three times a year, between my parents' (Indian) home in
California and my boarding school in England. Throughout my youth, I
never lived within 6000 miles [9660 km] of my nearest relative. From
the time I was a teenager, I took it for granted that I could take my
budget vacations (as I did) in Bolivia and Tibet, China and Morocco. It
never seemed strange to me that a girlfriend might be half a world (or
ten hours' flying time) away, or that my closest friends might be on the
other side of a continent or sea.

It was only recently that I realized that all these habits of mind and
life would scarcely have been imaginable in my parents' youth; that
the very facts and facilities that shape my world are all distinctly new
developments and mark me as a modern type.

It was only recently, in fact, that I realized I am an example of an entirely new breed of people, an intercontinental tribe of wanderers that is multiplying as fast as international phone lines and frequent-flier programs. We are the Transit Loungers, forever heading to the departure gate, forever orbiting the world. We enjoy our habits duty-free, we eat our food on plastic plates, we catch the world through rented headphones. We pass through countries as through revolving doors, resident aliens of the world, permanent residents of nowhere. Nothing is strange to us, and nowhere is foreign. We are visitors even in our own homes.

This is not, I think, a function of affluence so much as of simple circumstance. I am not, that is, a jet-setter pursuing vacations from Marbella to Phuket; I am simply a fairly typical product of a movable sensibility, living and working in a world that is itself increasingly small and increasingly mongrel. I am a multinational soul on a multi-cultural globe on which more and more countries are as polyglot and restless as airports. Taking planes seems as natural to me as picking up the phone or going to school; I fold up my self and carry it around with me as if it were an overnight bag.

This kind of life, of course, offers an unprecedented sense of free-dom and mobility: tied down to nowhere, I can pick and choose among locations. At the most basic level, this means that I can get on a plane in Los Angeles, get off a few hours later in Jakarta, check into a Hilton, order a cheeseburger in English, and pay for it all with an American Express card. At the next level, it means that I can meet, in the Hilton coffee shop, an Indonesian businessman who is as conversant as I am with Larry King and Magic Johnson and Madonna. At a deeper level, it means that I need never feel estranged. If all the world is alien to us, all the world is home.

I have learned, in fact, to love foreignness. In any place I visit, I have the privileges of an outsider: I am an object of interest and even fascination; I am a person set apart, able to enjoy the benefits of the place without paying the taxes. Distance—on both sides—lends enchantment: police officers let me out of speeding tickets, women want to hear the story of my life, pedestrians will gladly point me to the nearest golden arches.

People like me learn to exult in the blessings of belonging to what feels like a whole new race. It is a race, as Salman Rushdie has said, of "people who root themselves in ideas rather than places, in memories as much as in material things; people who have been obliged to define themselves—because they are so defined by others—by their otherness; people in whose deepest selves strange fusions occur, unprecedented unions between what they were and where they find themselves." And when people argue that our very notion of wonder is eroded, that alienness itself is as seriously endangered as the wilderness, that more and more of the world is turning into a single synthetic monoculture, I reply that I am not worried: a Japanese version of a French fashion is something new, I say, not quite Japanese and not truly French. Hybrids are the art form of the time.

And yet, sometimes, I stop myself and think, What kind of heart is being produced by these new changes? And how does one fix a moving object on a map? I am not an exile, really, or an immigrant; not deracinated, I think, any more than I am rooted. I have not fled the oppression of war, or found ostracism in the places where I do alight; I can scarcely feel severed from a home I have scarcely known. But when the cabin attendant comes down the aisle with disembarkation forms, what do I fill in?...

We airport-hoppers can go through the world as through a house of wonders, picking up something at every stop and taking the whole globe as our playpen or our supermarket. We don't have a home; we have a hundred homes. And we can mix and match as the situation demands. "Nobody's history is my history," the Japanese-English novelist Kazuo Ishiguro, a great spokesman for the privileged homeless, once said to me. "Whenever it was convenient for me to become very Japanese, I could become very Japanese, and then, when I wanted to drop it, I would just become this ordinary Englishman." Instantly, I felt a shock of recognition: I have a wardrobe of selves from which to choose. And I savor the luxury of being able to be an Indian in Cuba or an American in Thailand; to be an Englishman in New York.

And so we go on circling the world, six miles above the ground. We listen to announcements given in three languages. We confirm our reservations at every stop. We disembark at airports that are self-sufficient communities, with hotels, gymnasiums, and places of worship. At customs we have nothing to declare but ourselves.

But what is the price we pay for all of this? What is the new kind of soul that is being born out of this new kind of life? For us in the transit lounge, affiliation is as alien as disorientation. We become professional observers, able to see the merits and deficiencies of anywhere, to balance our parents' viewpoints with their enemies' positions. Yes, we say, of course it's terrible, but look at the situation from Saddam's point of view. I understand how you feel, but the Chinese had their own cultural reasons for Tiananmen Square. Fervor comes to seem to us the most foreign place of all.

Seasoned experts at the aerial perspective, we are less good at touching down. Unable to be stirred by the raising of a flag, we are often unable to see how anyone could be stirred. I sometimes think that this is how Rushdie, the great analyst of this condition, became its victim. He had juggled homes for so long, so adroitly, that he forgot how the world looks to someone who is rooted—in country or belief. He had chosen to live so far from affiliation that he could no longer see why people choose affiliation in the first place. Besides, being part of no society means one is accountable to no one and need respect no laws outside one's own.

We become, in fact, strangers to belief itself, unable to comprehend many of the rages and dogmas that animate (and unite) people. Conflict itself seems inexplicable to us sometimes, simply because partisanship is; we have the agnostic's inability to retrace the steps of faith. I cannot begin to fathom why some Muslims would think of murder after hearing about *The Satanic Verses,* yet sometimes I force myself to recall that it is we, in our floating skepticism, who are the exceptions, that in China or Iran, in Korea or Peru, it is not so strange to take life—or give it up—for local principles.

We tell ourselves, self-servingly, that nationalism breeds monsters, and we choose to ignore the fact that internationalism breeds them, too. Ours is the culpability not of the assassin but of the bystander who takes a snapshot of the murder. Or, when the revolution catches fire, hops on the next plane out.

Sometimes, though, I am brought up short by symptoms of my condition. They are not major things, but they are peculiar ones, and ones that would not have been so common fifty years ago. I have never bought a house of any kind. I have never voted. I have never supported a nation (in the Olympic Games, say) or represented "my country" in anything. Even the name I go by is weirdly international, because my "real name" (a polysyllabic, unpronounceable Indian one) makes sense only in the home where I have never lived.

I wonder, sometimes, if this new kind of nonaffiliation may not be alien to something fundamental in the human state. The refugee at least harbors passionate feelings about the world he has left; the exile at least is propelled by some kind of strong emotion away from the old country and toward the new—indifference is not an exile's emotion. But what does the Transit Lounger feel? What are the issues that we would die for? What are the passions that we would live for?

Airports are among the only sites in public life where emotions are hugely sanctioned. We see people weep, shout, kiss in airports; we see them at the furthest edges of excitement and exhaustion. Airports are privileged spaces where we can see the primal states—fear, recognition, hope—writ large. But there are some of us, perhaps, sitting at the departure gate, boarding passes in hand, watching the destinations ticking over, who feel neither the pain of separation nor the exultation of wonder; who alight with the same emotions with which we embarked; who go down to the baggage carousel and watch our lives circling, circling, circling, waiting to be claimed.

# Maps to Anywhere

### BY

### BERNARD

### COOPER

T he proprietress of Maps to Anywhere begins to spin in her swivel chair. The walls are covered with time zones and oceans, the room filled with dozens of globes scattered in shafts of dusty sunlight. She grips the seat and shoves off the floor to propel herself faster and faster. Her head tilts back. Her eyes close. The million lavender threads of her sweater swathe her like an atmosphere. She sings a song about strange places, an anthem improvised under her breath:

> Oh, Yalta and Bulgaria,
> dum, dum, la, la, la
> Oahu and...Mozambique...
> Helsinki and...Baja.

Despite her stock of atlases, it's safe to say this woman is lost, at least for several delirious minutes. She doesn't even notice that I'm standing at the door.

Whenever I've dropped a cufflink or a key and groped on the floor unable to find it, I could feel the world turn, buildings dimming in the dusk, the continent slipping into the dark, the planet trapped like a roast on a rotisserie, relentless rotations of night and day. Within this onslaught of time, I'd reach beneath the dresser, the bed, stirring up flimsy galaxies of dust, retrieving nothing, astonished and alone.

The whirling proprietress puts on her brakes, digs her high heels into the carpet. She tries to steady her lavender torso, clutches her churning head in her hands. Maps to everywhere must be in motion, latitudes and longitudes undulating before her eyes, hundreds of small pastel countries whizzing by like pricked balloons, the names of rivers and towns and mountains smeared and indecipherable.

A minute passes. Nothing but the shush of traffic and motes tumbling through shafts of light.

"Sorry," she blurts, blushing up at me. Wobbling, cordial, she rises from her chair, straightens her collar, smooths her skirt. "Mazel," she says, extending her hand, "Mrs. Mazel. And how may I help you?"

Her hand in mine is soft and hot. "I'm looking for a globe. Just something simple. How about those?" I point to a group of globes on the floor.

"Replogle globes. Model two-fourteen." She furrows her forehead, bites her lip. "Nice. But the colors are dull, don't you think?"

Before I can answer, Mrs. Mazel has crossed the room, her blonde bouffant as big as the sun among these excess earths.

"Now this," she says, "is the Dexter Special." She holds up a heavier, darker globe, raps her knuckle along its equator. That world resounds with a muffled thud. "Solid. Comes with a two-year warranty. Guaranteed not to dent or fade."

I've made up my mind. The Replogle is perfect. But Mrs. Mazel is over in a corner, jumping at a globe on the highest shelf. It almost drops as she drags it down. Walking briskly back to me, she grazes an entire table of globes which creak through a chorus of revolutions.

"Feel it," she says, thrusting this one up to my face. "Close your eyes and feel it."

"Mrs. Mazel, I'm in a hurry."

The planet before me starts to sink, and there, huge behind it, is the face of Mrs. Mazel.

"I wanted to be of assistance," she whispers.

There have been mornings, walking to work, when the heads of pedestrians looked like planets, every face encased in its weather, flushed cheeks, cold noses, all that shifting geography, the mumbling lips, the nervous tics. Today I get stranded on planet Mazel. Her topography amazes me: hazel eyes enmeshed in wrinkles, large dark nostrils, pointed chin.

I look to make sure no one is watching and I wipe my palms on my woolen pants and I close my eyes and I feel the globe till I reach a part that's raised.

"What a relief," jokes Mrs. Mazel, her voice deep from cigarettes. "And what mountain range is that?" she asks, slowly, as though I'm her hopeless pupil. She tilts the peaks to meet my fingers. I can hear her breathing through her nose. "Now keep those eyes of yours closed," she intones. "No cheating allowed, Mr. ———?"

The world feels chilly and sad and small, metallic and hollow and inconsequential, and I can't, for the life of me, recollect my name, or the name of the minuscule mountain range plunged into darkness beneath my palm. I let my right index finger fall off a shallow coast and flounder. Whatever ocean this is, is calm, except for an archipelago's braille, abstract and hard as rock.

"Stone," I can barely hear myself say. From far away, from within the dark, I lie. "Mr. Stone."

Mrs. Mazel keeps turning the world, very carefully, around and around. Strange terrain slides under my hands. My fingers, reaching beyond the horizon, are swept by the trade winds of Mrs. Mazel's breath.

I have to pry my eyes open, and what I find is blinding: Mrs. Mazel standing before me and beaming with authority. I'd forgotten how this place is cramped, typewriters shrouded in plastic covers, stacks of mail about to topple. It seems like days since I passed through that door.

"This is my lunch hour, Mrs. Mazel. Please, pack the Replogle."

Mrs. Mazel turns quickly officious. She scoops a globe up off the floor. She drops my purchase into a box, presses in crescents of styrofoam which squeak like tiny lives in pain. "There," she announces, handing me the box. Its sides are bulging. "Will that be cash or charge, Mr. Stone?"

Last week they drained the Echo Park lake and every possession I'd ever lost seemed to be strewn in its muddy dregs: an algae-covered credit card, a fountain pen, puckered shoes. And radiating out from the lake were palm trees posted with notices: missing parrot, blue and orange, eats sunflower seeds, answers to "George"; schnauzer, big, shy, reward; calico kitten with white paws, blind in one eye, please call. On the road, traffic roared and retreated. On the sidewalk, newspapers blew away. All things on earth were lost or leaving.

Walking back to the earth with the globe, I'm jostled by people who rush toward the park to claim a place on the grass to have lunch. The winter sun is low but warm. Everyone wants to feel it on their faces. They all crane in the same direction, planets leaning their cheeks to the light. And there at the center of their basking lies the lake, filled again, clear as a mirror. Huge, fluid clouds move through it, blown to Brussels, Paraguay, Perth.

# The Toynbee
# Convector

~

BY

RAY

BRADBURY

ood! Great! Bravo for me!"

Roger Shumway flung himself into the seat, buckled himself in, revved the rotor and drifted his Dragonfly Super-6 helicopter up to blow away on the summer sky, heading south toward La Jolla.

"How lucky can you get?"

For he was on his way to an incredible meeting.

The time traveler, after 100 years of silence, had agreed to be interviewed. He was, on this day, 130 years old. And this afternoon, at four o'clock sharp, Pacific time, was the anniversary of his one and only journey in time.

Lord, yes! One hundred years ago, Craig Bennett Stiles had waved, stepped into his *Immense Clock*, as he called it, and vanished from the present. He was and remained the only man in history to travel in time. And Shumway was the one and only reporter, after all these years, to be invited in for afternoon tea. And? The possible announcement of a second and final trip through time. The traveler had hinted at such a trip.

"Old man," said Shumway, "Mr. Craig Bennett Stiles—here I come!"

The Dragonfly, obedient to fevers, seized a wind and rode it down the coast.

The old man was there waiting for him on the roof of the Time Lamasery at the rim of the hang gliders' cliff in La Jolla. The air swarmed with crimson, blue, and lemon kites from which young men shouted, while young women called to them from the land's edge.

Stiles, for all his 130 years, was not old. His face, blinking up at the helicopter, was the bright face of one of those hang-gliding Apollo fools who veered off as the helicopter sank down.

Shumway hovered his craft for a long moment, savoring the delay.

Below him was a face that had dreamed architectures, known incredible loves, blueprinted mysteries of seconds, hours, days, then dived in to swim upstream through the centuries. A sunburst face, celebrating its own birthday.

For on a single night, one hundred years ago, Craig Bennett Stiles, freshly returned from time, had reported by Telstar around the world to billions of viewers and told them their future.

"We made it!" he said. "We did it! The future is ours. We rebuilt the cities, freshened the small towns, cleaned the lakes and rivers, washed the air, saved the dolphins, increased the whales, stopped the wars, tossed solar stations across space to light the world, colonized the moon, moved on to Mars, then Alpha Centauri. We cured cancer and stopped death. We did it—Oh Lord, much thanks—we did it. Oh, future's bright and beauteous spires, arise!"

He showed them pictures, he brought them samples, he gave them tapes and LP records, films and sound cassettes of his wondrous roundabout flight. The world went mad with joy. It ran to meet and make that future, fling up the cities of promise, save all and share with the beasts of land and sea.

The old man's welcoming shout came up the wind. Shumway shouted back and let the Dragonfly simmer down in its own summer weather.

Craig Bennett Stiles, 130 years old, strode forward briskly and, incredibly, helped the young reporter out of his craft, for Shumway was suddenly stunned and weak at this encounter.

"I can't believe I'm here," said Shumway.

"You are, and none too soon," laughed the time traveler. "Any day now, I may just fall apart and blow away. Lunch is waiting. Hike!"

A parade of one, Stiles marched off under the fluttering rotor shadows that made him seem a flickering newsreel of a future that had somehow passed.

Shumway, like a small dog after a great army, followed.

"What do you want to know?" asked the old man as they crossed the roof, double time.

"First," gasped Shumway, keeping up, "why have you broken silence after a hundred years? Second, why to *me*? Third, what's the big announcement you're going to make this afternoon at four o'clock, the very hour when your younger self is due to arrive from the past— when, for a brief moment, you will appear in two places, the paradox: the person you were, the man you are, fused in one glorious hour for us to celebrate?"

The old man laughed. "How you *do* go on!"

"Sorry." Shumway blushed. "I wrote that last night. Well. Those are the questions."

"You shall have your answers." The old man shook his elbow gently. "All in good—time."

"You must excuse my excitement," said Shumway. "After all, you *are* a mystery. You were famous, world-acclaimed. You went, saw the future, came back, told us, then went into seclusion. Oh, sure; for a few weeks, you traveled the world in ticker-tape parades, showed yourself on TV, wrote one book, gifted us with one magnificent two-hour television film, then shut yourself away here. Yes, the time machine is on exhibit below, and crowds are allowed in each day at noon to see and touch. But you yourself have refused fame—"

"Not so." The old man led him along the roof. Below in the gardens, other helicopters were arriving now, bringing TV equipment from around the world to photograph the miracle in the sky, that moment when the time machine from the past would appear, shimmer, then wander off to visit other cities before it vanished into the past. "I have been busy, as an architect, helping build that very future I saw when, as a young man, I arrived in our golden tomorrow!"

They stood for a moment watching the preparations below. Vast tables were being set up for food and drink. Dignitaries would be arriving soon from every country of the world to thank—for a final time, perhaps, this fabled, this almost mythic traveler of the years.

"Come along," said the old man. "Would you like to come sit in the time machine? No one else ever has, you know. Would you like to be the first?"

No answer was necessary. The old man could see that the young man's eyes were bright and wet.

"There, there," said the old man. "Oh, dear me; there, there."

A glass elevator sank and took them below and let them out in a pure white basement at the center of which stood—

The incredible device.

"There." Stiles touched a button and the plastic shell that had for one hundred years encased the time machine slid aside. The old man nodded. "Go. Sit."

Shumway moved slowly toward the machine.

Stiles touched another button and the machine lit up like a cavern of spider webs. It breathed in years and whispered forth remembrances. Ghosts were in its crystal veins. A great god spider had woven its tapestries in a single night. It was haunted and it was alive. Unseen tides came and went in its machinery. Suns burned and moons hid their seasons in it. Here, an autumn blew away in tatters; there, winters arrived in snows that drifted in spring blossoms to fall on summer fields.

The young man sat in the center of it all, unable to speak, gripping the armrests of the padded chair.

"Don't be afraid," said the old man gently. "I won't send you on a journey."

"I wouldn't mind," said Shumway.

The old man studied his face. "No, I can see you wouldn't. You look like me one hundred years ago this day. Damn if you aren't my honorary son."

The young man shut his eyes at this, and the lids glistened as the ghosts in the machine sighed all about him and promised him tomorrows.

"Well, what do you think of my *Toynbee Convector*?" said the old man briskly, to break the spell.

He cut the power. The young man opened his eyes.

"The *Toynbee Convector*? What—"

"More mysteries, eh? The great Toynbee, that fine historian who said any group, any race, any world that did not run to seize the future and shape it was doomed to dust away in the grave, in the past."

"Did he say *that*?"

"Or some such. He did. So, what better name for my machine, eh? Toynbee, wherever you are, here's your future-seizing device!"

He grabbed the young man's elbow and steered him out of the machine.

"Enough of that. It's late. Almost time for the great arrival, eh? And the earth-shaking final announcement of that old time traveler Stiles! Jump!"

Back on the roof, they looked down on the gardens, which were now swarming with the famous and the near famous from across the world. The nearby roads were jammed; the skies were full of helicopters and hovering biplanes. The hang gliders had long since given up and now stood along the cliff rim like a mob of bright pterodactyls, wings folded, heads up, staring at the clouds, waiting.

"All this," the old man murmured, "my God, for *me*."

The young man checked his watch.

"Ten minutes to four and counting. Almost time for the great arrival. Sorry; that's what I called it when I wrote you up a week ago for the *News*. That moment of arrival and departure, in the blink of an eye, when, by stepping across time, you changed the whole future of the world from night to day, dark to light. I've often wondered—"

"What?"

Shumway studied the sky. "When you went ahead in time, did *no one* see you arrive? Did anyone at all happen to look up, do you know, and see your device hover in the middle of the air, here and over Chicago a bit later, and then New York and Paris? *No one*?"

"Well," said the inventor of the *Toynbee Convector*, "I don't suppose anyone was *expecting* me! And if people saw, they surely did not know what in blazes they were looking at. I was careful, anyway, not to linger too long. I needed only time to photograph the rebuilt cities, the clean seas and rivers, the fresh, smog-free air, the unfortified nations, the saved and beloved whales. I moved quickly, photographed swiftly and ran back down the years home. Today, paradoxically, is different. Millions upon millions of mobs of eyes will be looking up with great expectations. They will glance, will they not, from the young fool burning in the sky to the old fool here, still glad for his triumph?"

"They will," said Shumway. "Oh, indeed, they *will*!"

A cork popped. Shumway turned from surveying the crowds on the nearby fields and the crowds of circling objects in the sky to see that Stiles had just opened a bottle of champagne.

"Our own private toast and our own private celebration."

They held their glasses up, waiting for the precise and proper moment to drink.

"Five minutes to four and counting. Why," said the young reporter, "did no one else ever travel in time?"

"I put a stop to it myself," said the old man, leaning over the roof, looking down at the crowds. "I realized how dangerous it was. I was reliable, of course, no danger. But, Lord, think of it—just *anyone* rolling about the bowling-alley time corridors ahead, knocking tenpins headlong, frightening natives, shocking citizens somewhere else, fiddling with Napoleon's life line behind or restoring Hitler's cousins ahead? No, no. And the government, of course, agreed—no, insisted—that we put the *Toynbee Convector* under sealed lock and key. Today, you were the first and the last to fingerprint its machinery. The guard has been heavy and constant, for tens of thousands of days, to prevent the machine's being stolen. What time do you have?"

Shumway glanced at his watch and took in his breath.

"One minute and counting down—"

He counted, the old man counted. They raised their champagne glasses.

"Nine, eight, seven—"

The crowds below were immensely silent. The sky whispered with expectation. The TV cameras swung up to scan and search.

"Six, five—"

They clinked their glasses.

"Four, three, two—"

They drank.

"One!"

They drank their champagne with a laugh. They looked to the sky. The golden air above the La Jolla coast line waited. The moment for the great arrival was here.

"Now!" cried the young reporter, like a magician giving orders.

"Now," said Stiles, gravely quiet.

Nothing.

Five seconds passed.

The sky stood empty.

Ten seconds passed.

The heavens waited.

Twenty seconds passed.

Nothing.

At last, Shumway turned to stare and wonder at the old man by his side.

Stiles looked at him, shrugged and said:

"I lied."

"You what?" cried Shumway.

The crowds below shifted uneasily.

"I lied," said the old man simply.

"No!"

"Oh, but yes," said the time traveler. "I never went anywhere. I stayed but made it seem I went. There is no time machine—only something that *looks* like one."

"But why?" cried the young man, bewildered, holding to the rail at the edge of the roof. "Why?"

"I see that you have a tape-recording button on your lapel. Turn it on. Yes. There. I want everyone to hear this. Now."

The old man finished his champagne and then said:

"Because I was born and raised in a time, in the sixties, seventies, and eighties, when people had stopped believing in themselves. I saw that disbelief, the reason that no longer gave itself reasons to survive, and was moved, depressed and then angered by it.

"Everywhere, I saw and heard doubt. Everywhere, I learned destruction. Everywhere was professional despair, intellectual ennui, political cynicism. And what wasn't ennui and cynicism was rampant skepticism and incipient nihilism."

The old man stopped, having remembered something. He bent and from under a table brought forth a special bottle of red Burgundy with the label 1984 on it. This, as he talked, he began to open, gently plumbing the ancient cork.

"You name, it, we had it. The economy was a snail. The world was a cesspool. Economics remained an insolvable mystery. Melancholy was the attitude. The impossibility of change was the vogue. End of the world was the slogan.

"Nothing was worth doing. Go to bed at night full of bad news at eleven, wake up in the morn to worse news at seven. Trudge through the day underwater. Drown at night in a tide of plagues and pestilence. Ah!"

For the cork had softly popped. The now-harmless 1984 vintage was ready for airing. The time traveler sniffed it and nodded.

"Not only the four horsemen of the Apocalypse rode the horizon to fling themselves on our cities but a fifth horseman, worse than all the rest, rode with them: Despair, wrapped in dark shrouds of defeat, crying only repetitions of past disasters, present failures, future cowardices.

"Bombarded by dark chaff and no bright seed, what sort of harvest was there for man in the latter part of the incredible twentieth century?

"Forgotten was the moon, forgotten the red landscapes of Mars, the great eye of Jupiter, the stunning rings of Saturn. We refused to be comforted. We wept at the grave of our child, and the child was *us*."

"Was that how it was," asked Shumway quietly, "one hundred years ago?"

"Yes." The time traveler held up the wine bottle as if it contained proof. He poured some into a glass, eyed it, inhaled, and went on. "You have seen the newsreels and read the books of that time. You know it all.

"Oh, of course, there were a few bright moments. When Salk delivered the world's children to life. Or the night when *Eagle* landed and that one great step for mankind trod the moon. But in the minds and out of the mouths of many, the fifth horseman was darkly cheered on. With high hopes, it sometimes seemed, of his winning. So all would be gloomily satisfied that their predictions of doom were right from day one. So the self-fulfilling prophecies were declared; we dug our graves and prepared to lie down in them."

"And you wouldn't allow that?" said the young reporter.

"You know I couldn't."

"And so you built the *Toynbee Convector*—"

"Not all at once. It took years to brood on it."

The old man paused to swirl the dark wine glass, gaze at it and sip, eyes closed.

"Meanwhile, I drowned, I despaired, wept silently late nights thinking, What can I do to save us from ourselves? How to save my friends, my city, my state, my country, the entire *world* from this obsession with doom? Well, it was in my library late one night that my hand, searching along shelves, touched at last on an old and beloved book by H.G. Wells. His time device called, ghostlike, down the years. I *heard!* I understood. I truly listened. Then I blueprinted. I built. I traveled, or so it *seemed*. The rest, as you know, is history."

The old time traveler drank his wine, opened his eyes.

"Good God," the young reporter whispered, shaking his head. "Oh, dear God. Oh, the wonder, the wonder—"

There was an immense ferment in the lower gardens now and in the fields beyond and on the roads and in the air. Millions were still waiting. Where was the great arrival?

"Well, now," said the old man, filling another glass with wine for the young reporter. "Aren't I something? I made the machines, built miniature cities, lakes, ponds, seas. Erected vast architectures against crystal-water skies, talked to dolphins, played with whales, faked tapes, mythologized films. Oh, it took years, years of sweating work and secret preparation before I announced my departure, left and came back with good news!"

They drank the rest of the vintage wine. There was a hum of voices. All of the people below were looking up at the roof.

The time traveler waved at them and turned.

"Quickly, now. It's up to you from here on. You have the tape, my voice on it, just freshly made. Here are three more tapes, with fuller data. Here's a film-cassette history of my whole inspired fraudulence. Here's a final manuscript. Take, take it all, hand it on. I nominate you as son to explain the father. Quickly!"

Hustled into the elevator once more, Shumway felt the world fall away beneath. He didn't know whether to laugh or cry, so gave, at last, a great hoot.

The old man, surprised, hooted with him, as they stepped out below and advanced upon the *Toynbee Convector*.

"You see the point, don't you, son? Life has *always* been lying to ourselves! As boys, young men, old men. As girls, maidens, women, to gently lie and prove the lie true. To weave dreams and put brains and ideas and flesh and the truly real beneath the dreams. Everything, finally, is a promise. What seems a lie is a ramshackle need, wishing to be born. Here. Thus and so."

He pressed the button that raised the plastic shield, pressed another that started the time machine humming, then shuffled quickly in to thrust himself into the *Convector's* seat.

"Throw the final switch, young man!"

"But—"

"You're thinking," here the old man laughed, "if the time machine is a fraud, it won't work, what's the use of throwing a switch, yes? Throw it anyway. *This* time, it *will* work!"

Shumway turned, found the control switch, grabbed hold, then looked up at Craig Bennett Stiles.

"I don't understand. Where are you *going*?"

"Why, to be one with the ages, of course. To exist now, only in the deep past."

"How can that *be*?"

"Believe me, this time it will happen. Goodbye, dear, fine, nice young man."

"Goodbye."

"Now. Tell me my name."

"What?"

"Speak my name and throw the switch."

"Time traveler?"

"Yes! *Now!*"

The young man yanked the switch. The machine hummed, roared, blazed with power.

"Oh," said the old man, shutting his eyes. His mouth smiled gently. "Yes."

His head fell forward on his chest.

Shumway yelled, banged the switch off and leaped forward to tear at the straps binding the old man in his device.

In the midst of so doing, he stopped, felt the time traveler's wrist, put his fingers under the neck to test the pulse there and groaned. He began to weep.

The old man had, indeed, gone back in time, and its name was death. He was traveling in the past now, forever.

Shumway stepped back and turned the machine on again. If the old man were to travel, let the machine—symbolically, anyway—go with him. It made a sympathetic humming. The fire of it, the bright sun fire, burned in all of its spider grids and armatures and lighted the cheeks and the vast brow of the ancient traveler, whose head seemed to nod with the vibrations and whose smile, as he traveled into darkness, was the smile of a child much satisfied.

The reporter stood for a long moment more, wiping his cheeks with the backs of his hands. Then, leaving the machine on, he turned, crossed the room, pressed the button for the glass elevator, and, while he was waiting, took the time traveler's tapes and cassettes from his jacket pockets and, one by one, shoved them into the incinerator trash flue set in the wall.

The elevator doors opened, he stepped in, the doors shut. The elevator hummed now, like yet another time device, taking him up into a stunned world, a waiting world, lifting him up into a bright continent, a future land, a wondrous and surviving planet...

That one man with one lie had created.

# Map

**BY**

**SARAH**

**KLASSEN**

The map you cling to is a construct
of tenacious imagination. It permits no room
for confusion. Clear-cut lines
lead travellers through gentle, pastel spaces,
home. You know where you are or should be.
Everyone arrives on time.

This map refuses to mark the basswood forest
where your cry for help gets caught
in forked branches, your alarmed breathing
dissolves in a tangle of sinister undergrowth.
Boulders you should sidestep, the treacherous
river crossings are simply omitted.

It withholds warning: not all roads
lead home. Fellow travellers
are not so much alien as mute and dead-tired.
Lost like you in the shadows, unable to name
one single city.

Blurred borders are never mentioned. The
    longed-for
destination remains a dream. The distance
from here to there
nothing
but a fabulous mirage.

# Questions of Travel

## BY ELIZABETH BISHOP

There are too many waterfalls here; the crowded streams
hurry too rapidly down to the sea,
and the pressure of so many clouds on the mountaintops
makes them spill over the sides in soft slow-motion,
turning to waterfalls under our very eyes.
—For if those streaks, those mile-long, shiny, tearstains,
aren't waterfalls yet,
in a quick age or so, as ages go here,
they probably will be.
But if the streams and clouds keep travelling, travelling,
the mountains look like the hulls of capsized ships,
slime-hung and barnacled.

Think of the long trip home.
Should we have stayed at home and thought of here?
Where should we be today?
Is it right to be watching strangers in a play
in this strangest of theatres?
What childishness is it that while there's a breath of life
in our bodies, we are determined to rush
to see the sun the other way around?
The tiniest green hummingbird in the world?
To stare at some inexplicable old stonework,
inexplicable and impenetrable,
at any view,
instantly seen and always, always delightful?
Oh, must we dream our dreams
and have them, too?
And have we room
for one more folded sunset, still quite warm?

But surely it would have been a pity
not to have seen the trees along this road,
really exaggerated in their beauty,
not to have seen them gesturing
like noble pantomimists, robed in pink.
—Not to have had to stop for gas and heard
the sad, two-noted, wooden tune
of disparate wooden clogs
carelessly clacking over
a grease-stained filling-station floor.
(In another country the clogs would all be tested.
Each pair there would have identical pitch.)
—A pity not to have heard
the other, less primitive music of the fat brown bird
who sings above the broken gasoline pump
in a bamboo church of Jesuit baroque:
three towers, five silver crosses.
—Yes, a pity not to have pondered,
blurr'dly and inconclusively,
on what connection can exist for centuries
between the crudest wooden footwear
and, careful and finicky,
the whittled fantasies of wooden cages.
—Never to have studied history in
the weak calligraphy of songbirds' cages.
—And never to have had to listen to rain
so much like politicians' speeches:
two hours of unrelenting oratory
and then a sudden golden silence
in which the traveller takes a notebook, writes:

*"Is it lack of imagination that makes us come*
*to imagined places, not just stay at home?*
*Or could Pascal have been not entirely right*
*about just sitting quietly in one's room?*

*Continent, city, country, society:*
*the choice is never wide and never free.*
*And here, or there...No. Should we have stayed at home,*
*wherever that may be?"*

# ACKNOWLEDGEMENTS

Care has been taken to trace ownership of copyright material contained in this text. The publishers will gladly accept any information that will enable them to rectify any reference or credit in subsequent editions.

## TEXT

**p. 1** Excerpt from "Traveller, Conjuror, Journeyman" by P.K. Page © P.K. Page, 1970. Reprinted by permission of the author; Excerpt from *Blue Highways* by William Least Heat Moon. Copyright © 1982 by William Least Heat Moon. By permission of Little, Brown and Company; Excerpt from *Traveller's Prelude* by Freya Stark. Reprinted by permission of John Murray (Publishers) Ltd.; Excerpt from *My Travels Around the World* by Nawal el Saadawi. Reprinted by permission of Methuen London. **p. 6** "Peopling the Landscape" by Mark Salzman. Reprinted by permission of Donadio & Ashworth, Inc. Copyright 1991 by Mark Salzman; **p. 14** "Passports to Understanding" by Maya Angelou. From *Wouldn't Take Nothin For My Journey Now* by Maya Angelou. Copyright © 1993 by Maya Angelou. Reprinted by permission of Random House, Inc.; **p. 15** Excerpt from *Sunrise with Seamonsters* by Paul Theroux. Copyright © 1985 by Cape Cod Scriveners Company. Reprinted by permission of Houghton Mifflin Company. All rights reserved; **p. 18** "The Terminal Man" by Alberto Manguel © 1990 Alberto Manguel; **p. 21** "The Return" by Alistair MacLeod. From *The Lost Salt Gift of Blood* by Alistair MacLeod. Used by permission of the Canadian Publishers, McClelland & Stewart; **p. 34** "Why You Travel" by Gail Mazur will appear in her third book, *The Common*, University of Chicago Press, 1995; **p. 36** "The Returning" by Gail Tremblay is reprinted by permission of the publisher from *Indian Singing in Twentieth Century America* (CALYX Books, © 1990); **p. 38** "An Interview with Alison Tilley" by Gillda Leitenberg. By permission of Alison Tilley. "Packing Tips" from *Tilley Travel Tips for Safe, Easy, Worry-Free Travelling* by Alison Tilley. Reprinted courtesy of Alison Tilley; **p. 47** "A Trio Who Travel at the Drop of a Hat" by Judy Ross. Reprinted with permission from Judy Ross; **p. 53** From *The Accidental Tourist* by Anne Tyler. Copyright © 1985 by Anne Tyler Modarressi. Reprinted by permission of Alfred A. Knopf Inc.; **p. 62** "Trickster Time" by Jeannette Christine Armstrong. Originally published in *Voices: Being Native in Canada*, L. Jaine and D. Taylor (eds.), Extension Division, University of Saskatchewan; **p. 67** "Wide Horizons" by Peter E. Tarlow and Mitchell J. Muehsam from *The Futurist* (September-October 1992). Reproduced with permission from the World Future Society, 7910 Woodmont Avenue, Suite 450, Bethesda, Maryland 20814 USA; **p. 74** "We Need to Limit Tourism" by Wallace Immen. By permission of *The Globe and Mail*; **p. 78** "On Holiday" by Shaunt Basmajian. From *And Other Travels* (Moonstone Press, 1988); **p. 80** "Letters from India" by Jennifer Lewis. By permission of Jennifer Lewis; **p. 83** "Walking the Line" by Marian Botsford Fraser. Excerpted from *Walking the Line* © 1989 by Marian Botsford Fraser, published by Douglas & McIntyre. Reprinted by permission; **p. 88** "Only in Canada, We Say!" by Valerie Wyatt. Reprinted by permission of Valerie Wyatt; **p. 92** "RV's" by Tom Wayman. From *In a Small House on the Outskirts of Heaven* by Tom Wayman (Harbour Publishing, 1989); **p. 94** "Algonquin Idyll" by John Bemrose. Reprinted by permission of John Bemrose; **p. 99** "Forced to Have Fun" by David Owen © 1993 by David Owen. Reprinted from *The Atlantic Monthly*; **p.102** "Thirsty Dreams" by Sue MacLeod. Sue MacLeod is a poet, researcher and editor living in Halifax. This poem first appeared in the Atlantic Canadian literary journal, *The Pottersfield Portfolio*; **p. 104** "The Misfortune in Men's Eyes" by Eddy L. Harris. Copyright © 1992 by Eddy Harris. Reprinted by permission of Simon & Schuster, Inc.; **p. 110** "African Journey" by Nawal el Saadawi. From *My Travels Around the World* by Nawal el Saadawi, Methuen London; **p. 120** "Provincial" by Miriam Waddington. From *Collected Poems* by Miriam Waddington. Copyright © Miriam Waddington 1986. Reprinted by permission of Oxford University Press Canada; **p. 122** "Pilgrimage to Sighet, a Haunted City" by Elie Wiesel. Copyright © 1984 by The New York Times Company. Reprinted by permission; **p. 127** "Because of You, Kyushu" by Rita Ariyoshi reprinted from *Islands*, May/June 1991. Copyright © 1991 Islands Publishing Company. Reprinted by permission; **p. 137** "And I Remember" by Afua Cooper. Reprinted from *Memories Have Tongue* by Afua Cooper, 1992 (Sister Vision Press, Canada); **p. 140** "A Father's Journey" by Paul Hawryluk © 1993 by Paul Hawryluk, *Canadian Living* (June '93) Toronto, Ontario; **p. 146** "Great Explorations" by Jesse Birnbaum. Copyright 1993 Time Inc. Reprinted by permission; **p. 154** "Arctic Storm" from *Polar Dreams* by Helen Thayer. Copyright by Helen Thayer. Reprinted by permission of Simon & Schuster, Inc.; **p. 162** From *Travels* by Michael Crichton. Copyright © 1988 by Michael Crichton. Reprinted by permission of Alfred A. Knopf Inc.; **p. 171** "Italy Possible? Si!" by Lynn Atkinson. By permission of Lynn Atkinson. Lynn Atkinson publishes the quarterly newsletter "We're Accessible: News for Disabled and Elderly Travellers"; **p. 175** "Creating Your Own Journey" (Kathleen Saadat's Story) from *A Journey of One's Own: Uncommon Advice for the Independent Woman Traveller* by Thalia Zepatos, The Eighth Mountain Press, Copyright © 1993 by Thalia Zepatos. Reprinted by permission of the publisher and author; **p. 179** "A Winter June" by Elizabeth Haynes. Previously published in *Alberta Rebound* by NeWest Press (1990). Reprinted by permission of Elizabeth Haynes; **p. 189** "Distant Intimacies" by Gary Ross © 1988 Gary Ross Consulting Inc.; **p. 197** "Edinburgh or Bust" by Rohinton Mistry. This is an excerpt from "Searching for Stevenson" which appeared in *Writing Away* (McClelland & Stewart, 1994); **p. 204** "The Personal Touch" by David Dale. Reprinted from *The Obsessive Traveller or Why I Don't Steal Towels From Great Hotels Any More* by David Dale (HarperCollins Publishers Australia). Copyright David Dale 1991; **p. 209** Excerpt from *Equator: A Journey* by Thurston Clarke. Copyright © 1988 by Thurston Clarke. By permission of William Morrow and Company, Inc.; **p. 217** "The Soul of an Intercontinental Wanderer" by Pico Iyer © Pico Iyer; **p. 223** "Maps to Anywhere" by Bernard Cooper. From *Maps to Anywhere* by Bernard Cooper © 1990 Bernard Cooper. Reprinted by permission of the University of Georgia Press; **p. 227** "The Toynbee Convector" by Ray Bradbury. Reprinted by permission of Don Congdon Associates, Inc. Copyright © 1988 by Ray Bradbury; **p. 237** "Map" by Sarah Klassen. Reprinted with the permission of the author. From Sarah Klassen, *Borderwatch* (Windsor, Ont.: Netherlandic Press, 1993), p. 39; **p. 239** "Questions of Travel" from *The Complete Poems 1927–1979* by Elizabeth Bishop. Copyright © 1979, 1983 by Alice Helen Methfessel. Reprinted by permission of Farrar, Straus & Giroux, Inc.

## PHOTOGRAPHS

**p. 3** Joe Talirunili (Pavungnituk) 1899-1976 *Migration* c. 1976, grey stone, wood, hide, and string 29 x 31 x 18 cm, Art Gallery of Ontario, Toronto. Gift of the Klamer family, 1978; **p. 5** Lynda Powell; **p. 11** Robert Garrard; **p. 20** Provincial Archives of Alberta A 2017; **p. 37** Dick Hemingway; **p. 39** Alison Tilley; **p. 48** Wally Moss Photography; **p. 61**